Studies in

AFRICAN AMERICAN HISTORY AND CULTURE

edited by

GRAHAM HODGES
COLGATE UNIVERSITY

A GARLAND SERIES

Running for Freedom

Slave Runaways in North Carolina 1775–1840

FREDDIE L. PARKER

GARLAND PUBLISHING, INC.
NEW YORK & LONDON 1993

Library of Congress Cataloging-in-Publication Data

Parker, Freddie L., 1953–
    Running for freedom : slave runaways in North Carolina, 1775–1840 /
Freddie L. Parker.
        p.   cm. — (Studies in African American history and culture)
    Includes bibliographical references and index.
    ISBN 0–8153–1005–6
    1. Fugitive slaves—North Carolina—History. 2. Fugitive slaves—North Carolina—
Statistics. 3. North Carolina—Population—History.   4. North Carolina—
Population—Statistics.   I. Title. II. Series.
E445.N8P35   1993
973.7'115—dc20   92-38603
                                                                                CIP

Printed on acid-free, 250-year-life paper
Manufactured in the United States of America

To my wife Debra, my son Quinton,
my parents Alvin "Bud" and Sarah,
and to the loving memory of Harold

Contents

Preface   xiii

Chapter One
Origins, Growth, and Distribution
of the Black Population   3

Chapter Two
Slaveowners, Runaways, and the Law   29

Chapter Three
Runaway Slaves: A Physical Portrait   65

Chapter Four
Slave Personalities   123

Chapter Five
Flight, Destination, and Rewards   173

Summary and Conclusions   211

Bibliography   219

Index   237

Illustrations

Figures

1. Runaways Slaves by Sex 70

2. Grouped Frequency Distribution of
   Runaways by Ages and Sex 74

3. Runaway Slaves by Complexion 81

4. Complexion of Runaway Slaves
   Passing as Free 84

5. Complexion of Runaway Slaves With a Pass 87

6. Number of Slaves Who Had More Than
   One Owner 177

7. Frequency Distribution of Runaways
   by Month 185

8. Frequency Distribution of Runaways
   by Season of the Year 186

9. Grouped Frequency Distribution of
   Rewards Offered for Runaways 200

Following page 95

Selected Newspaper Advertisements for Runaway Slaves

x

Maps

1. North Carolina Census Districts in 1800   13

2. North Carolina Census Districts in 1840   15

3. The Great Dismal Swamp in Eastern Virginia
   and Eastern North Carolina   34

4. Edenton, New Bern, and Wilmington,
   Slave Harboring Towns   46

Tables

1. The White and Black Populations in
   North Carolina, 1770-1840   9

2. The North Carolina Population by
   District in 1800   14

3. The North Carolina Population by
   District in 1840   16

4. Black Population and Percentage
   in North Carolina Counties in 1800
   and 1840   18

5. Frequency Distribution of
   Runaways by Age and Sex   77

6. Description of Slave Runaways
   Based on Scars   94

7. Diseases and Maladies from which
   Slaves Suffered   98

8. Slaves with Speech Disorders
   in Skilled Occupations   134

9. Occupations of Skilled Runaways
   with Speech Disorders   135

10. Occupational Breakdown of Slave Runaways
    in North Carolina, 1775 to 1840   144

11. Destinations of Runaway Slaves Leaving
    North Carolina   182

12. Frequency Distribution of Slaves Who
    Ran Away in Groups   188

13. Composition of Groups of Runaways   189

14. Frequency Distribution of Runaways by
    County, Sex, and Children Taken   192

15. Frequency Distribution of Rewards Offered
    for Runaways by Sex   198

Preface

Over the past twenty-five years, North Carolina's northern neighbor, Virginia, and its southern neighbor, South Carolina, have been the focus of extensive research efforts on the subject of slavery. Many of these efforts have centered on the issue of slave resistance. North Carolina, on the other hand, has only received scant attention on the subject of slavery and slave protest. But many slaves in North Carolina, like those in other Southern states, exhibited their hatred of slavery in a number of ways. One form of resistance was the act of running away. It is a subject that has received little attention by students of slavery in North Carolina. Except for Marvin Kay and Lorin Cary, who profiled 134 fugitive slaves in North Carolina between 1748 and 1775, and Eddie Marie Ervin's Master's thesis written at North Carolina College at Durham in 1946, little else has been written on slave runaways in North Carolina. To date, no study has analyzed quantifiable data on fugitive slaves in North Carolina, between 1775 and 1840.

This study is an attempt to help fill that void. By far, the best sources available for a study on slave runaways are eighteenth- and nineteenth-century North Carolina newspaper advertisements. The advertisements for runaways yield significant pieces of information about slaves. Vivid descriptions were sometimes provided by slaveowners to make citizens aware of their absconded property. Owners disclosed such information as the slave's name, age, sex, weight, height, complexion, language and speech patterns, when and why they fled, and possible destinations. So much of what we read about the slavery era in American history is about the institution of slavery, and not about the men, women, and children who were slaves. This study is basically a profile of nearly 2,800 slaves who ran away from their owners between 1775 and 1840. It is about men, women, and children who had names; and about human beings who could be identified by certain physical scars, impairments, afflictions, and numerous personality traits that characterized the total individual.

The year 1775 was surely a watershed in American Colonial history. It marked the beginning of the American Revolution and of tremendous slave unrest in North Carolina and throughout the South. Slaves seized the opportunity afforded them by strife between the colonists and Great Britian. I selected the year 1775 as a starting point to assess the impact of the Revolution on slave flight. The year 1840 was important in North Carolina's history. The state had begun to awaken from a restful sleep of political, cultural, economic, and educational lag. By 1820, the state was referred to as the "Rip Van Winkle State." During the 1830s, the state had to deal with increasing slave unrest. Currents were being generated by the abolitionist campaign and Nat Turner's revolt in Southampton County, Virginia located just across the North Carolina border. The question is, did the activities of the 1830s influence slave flight? So, 1840 too was a watershed year in the state's history—the culmination of affairs in a state that was in transition in a number of ways.

Chapter 1 is a demographic analysis of the black and white populations in North Carolina from the 1660s to 1840. It concentrates on the slave population, and compares the growth of slavery in North Carolina with its growth in South Carolina. Chapter 2 addresses the legislation passed in North Carolina between 1699 and 1835 governing the problem of slave flight. For example, nearly 38 percent of the articles in the 1741 Slave Code were devoted to runaway slaves. The third chapter is an analysis of the fugitives' physical make-up. It examines age, gender, complexion, physical impairments, clothing, and other components of the runaways' physical being. Chapter 4 is a discussion of slave personality. Speech patterns, their facility in English, speech defects, behavioral and emotional characteristics, occupational skills, and literacy, are some of the themes discussed in this chapter. The last chapter, "Flight, Destination, and Rewards," examines why slaves ran away, where owners believed their slaves were going, when they fled, group and individual flight, areas in the state where flight was most common, and finally, the rewards that owners offered for the return of their slaves.

Along the way, a number of people have been helpful to me. I am especially grateful to the staff of the North Carolina Collection, Wilson Library, at the University of North Carolina at

Chapel Hill. Alice, Jeff, Harry, and other staff members often went beyond the "call of duty." Many dedicated staffers at the Division of Archives and History in Raleigh, and the Duke University Manuscript Division were extremely helpful. A Carolina Minority Postdoctoral Fellowship at the University of North Carolina at Chapel Hill provided me the time and financial support to bring this work to an end. Dr. Mary Sue Coleman and her staff were more than gracious. I am also grateful to administrators and chairpersons at my home institution, North Carolina Central University, for their generous support during my two year leave-of-absence. I also wish to express my sincere thanks to Professor Colin Palmer, a friend and adviser at the University of North Carolina at Chapel Hill, for his support and guidance. The seed for this research was planted when I was a Master's student in Professor George Reid's North Carolina History class at North Carolina Central University. In the early stages, he helped nurture the seed; he has been a friend, and has provided encouragement over the years. And I am grateful to my wife Debra for statistical help, but more than that, her sacrifices, love, support, and encouragement that surely made this undertaking a more pleasant one.

Running for Freedom

CHAPTER ONE

Origins, Growth, and Distribution of the Black Population

In 1663, three years after being restored to the English throne, King Charles II granted a stretch of land in colonial America to eight men who had remained loyal to him while he was in exile.[1] The land, named Carolina, in honor of Charles II, was located between thirty-one degrees and thirty-six degrees north latitude. Because some earlier settlers in Carolina were not included in the 1663 charter, King Charles issued a second charter dated June 30, 1665. The new charter enlarged Carolina by extending the boundaries by thirty minutes to the north and by two degrees to the south. Carolina's boundaries, then, stretched from twenty-nine degrees to thirty-six degrees and thirty minutes north latitude, between the northern border of Florida to the south and the southern border of Virginia to the north.[2] The eight Proprietors were Edward Hyde, Lord of Clarendon; George Monck, Duke of Albemarle; William Craven, Earl of Craven; John Lord Berkeley; Anthony Ashley Cooper; Sir George Carteret, Knight and Baronet; Sir William Berkeley, and Sir John Colleton.[3]

Within a few months of King Charles's grant to the Proprietors, efforts had begun to promote the settlement of Carolina. Promotional literature was used in many instances to stimulate interest in the settlement of the new colony. The literature referred to the beauty of Carolina, often describing the plant and animal life, and the pleasant climate. The Proprietors also made personal appeals to encourage the settlement of the new province.[4]

The earliest settlers in Carolina moved into the Albemarle Sound region south of the Virginia border in the northeastern section of the colony. These early immigrants to Carolina were from Virginia.[5] Not only was there an appeal to Virginians to move into the new province, but the Proprietors also issued a call to Barbadians to immigrate to Carolina. Barbadians did not settle immediately, but in late 1663, Anthony Long, William Holton, and Peter Fabian explored the Cape Fear River in the southeastern section of North Carolina.[6] No settlement, however, was planted there by these men representing Barbadian interest in the colony. It was not until 1670 that Barbadians began moving into Carolina, settling in what is now South Carolina.

Settlers from Virginia and Barbados took their black slaves with them, or purchased slaves after they settled. The Proprietors realized early that slavery was essential to the growth and the development of their province. The use of black slave labor was discussed by the Proprietors early in the colony's history.[7] However, it was not until 1665 that the Proprietors officially announced their position regarding slavery in the colony. Under "The Concessions and Agreement," the Proprietors promised fifty acres of land to a master or mistress...for every weaker Servant...brought or sent or bring or send...as women, children, and slaves above" fourteen years of age.[8] The language in the "Concessions and Agreement" was vague and imprecise as it related to headrights and slavery, but by 1669, the language was much more precise and definitive.

The Fundamental Constitutions drafted by John Locke, secretary to Ashley Cooper, firmly legalized slavery in Carolina. The document written in 1669 assured whites that "Every freeman of Carolina, shall have absolute power and authority over his negro slaves, of what opinion or religion soever."[9] Although it was lawful for slaves as well as others, "to enter themselves and be of what church or profession any of them shall think best, and thereof be as fully members as freeman," black slaves were not exempt from the harsh realities of enslavement.[10] As Virginians moved into North Carolina and Barbadians into South Carolina, the slave population gradually increased.[11] Unfortunately, the colony of North Carolina did not take official population censuses during the colonial period.[12] Population estimates, however, were made based on tax records. For instance, in 1663, it was reported that 300 families lived in North Carolina; but no estimate of the slave population was given at that time. Fourteen years later, in 1677, there were 1400 tithables, "a third part whereof at least being Indians, Negros and women..."[13] The total population in the colony was placed at 4,000.[14]

The growth of slavery in North Carolina was slow relative to its growth in South Carolina. Rosser H. Taylor, a historian of North Carolina slavery, pointed out that during "the proprietary period and in some degree to the close of the eighteenth century slave labor was not, as a rule, quite so efficient as it came to be at a later date."[15] For this reason, the Proprietors turned most of their attention to the thriving slave economy in South Carolina by the end of the seventeenth century. North Carolina's geographical position handicapped its "ease and access" to ocean going trade. Poor harbors and a jagged coastline prevented the colony from developing to the extent that her neighbors to the north and to the south developed.[16]

The contrast between the two colonies was evident in the number of blacks in each colony during the first decade of the eighteenth century. In 1705, the black population in North Carolina was about 1,000, which was 20 percent of the 5,000 inhabitants. In 1708, South Carolina had a population of 9,580 "souls," of whom 4,100 were black, and the remainder were Indian slaves, and whites.[17] In 1715, South Carolina had nearly 7,000 more slaves than her northern neighbor, and almost one-third more total inhabitants. There were 16,750 people in South Carolina, of whom 10,500 were black, while at the same time North Carolina had a total population of 11,200, of whom 3,700 were black. The percentage of the black population at that time in each colony was 62.4 percent and 24.8 percent, respectively.[18]

By the end of the Proprietary period in 1729, both colonies had developed economies based on slave labor. North Carolina's economy was based on the production of tobacco, wheat, and corn; and in the Lower Cape Fear region—in addition to the aforementioned—naval stores (tar, pitch, and turpentine) proved to be important to that region's economy. As early as the 1720s, slave labor was employed in the production of naval stores.[19]

On the other hand, South Carolina's economy was based on rice production. Recent scholarship has shown the correlation between the introduction of rice and the growth of the slave population in South Carolina after 1700. African laborers proved indispensable in teaching whites how to grow the crop. Daniel Littlefield wrote in his book, *Rice and Slaves* that: "Carolinians may well have gone to Gambia as students and brought Africans back as teachers, making the African influence on the development of rice cultivation in Carolina a decisive one."[20] The same expertise was undoubtedly used in the Lower Cape Fear region (New Hanover and Brunswick counties) of North Carolina where there was small-scale rice production by a small number of slaveholders.[21] The slaves in that region of the state were transshipped, primarily, from South Carolina. Many of the slaves who were employed in the rice fields of South Carolina eventually ended up in the Lower Cape Fear Valley in North Carolina. The state, however, could not compete with its neighbor to the south, and rice production in the colony hardly existed by the end of the colonial period.[22]

The population in both colonies continued to grow during the 1720s and the 1730s. In his 1733 report on the "Present State And Condition" of North Carolina, Governor George Burrington calculated that there were 30,000 whites and 6,000 blacks in the colony.[23] On the other hand, there were 39,155 blacks and 20,000 whites in South Carolina by the end of the same decade.[24] The bulk of the slaves brought into South Carolina in the eighteenth century were imported directly from Africa and the West Indies.[25] Most of the slaves who entered North Carolina in the eighteenth century were imported via land routes from Virginia and South Carolina. It has been well established that slave imports to North Carolina by sea were minimal relative to slave imports to Virginia and to South Carolina.[26]

There is some controversy, however, over the assertion that natural increase best explains the growth of the slave population in eighteenth-century North Carolina. The black population grew dramatically between 1730 and 1755. It rose from 6,000 to 18,532, a 209 percent increase. By 1767, the number of blacks more than doubled to 40,641—a 111 percent increase between 1755 and 1767—making blacks almost one-fourth of the population in North Carolina.[27]

Marvin L. Michael Kay and Lorie L. Lee Cary argue that the astounding increase in the black population between 1730 and 1767 was due, in part, to slave imports by sea and by land. They refute the notion advanced by some scholars "that the scattered extant records of entries of slaves through North Carolina's seaports indicate that "even in the busiest years" relatively few slaves, perhaps no more than one or two hundred per year, entered North Carolina directly from Africa or from the West Indies prior to the Revolution."[28] They also contend that, in general, scholars agree that the growth of the white population in North Carolina in the eighteenth century is best explained by immigration and natural increase. The growth rate was even higher among blacks, yet most scholars continued to maintain that natural increase was responsible for such a high rate of growth. Kay and Cary further maintained that "lax record-keeping" practices by North Carolina officials did not account for many slave imports by sea. Often newspaper advertisements for imported slaves exceeded the number that was reported by officials at the colony's ports of entry.[29]

Using extensive tax lists for North Carolina and newspaper advertisements for slaves imported into the province, Kay and Cary projected that about 3,600 slaves entered North Carolina by sea routes between 1755 and 1767. A total of 8,400 entered the province via land routes, while 10,109 blacks were born in North Carolina between 1755 and 1767. "Recent black immigrants to North Carolina, therefore, whatever their immediate geographical origins and whether Africans or Creoles, made up a sizable proportion of North Carolina's population in the 1750s and the 1760s."[30]

This new interpretation of the growth of the black population in North Carolina for the years 1755 to 1767 should be looked at closely, but with reservations. First, the authors extrapolated from the 50 slaves who were imported during a two-month period in the fall of 1764 to reach their conclusion that 3,600 slaves must have entered the state by sea between 1755 and 1767. These figures, then, are projections that may or may not hold true. The overland trade from South Carolina and Virginia, and natural increase, perhaps best explain the growth of the black population in North Carolina before, during, and after the 1755 to 1767 period.[31]

At the beginning of the decade of the American Revolution, North Carolina's population stood at 266,000, of whom 69,600, or 26 percent were black (see table 1). In ten years, the population grew by 35 percent, to 270,133 whites and 91,000 blacks. Slaves made up 21.5 percent of the population.[32] According to the first Federal Census of 1790, there were 288,204 whites, 100,572 slaves, and 5,041 free blacks in North Carolina.[33] The free black population in North Carolina had been almost non-existent before the American Revolution.

However, after 1775, a number of political, social, and legal ramifications combined and contributed to the growth of the free black population in North Carolina. The political currents generated by the American Revolution, coupled with the struggle by the Quakers and other religious groups to end slavery, contributed to the increase in the number of free blacks in North Carolina by the end of the eighteenth century. Quakers, for example, purchased slaves and set them free. This action by the Quakers, forced the North Carolina

Table 1

The White and Black Populations in North Carolina, 1770-1840

Year	White	% of Increase	% of Pop.	Slave	% of Increase	% of Pop.	Free Blacks	% of Increase	% of Pop.	Total Pop.
1770	197,200	—	74.0	69,000	—	26.0	—	—	—	266,800
1780	270,133	36.98	74.8	91,000	30.74	25.2	—	—	—	361,133
1790	288,204	6.68	73.2	100,572	10.5	25.5	5,041	—	1.28	393,751
1800	337,764	17.19	70.6	133,296	32.53	27.8	7,043	39.71	1.47	478,103
1810	376,410	11.44	67.7	168,824	26.65	30.3	10,266	45.76	1.84	555,500
1820	419,200	12.66	65.6	205,017	21.43	32.1	14,612	42.33	2.28	638,829
1830	472,843	12.79	64.1	245,601	16.56	33.2	19,543	33.74	2.65	737,987
1840	484,870	2.54	64.3	245,817	.08	32.6	22,732	16.31	3.02	753,419

Sources: United States Department of Commerce, *Historical Statistics of the United States: Colonial Times to 1970*; Department of Commerce, *Negro Population, 1790-1915*; Bureau of the Census, *Return of the Whole Numbers of Persons Within the Several Districts, 1790*; Department of State, *Return of the Whole Number of Persons Within the Several Districts, 1800*; Department of State, *Census for 1820*; U.S. Census Office, *Schedule of the Number of Persons Within the Several Districts of the United States, 1830*; Department of State, *Compendium of the Enumeration of the Inhabitants and Statistics of the United States, From the Returns of the Sixth Census*.

General Assembly to pass a law to prevent the manumission of slaves, except for meritorious services. Hundreds of North Carolina slaves were freed by the county courts for meritorious services, while other slaves found freedom by running away, acquiring free papers, and simply passing as free.[34]

Between 1790 and 1800, the number of free blacks grew by 2,000, or almost 40 percent, outpacing the growth rates of both the white and black populations. At the same time the white and slave populations grew by 17.19 percent and 32.53 percent, respectively. Of the 478,103 people in North Carolina in 1800, 133,296 were black slaves.[35]

As Table 1 shows, slaves made up no less than 30 percent of the population in North Carolina between 1810 and 1840. Their percent of increase, however, dwindled over the thirty year period from 26.7 percent between 1800 and 1810 to .08 percent between 1830 and 1840. Between 1830 and 1840, for instance, the slave population grew only by 216, from 245,601 to 245,817. The degree of increase in the white population was also relatively small. That population grew only by 2.54 percent, or 12,027, from 472,843 to 484,870.[36] This small increase in the black and the white populations between these years was due to the exodus of North Carolina farmers and planters to Georgia, Alabama, and Mississippi, and other southern and western states. The rich soils of the Lower South drew thousands of Carolinians during the 1820s and the 1830s. Large, as well as small farmers and planters abandoned the exhausted soils in eastern North Carolina and moved into the deep South. It was common to see a white man, his family, and his slaves in a wagon caravan en route to one of the lower southern states.[37]

The number of families that owned slaves in North Carolina grew substantially between 1790 and 1840. According to the 1790 Census, 31 percent of North Carolina's families held slaves. On the other hand, the percentage of whites who owned slaves in Virginia and South Carolina was somewhat higher. Almost 45 percent of

Virginia's families owned slaves, while 34.2 percent of the families in South Carolina held blacks in bondage. The number of slaves per slaveholding family in North Carolina was also lower than those in Virginia and South Carolina. North Carolina families owned an average of 6.7 slaves, whereas slaveholding families in Virginia and South Carolina averaged 8.5 and 12.1 slaves, respectively.[38]

Although the average number of slaves per slaveholding family in North Carolina was 6.7 in 1790, most families owned between 1 and 9 slaves. For example, about 27 percent of the 14,973 slaveholding families owned 1 slave; 33 percent owned 2 to 4 slaves; and 22.6 percent owned 5 to 9 slaves. Only about 12 percent of the families owned between 10 and 19 slaves in 1790. Plantations with 20 or more slaves were uncommon in North Carolina. Based on the 1790 Census, only 804 (5.3 percent) families held more than 20 slaves; most of these slaveholders, 87 percent, owned between 20 and 49 slaves. Ninety families, or 0.6 percent of all slaveholding families owned between 50 and 99 slaves, while 13 families claimed between 100 and 299 slaves.[39] Four such "heads of families" were, Herbert Haynes, Thomas Eaton, William Alston—all of Warren County—and Whitinall Hill of Bertie County. Haynes and Eaton held 138 slaves each; Alston owned 105, and Hill 130.[40] At the same time, there were 34,026 slaveholding families in Virginia and 8,859 in South Carolina. Virginia slaveholders owned more slaves in every category except in the 1 slave category, while South Carolinians owned more slaves in the 20 or more slaves categories.

Slaveholding families in North Carolina grew between 1790 and 1840, and so did the average number of slaves on individual units of production. By 1850, for instance, the number of slaveholding families had nearly doubled to 28,303. Slaveholding families owned an average of nearly 10.2 slaves. While nearly 27 percent of the families held only one slave in 1790, by 1850 just 3.6 percent of slaveowning families owned one slave.[41] This marked increase in the number of families owning two or more slaves was the result of greater dependence on slave labor due to increased production in most sectors of the North Carolina economy.[42]

The paths of settlement in North Carolina began in the northeastern section of the state in the 1660s, down to the southeast, across the northern tier counties, and westward across the state. In 1800, North Carolina, like the other states was divided into districts for enumeration purposes. The state's sixty counties were placed into the following Census districts: Morgan, Salisbury, Hillsborough, Edenton, Newbern, Wilmington, and Fayetteville. Slavery existed in every district in the state. Map 1 shows the eight census districts in 1800; each district was composed of between five and ten counties. Table 2 indicates North Carolina's total population, slave population, and the percentage of slave's in each district.

Halifax, Edenton, Newbern, and Wilmington districts contained 63.6 percent of the slaves in the state. In all four districts, blacks made up more than one-third of the total population. The slave population in the remaining four districts did not exceed 30 percent of the total population. The Morgan District—located in the western part of the state—contained the smallest slave population. According to the 1800 Census returns, that district had 4,643 slaves, or 9.4 percent of the total population, while Halifax, the district that held the largest number of slaves, had 31,445, or 45.4 percent of the population. The Halifax district alone, contained almost 24 percent of the state's slave population in 1800.[43]

The North Carolina slave population grew by 84.4 percent between 1800 and 1840, from 133,296 to 245,817. Map 2 shows the Census districts as they appeared in 1840. There was an increase of eight counties between 1800 and 1840. Cherokee, Macon, Haywood, Henderson, and Yancey counties were formed from Buncombe and Burke counties in the Morgan district; Davie and Davidson Counties were formed from Rowan County in the Salisbury district; and Columbus County was formed from Bladen and Brunswick counties in the Wilmington district.[44] Table 3 shows that by 1840 slaves made up at least one-third of the population in

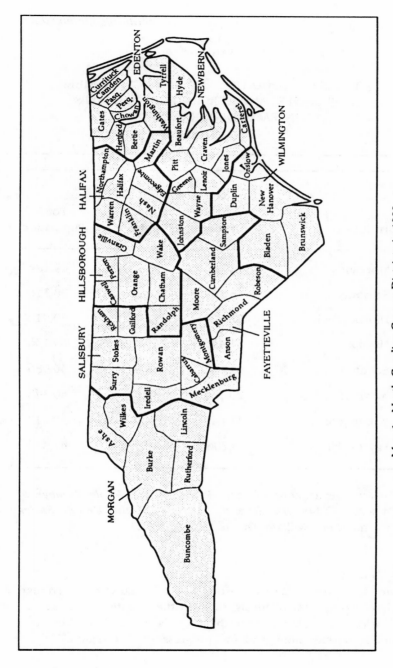

Map 1. North Carolina Census Districts in 1800

TABLE 2

THE N.C. POPULATION BY DISTRICT, NUMBER
OF SLAVES, AND PERCENTAGE OF SLAVES
IN EACH DISTRICT IN 1800

District	No. of Slaves	% of Population	Total Population
Morgan	4,643	9.4	49,184
Salisbury	13,389	14.8	90,376
Hillsborough	22,198	27.7	80,012
Halifax	31,445	45.4	69,136
Edenton	21,632	38.0	56,986
Newbern	20,134	33.3	60,343
Wilmington	11,649	38.0	30,617
Fayetteville	8,206	19.9	41,358

Source: Department of State, *Return of the Whole Number of
Persons Within the Several Districts of the United States*
(Washington: William Duane, 1802), 22-23.

all but two districts—Morgan and Salisbury. Though
slaveholding was relatively small in the counties in those two
districts, slave labor, nevertheless, played an important role
in the development and the progress of that region.[45]

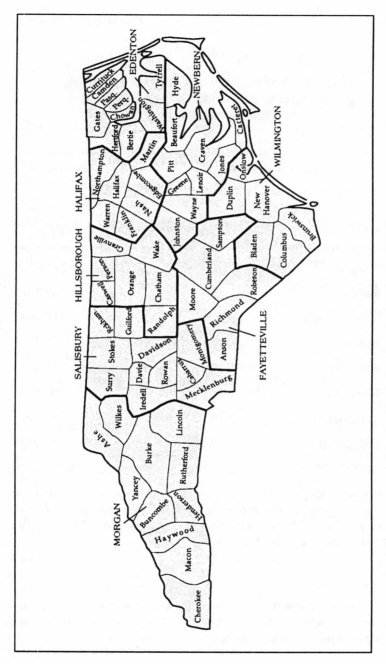

Map 2. North Carolina Census Districts in 1840

TABLE 3

THE N.C. POPULATION BY DISTRICT, NUMBER
OF SLAVES, AND PERCENTAGE OF SLAVES
IN EACH DISTRICT IN 1840

District	No. of Slaves	% of Population	Total Population
Morgan	16,250	14.4	114,651
Salisbury	34,174	22.4	152,156
Hillsborough	41,755	35.4	117,891
Halifax	43,636	50.4	89,525
Edenton	29,963	41.6	71,918
Newbern	36,001	39.4	91,244
Wilmington	20,410	41.4	49,249
Fayetteville	23,358	33.4	69,785

Source: Department of State, *Compendium of the Enumeration of the Inhabitants and Statistics of the United States, from The Returns to the Sixth Census* (Washington: Blair and Rives, 1841), 218-223.

Slaves constituted 50.4 percent of the population in the Halifax district, but that district's share of the state's slave population dropped from nearly 24 percent in 1800 to almost 18 percent in 1840. As newcomers migrated to the state and moved westward, slavery began to grow in the counties making up the Hillsborough and Fayetteville districts. Slavery, then, was more evenly distributed across the state in 1840, yet almost 53 percent of the slaves were in the districts of Halifax, Edenton, Newbern, and Wilmington.[46]

It is interesting to note the number of slaves in selected counties in the state in 1800 and 1840. Two counties reported less than 500 slaves in 1800; thirty-three counties had between 501 and 2,000 slaves; and four had between 5,000 and 7,500 slaves. Four counties—Halifax, Warren, Northampton, and New Hanover—had more slaves than whites. Slaves made up 52 percent of the population in Halifax; 53.2 percent in Warren; 50.2 percent in Northampton; and 57.5 percent in New Hanover County. All four were heavy cotton and tobacco producing counties, requiring large numbers of slaves[47] (see table 4).

By 1840, three other counties, Bertie and Chowan, located in the northeastern section of the state, and Jones County located in the southeast contained more slaves than whites. Slaves represented 55.2 percent of the population in Bertie County; in Chowan County, they were 54.7 percent; and in Jones, slaves were 57 percent of the population. Six counties—all located in the mountains—contained less than 500 slaves. There was a substantial decrease in the number of counties holding 501 to 2,000 slaves, and an increase in the number of counties containing 2001 to 5000 slaves. The 1840 Census indicated that only eleven counties contained 501 to 2,000 slaves, while thirty-one counties reported 2,001 to 5,000 slaves in 1840. The number of counties that held 5,000 slaves or more also rose. Eighteen counties had between 5,000 and 9,500 slaves in 1840. Cherokee County, the smallest slaveholding county reported 199 slaves, while Halifax County, consistently the largest slaveholding county in the state, contained 9,405 slaves.[48]

Though North Carolina did not enjoy the luster of importing large numbers of slaves directly from Africa and the West Indies, slavery, nevertheless grew, and like Virginia

Table 4

Black Population and Percentage in
North Carolina Counties in 1800 and 1840

County	Pop. 1800	% of Total Pop.	Pop. 1840	% of Total Pop.
Anson	1,290	15.8	5,304	35.2
Ashe	85	3.0	497	6.6
Beaufort	2,044	32.7	4,472	36.6
Bertie	5,512	49.0	6,728	55.2
Bladen	2,299	32.7	3,413	42.5
Brunswick	1,614	39.3	2,110	40.0
Buncombe	347	6.0	1,196	11.9
Burke	878	8.8	3,216	20.4
Cabarrus	699	13.7	2,179	23.6
Camden	1,170	28.0	1,661	29.3
Carteret	796	20.0	1,360	20.6
Caswell	2,788	32.0	7,024	47.8
Chatham	2,809	23.7	5,316	32.7
Cherokee	—	—	199	5.8
Chowan	2,473	48.1	3,665	54.7
Columbus	—	—	1,086	27.8
Craven	4,161	40.6	5,702	42.4
Cumberland	2,723	29.3	5,392	35.3
Currituck	1,530	22.0	2,100	31.3
Davidson	—	—	2,538	17.4
Davie	—	—	1,888	25.9
Duplin	1,864	27.4	4,677	41.8

Table 4 (cont'd)

County	Pop. 1800	% of Total Pop.	Pop. 1840	% of Total Pop.
Edgecombe	3,905	37.5	7,439	47.4
Franklin	3,698	43.4	5,320	48.4
Gates	2,688	45.7	3,642	44.6
Granville	6,106	43.6	8,707	46.2
Greene	1,496	35.5	2,971	45.0
Guilford	905	9.6	2,647	13.8
Halifax	7,239	52.0	9,405	55.8
Haywood	—	—	304	6.1
Henderson	—	—	466	9.0
Hertford	2,864	42.7	3,298	44.0
Hyde	1,404	29.0	2,198	34.0
Iredell	1,508	17.0	3,716	23.7
Johnston	1,763	28.0	3,476	32.8
Jones	1,949	45.0	2,818	57.0
Lenoir	1,526	38.1	3,683	48.4
Lincoln	1,523	12.0	5,386	21.4
Macon	—	—	368	7.6
Martin	1,773	31.9	2,816	36.9
Mecklenburg	1,988	19.0	6,322	34.6
Montgomery	1,373	17.9	2,467	22.9
Moore	608	12.8	1,472	18.4
Nash	2,596	37.2	3,697	40.9
New Hanover	4,058	57.5	6,376	47.9

Table 4 (cont'd.)

County	Pop. 1800	% of Total Pop.	Pop. 1840	% of Total Pop.
Northampton	6,209	50.2	6,729	50.3
Onslow	1,814	32.3	2,739	36.4
Orange	3,565	21.8	6,954	28.6
Pasquotank	1,755	32.6	2,788	32.7
Perquimans	2,020	35.4	2,543	34.6
Person	2,082	32.5	4,351	44.4
Pitt	2,885	31.8	5,618	47.6
Randolph	607	6.6	1,357	10.5
Richmond	875	15.6	3,880	43.6
Robeson	998	14.6	2,885	27.8
Rockingham	1,633	19.7	4,512	33.6
Rowan	2,839	14.1	3,365	27.8
Rutherford	1,072	10.0	3,201	29.2
Sampson	1,712	25.5	4,425	36.4
Stokes	1,439	13.0	2,682	16.5
Surry	1,005	10.6	1,778	11.8
Tyrrell	859	25.3	1,411	30.3
Wake	4,241	31.6	7,994	37.9
Warren	6,012	53.3	8,200	63.5
Wayne	1,988	29.3	3,673	33.7

Table 4 (cont'd)

County	Pop. 1800	% of Total Pop.	Pop. 1840	% of Total Pop.
Wilkes	790	11.0	1,430	11.4
Yancey	—	—	254	4.3

Sources: Department of State, *Return of the Whole Number of Persons Within the Several Districts of the United States* (Washington: William Duane, 1802), 22-23; Department of State, *Compendium of the Enumeration of the Inhabitants and Statistics of the United States, from The Returns to the Sixth Census* (Washington: Blair and Rives, 1841), 218-223.

and South Carolina, the state became a major slaveholding province in the South. Often leading the South in the production and the sell of major staples, North Carolina developed an economy that was based on black slave labor. The transshipment of slaves to North Carolina via land routes across Virginia and South Carolina shaped the character of slavery in North Carolina in the image of those two states. To a great extent, the institution of slavery in North Carolina reflected the institutions of its northern and southern neighbors.

Slaves were concentrated in those northeastern and southeastern counties bordering, or within 100 miles or so of Virginia and South Carolina. Tobacco, cotton, and naval stores were main staples produced in these areas. Census data show that North Carolina slaveholding families owned a small number of slaves relative to slaveholding families in Virginia and South Carolina. Eighty-three percent of the slaveholding families in North Carolina only owned between 1 and 9 slaves. By 1775, slavery was a well-entrenched institution in North Carolina that most whites wanted to keep. It was for that reason that white Carolinians continued the campaign to enact legislation to allay their fears of black rebellion, and to keep their slaves on the plantation.

Notes

1. William L. Saunders, ed. *The Colonial Records of North Carolina*, 10 vols. (Raleigh: P.M. Hale, 1886-1890), 1:20-25.

2. Ibid., I:2 for Charles's first charter, and 102-103 for his second charter; William S. Powell, *North Carolina Through Centuries* (Chapel Hill and London: The University of North Carolina Press, 1989), 53-54; William S. Powell, *The Proprietors of Carolina* (Raleigh: The Carolina Charter Tercentenuary Commission), 1-5; David L. Corbitt, *The Formation of the North Carolina Counties, 1663-1943* (Raleigh: State Department of Archives and History, 1950), xii.

3. Saunders, *Colonial Records*, I:20-21; Powell, The Proprietors, 12-49. Powell included a brief biography of each of the Proprietors, and the descent of the Carolina title to their heirs. See pages 6-49.

4. William S. Powell, "Carolina in the Seventeenth Century: An Annotated Bibliography of Contemporary Publications," *North Carolina Historical Review* (January 1964): 74-104; Susan Brinn," Blacks in Colonial North Carolina, 1660-1723" (Master's thesis, University of North Carolina at Chapel Hill, 1978), 5-6. Saunders, *Colonial Records*. See the letters of the Proprietors, 43-48 and 55-56.

5. John S. Bassett, *Slavery and Servitude in the Colony of North Carolina* (Baltimore: The Friedwell Co., Printers, 1898), 17-18; Harry Roy Merrens, *Colonial North Carolina in the Eighteenth Century* (Chapel Hill: The University of North Carolina Press, 1964), 19-20. William Berkeley, Governor of Virginia, and one of the Lords Proprietors were empowered to appoint governors of Carolina, "and all other necessary officers both military and civil, and to make, enact and ordayne Lawes by and with the advise and consent of the freeman..." Saunders, *Colonial Records*, I:48-50. It would stand to reason that as governor of Virginia and a Proprietor of Carolina, Berkeley would encourage Virginians to settle in the new province.

6. For the appeal to Barbadians to settle in Carolina, see Saunders, *Colonial Records*, I:47-48 and 57-59; for the exploration of the Cape Fear River, see the same volume,

"Report of Commissioners Sent From Barbadoes To Explore the River Cape Fear, In 1663," 67-71.

7. Saunders, *Colonial Records*, I:41; Bassett, *Slavery and Servitude*, 16-17. Most of the Proprietors were not strangers to black slavery. See Peter Wood, *Black Majority: Negroes in Colonial South Carolina From 1670 through the Stono Rebellion* (New York: Alfred A. Knopf, 1974), 15, note 4; John Colleton to Peter Carteret in William S. Powell, *Ye Countie of Albemarle in Carolina: A Collection of Documents, 1664-1675* (Raleigh: State Department of Archives and History, 1959), 6-8; Susan Brinn, *Blacks in Colonial North Carolina*, 9.

8. Saunders, *Colonial Records*, I:86.

9. Ibid., I:204; Hiram H. Hilty, *Toward Freedom for All: North Carolina Quakers and Slavery* (Richmond: Friends United Press, 1984), 11.

10. Saunders, *Colonial Records*, I:204.

11. For the migration of Barbadians to Charlestown during the 1670s, see W. Robert Higgins, "The Geographical Origins of Negro Slaves Colonial South Carolina," *South Atlantic Quarterly* LXXXI (1971): 35-36; Wood, *Black Majority*, 13-34.

12. Bureau of the Census, *A Century of Population Growth: From the First Census of the United States to the twelfth, 1790-1900* (Washington: Government Printing Office, 1909), 7. Although this volume is a compilation of census data from the first census to the twelfth, it also gives census information for the colonial period, based on censuses taken by some colonies, and estimates by scholars.

13. Saunders, *Colonial Records*, I:260; Evarts B. Green and Virginia D. Harrington, *American Population Before the Federal Census of 1790* (New York: Columbia University Press, 1935), 156.

14. United States Department of Commerce, *Historical Statistics of the United States: Colonial Times to 1970* (Washington: Bureau of the Census), Series Z 1-19, Part 2, 1168.

15. Rosser H. Taylor, *Slaveholding in North Carolina: An Economic View* (Chapel Hill: University of North Carolina Press, 1926, reprint ed., New York: Negro Universities Press, 1969), 10.

16. Jeffrey Crow, *The Black Experience in Revolutionary North Carolina* (Raleigh: Department of Cultural Resources,

Division of Archives and History), 1; Brinn, *Blacks in Colonial North Carolina*, 9-10.

17. Marvin L. Michael Kay and Lorin L. Cary, "A Demographic Analysis of Colonial North Carolina with Special Emphasis upon the Slave and Black Populations," in Jeffrey Crow and Flora J. Hatley, *Black Americans in North Carolina and the South* (Chapel Hill: The University of North Carolina Press, 1985), 73; Green and Harrington, *American Population*, 156; Bassett, *Slavery and Servitude*, 20, note 1. These important sources provide demographic data for North Carolina. For South Carolina, see Wood, *Black Majority*, 144, Table I.

18. Green and Harrington, *American Population*, 156 and 173.

19. Merrens, *Colonial North Carolina*, 85-92. Merrens provided an excellent account of the naval stores production in the Cape Fear region, and the necessity of slave labor in that production. According to Merrens, North Carolina led colonial America in tar, pitch, and turpentine production. In 1768, for instance, the colony exported 60 percent of all naval stores shipped out of British North America. Also, see Taylor, *Slaveholding in North Carolina*, 10-14; and Saunders, *Colonial Records*, 431, in which Governor Burrington recorded his impressions of the "Present State and Condition of North Carolina," January 1733. For an excellent description of how tar, pitch, and turpentine were made, and how slave labor was used in the production of these naval stores, see John Brickell, *The Natural History of North Carolina* (Dublin: Printed by James Carson, 1737; reprint ed., Murfreesboro, N.C. Johnson Publishing Co., 1968), 265-67.

20. Daniel Littlefield, *Rice and Slaves: Ethnicity and the Slave Trade in Colonial South Carolina* (Baton Rouge: Louisiana State University Press, 1981), 113-14. For information on rice production in Africa, the various species of rice, and the relationship that developed between rice growing areas of Africa and South Carolina, see 74-114. Also see Wood, *Black Majority*, 35-62.

21. Merrens, *Colonial North Carolina*, 125-33. See Table 12, 126 for rice imports from North and South Carolina.

22. Most of the scholarship on the slave trade indicates that North Carolina was left out of the direct commerce in slaves from Africa and the West Indies. See Higgins, Geographical Origins," 46-47. Taylor, *Slaveholding in North Carolina*, 20-29.

23. Saunders, *Colonial Records*, 3:433.

24. Wood, *Black Majority*, 152, Table IV.

25. See Higgins, "Geographical Origins," passim.

26. Scholars who discussed the slave trade to North Carolina reached this conclusion. See Bassett, *Slavery and Servitude*, 22-24; Taylor, *Slaveholding in North Carolina*, 20-21; Elizabeth Donnan, *Documents Illustrative of the Slave Trade to the United States*, 4 vols.(Washington: Carnegie Institute of Washington, 1930-1935), 4:235-37. Because of the dearth of documents related to the slave trade to North Carolina, Donnan did not devote a section to North Carolina. See Saunders, *Colonial Records*, III:430. See the comments of Governor Burrington who wrote: "Great is the loss this Country has sustained in not being supply'd by vessels from Guinea with Negroes; in any part of the Province the People are able to pay for a ships load; but as none come directly from Africa, we are under a necessity to buy, the refuse refractory and distemper'd Negroes, brought from other Governments; It is hoped some Merchants in England will speedily furnish this Colony with Negroes, to increase the Produce and its Trade to England."

27. Kay and Cary, "A Demographic Analysis," 73.

28. Ibid., 73.

29. Ibid., 73, 81, and 85.

30. Ibid., 86.

31. It is unfortunate that we do not have sufficient data for slave imports to North Carolina. Elizabeth Donnan pointed out that the overland trade to the colony was large, "and for these there are no reports comparable to customs entries or naval officers' lists," Donnan, *Documents*, IV:235; Higgins, "Geographical Origins," and Kay and Cary, "A Demographic Analysis," are in agreement with regard to the large overland trade from Virginia and South Carolina.

32. Department of Commerce, *Historical Statistics of the United States*, 1168.

33. The Bureau of the Census has published several population summaries. I examined the microfilm and published returns for the years, 1790-1840. For 1790, see *Return of the Whole Numbers of Persons Within The Several Districts* (Philadelphia: Printed by Childs and Swaine, 1791, 52-53; Department of Commerce, *Negro Population, 1790-1915* (Washington: Government Printing Office, 1918). Hilty, *Toward Freedom for All*, 28-37.

34. Ira Berlin, *Slaves Without Masters: The Free Negro in the Antebellum South* (New York: Pantheon Books, 1974), 36-38. John Hope Franklin, *The Free Negro in North Carolina, 1790-1860* (Chapel Hill: University of North Carolina Press, 1943; reprint ed. New York: W.W. Norton & Company, Inc., 1971), 11-12.

35. Department of State, *Return of the Whole Number of Persons Within The Several Districts of The United States* (Washington: Printed by William Duane, 1802), 73-76.

36. Census data for the years 1810 to 1840 can be found in the following sources: Department of Commerce, *Negro Population, 1790-1915*, 45; Department of State, *Census for 1820* (Washington: Printed by Gales and Seaton, 1821), 24-26; U.S. Census Office, *Schedule of The Number of Persons Within the Several Districts of the United States* (Washington: Duff Green, 1832), see *Aggregate Amount of each description of persons within the District of North Carolina Corrected at the Department of State*, 90-93; *Department of State, Compendium of the Enumeration of the Inhabitants and Statistics of the United States, From The Returns of the Sixth Census* (Washington: Printed by Blair and Rives, 1841), 40-42. The published Census schedules showed that there were 6,428 slaves in Bertie County. That number, however, is incorrect (no doubt, a misprint); the correct number of slaves in Bertie County was 6,728. See the *Sixth Census of the United States, 1840: Burke County, North Carolina, Population Schedule, microfilm of National Archives manuscript copy*, North Carolina Collection, University of North Carolina Library, Chapel Hill.

37. Powell, *North Carolina Through four Centuries*, 249-50; Johnson, *Antebellum North Carolina*, 38-41; Taylor, *Slaveholding in North Carolina*, 53-55. Consult Jane T. Censer, Southwestern

Migration among North Carolina Planter Families: "The Disposition to Emigrate, *Journal of Southern History* LVII (August 1991): 407-26 for an interesting quantitative analysis of the North Carolina migration during the 1820s and 1830s.

38. Census Bureau, *A Century of Population Growth*, 135.

39. Ibid., 135-36.

40. Walter Clark, ed., *The State Records of North Carolina: Names of Heads of Families, 1790 Census* (Goldsboro: Nash Brother, Book and Job Printers, 1905), 1195, 1192, 1188, and 281.

41. Census Bureau, *A Century of Population Growth*, 136.

42. Powell, *North Carolina Through Four Centuries*, 308-27.

43. Department of State, *Return of The Whole Number of Persons in 1800*, 73-76.

44. Corbitt, *Formation of North Carolina Counties*, 62, 140, 117, 120, 239, 88, 87, and 71.

45. For a new interpretation on the importance of slave labor in western North Carolina, see John C. Inscoe, "Mountain Masters: Slaveholding in Western North Carolina," *North Carolina Historical Review* LXI (April 1984); for a more detailed account, see John C. Inscoe, *Mountain Masters, Slavery, and the Sectional Crisis in Western North Carolina* (Knoxville: The University of Tennessee Press, 1989); Edward Phifer, "Slavery in Microcosm," *Journal of Southern History* XXVIII (May 1962).

46. Department of State, *Returns of the Sixth Census*, 40-42.

47. Department of State, *Return of Whole Number of Persons in 1800*, 73-76. For cotton and tobacco producing areas in North Carolina, see Johnson, *Antebellum North Carolina*, 470.

48. Department of State, *Returns of the Sixth Census*, 40-42.

CHAPTER TWO

Slaveowners, Runaways, and
The Law

Slaveowners in North Carolina fought a constant battle to secure legislation to combat the problem of runaway slaves. Slaves who left the plantations in North Carolina robbed owners of their primary source of labor. This was especially true of slaveholders who owned only one or two slaves.[1] In addition to owners losing the runaway's labor, they also expended time and money to retrieve their valuable property. Slaveowners and North Carolina citizens, in general, were confronted with the havoc that runaways often caused. Fugitive slaves did whatever it took to survive while they were in flight. Often, this meant robbing plantations, stealing horses, cattle, chickens, vegetables from gardens—which were both consumed and sold to free blacks and whites who traded with fugitive slaves. Besides stealing, which was a misdemeanor, and the most common slave crime, runaway slaves often committed felonies. Though arson and burglary were the two most common felonious crimes committed by runaways, they also were involved in the murder of both whites and other slaves.[2]

Slaveowners suffered an enormous economic loss when their slaves absconded. Added to this were the many problems that runaway slaves presented to the community at large. The crimes they committed in an effort to survive and to avoid capture, and the fact that slaves, free blacks, and whites often harbored, enticed and persuaded slaves to abscond—forced slaveholders and non-slaveholders alike to petition the General

Assembly of North Carolina to enact legislation to deal with runaway slaves. As early as the 1690s, North Carolina was looked at by Virginians as a sanctuary for fugitive slaves. Many Virginia citizens believed that North Carolinians concealed Virginia runaways. In response to charges by the Governor and the Attorney General of Virginia that runaway servants and slaves were harbored by North Carolina citizens, Governor Henderson Walker of North Carolina wrote the two men explaining to them that "diligent enquiry" had not turned up any runaways in North Carolina. He also assured them that a law had been passed in the colony to punish individuals who sheltered runaway slaves. The law to which Governor Walker referred was passed in 1699, the same year he responded to the indictment made by the governor and the attorney general of Virginia. Under the law, citizens found guilty of harboring runaways were fined ten shillings per night and any damages that could be proved by the owner of the fugitive.[3] So, as early as 1699, the North Carolina General Assembly took measures to deal with the problem of runaway slaves. Governor Walker vowed to recommend to the "next Assembly" that stiffer legislation be enacted to prevent the mischief of harboring runaways.[4]

The 1699 statute was directed primarily at whites who concealed runaway indentured servants and slaves. The law made no reference to the penalty that runaway slaves would suffer. Custom, however, dictated that the slave would be beaten, given more duties, possibly branded, or suffer the cropping of one or both ears. It was not until 1715 that North Carolina adopted its formal slave code. Using the Virginia and South Carolina slave codes as examples, North Carolina legislators enacted a number of laws that were to govern the activities of slaves and their relationship with whites and free blacks. It was also under the 1715 code that lawmakers sought to confront the growing threat that runaway slaves posed.[5]

The first clause in the new code reaffirmed the 1699 harboring law. The penalty of ten shillings, and all costs for damages remained in effect. Legislators also established the "pass" or "ticket" system, forbidding slaves to leave the plantation without written permission from the owner or overseer. The "pass" bore the slave's name, and points of origin and destination. Slaves accompanied by a white servant were exempt from carrying a pass. Slaveowners who allowed slaves to leave the plantation without a ticket were subject to a fine of five shillings and the cost of taking up the slave, who was then regarded a runaway.[6]

To get North Carolinians involved in the return of fugitive slaves, legislators specified that owners of runaways pay a reward to citizens who apprehended slaves. Because slaves often ran long distances from their owners, lawmakers wanted to reward captors for returning slaves across rough terrain, through bad weather, and for the general expense that it required to transport a slave back to the owner. Under the 1715 law, persons apprehending runaway slaves were allowed a minimum of five shillings; additionally, the owner was to pay one shilling per mile up to ten miles and three pence a mile above ten miles. If the owner was not known or could not be found, the apprehender was to carry the runaway to the local law enforcement authorities. They then paid the catcher; and the owner, if found, had to reimburse the county for the apprehension of the slave, and he had to pay six pence per day for the slave's lodging in jail.[7]

After 1715, the North Carolina General Assembly revised the slave code several times to meet the wishes of slaveholders and other citizens who pressed for more stringent laws to govern runaway slaves. Along with the pressures from slaveowners and other North Carolina citizens, the state lawmaking body responded to the rebellious activities of slaves in other colonies, and even to the activities of slaves as far away as Haiti. Typical of the many responses to outside slave unrest was the Stono, South Carolina rebellion of September 1739. Slaves revolted in that small town located south of Charleston, and killed at least twenty whites. During the following year, the South Carolina General Assembly strengthened the colony's slave code by passing the "Negro Act."[8] In 1741, borrowing heavily from the South Carolina code, the North Carolina General Assembly put into law what had long been a custom regarding what slaves could and could not do.

A major portion of the 1741 slave code was devoted to runaway slaves. Legislators were concerned most about securing legislation that would ensure the safe return of slaves to their rightful owner; and for that reason stiff penalties were given to individuals who impeded owners in retrieving their human property. Emphasis was placed again on the reward system "for encouragement of all persons to take up Runaways." Under the new law, slaveowners were required to pay captors of runaway slaves at least seven shillings and six pence if the slave were found less than ten miles from home, and three pence per mile above ten miles. These charges were levied against the owner, or against the Church Wardens if the owner was not found. When the owner came to claim his property, he of course, was required to reimburse the Church Wardens for the reward and the expense of holding the slave in jail.[9]

A large percentage of North Carolina's colonial runaways were African born. Their facility with English was poor—many could speak no English at all.[10] The 1741 law, therefore, included a section to address the problem that these runaways presented. The sheriff of the county in which the runaway was taken up was required to write a full description of the slave, including the fugitive's height, complexion, any marks on the body, and the clothing worn by the slave. He was then to give a copy to every church in the County; church officials were to place the notice in an "open and convenient place" every Sunday for two months so that church-goers would read the notice, and with any luck, provide the sheriff with any information they might have concerning the runaway's owner. To guard against the use of slaves by law enforcement authorities, sheriffs who failed to give notice were required to pay five pounds.[11]

If the runaway was not claimed during the two month period, the constable or jailor in the town in which the slave was taken was required to send the escaped slave from constable to constable until the slave reached the public jail. The law directed that each constable could whip the runaway, administering no more than thirty-nine lashes. If the owner of the slave was not found while the fugitive was in the public jail, the sheriff—with the approval of two Justices of the Peace—was empowered to hire the slave out to any person whom he approved. The money and/or commodities from the hire of the runaway were used to pay the expense of the slave's imprisonment, and take-up and maintenance fees. Runaway slaves hired out were forced to wear an iron collar around their neck bearing the letters P.G. (Public Gaol). After the slave was delivered to the hirer, the sheriff or keeper of the jail had no legal responsibility if the slave escaped. If the owner of the slave came to claim his property, the hirer was required to return the slave to the public jail. The owner then had to pay all charges if the hiring fees were not sufficient to cover any expenses the runaway had accrued.[12]

The North Carolina legislature enacted several laws to aid slaveowners in apprehending and securing their runaway slaves. Typical of the aid were the exemptions given to sheriffs and other law enforcement authorities who were saddled with the responsibility of jailing runaways, conveying them from one constable to another, returning them to their owner, and hiring them out. They, for example, were exempted from paying county and town taxes while in office. As further encouragement for law enforcement officials to exercise their duties regarding runaways, they had free passage on ferries—both ways—when transporting fugitive slaves to jail or returning them to their owner. Besides these exemptions, the law required that two shillings and six pence be paid to the sheriff or constable for keeping a runaway slave in jail twenty-four hours; and six pence per day thereafter. An additional two shillings and six pence were also required at the time the runaway was claimed by the owner.[13]

Slaves who deserted their masters often found refuge in the swamps of eastern North Carolina. Some hid out in the woods for months and even years. Creeks in Cumberland County and marshy areas in the southeastern section of the state—especially near Wilmington—also provided temporary sanctuaries for slave runaways. By far, the largest hideout, temporary quarters, and home for thousands of runaway slaves was the Great Dismal Swamp. The Dismal Swamp, located in southeastern Virginia and northeastern North Carolina, provided shelter, food, and refuge for slaves for more than two-hundred years.[14] (See map 3)

Slave runaways established maroon societies deep inside the Swamp—an area that was virtually impenetrable. Once a runaway slave reached the Swamp, "...unless he was betrayed, it would be a matter of impossibility to catch him."[15] Slaveowners lost several hundred thousand dollars in slave property yearly to the Dismal Swamp.[16] Citizens in both Virginia and North Carolina feared venturing near or into the Dismal Swamp due to the presence

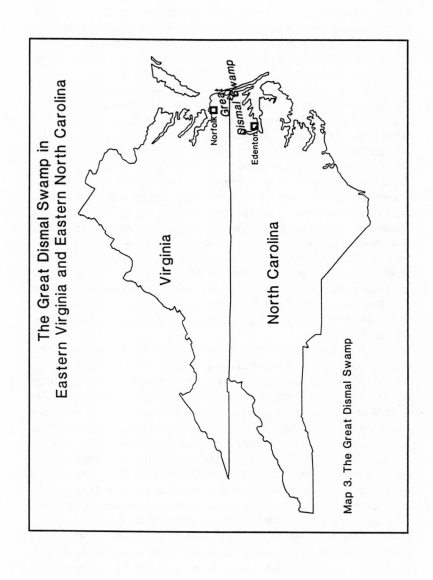

The Great Dismal Swamp in
Eastern Virginia and Eastern North Carolina

Virginia

North Carolina

Great Dismal Swamp

Norfolk

Edenton

Map 3. The Great Dismal Swamp

of so many runaway slaves. Samuel H. Perkins, an 1817 Yale College graduate, spent a year in North Carolina tutoring the children of Dr. Hugh Jones of Hyde County. Perkins chronicled his impressions of Carolinians and the South in a daily journal. An entry of February 24, 1817 revealed his fear of runaway slaves in the Dismal Swamp. While traveling from Norfolk, Virginia to Elizabeth City, North Carolina, he wrote that: "Traveling here without pistols is considered very dangerous owing to the great number of runaway Negroes. They conceal themselves in the woods & swamps by day and frequently plunder by night." Perkins went on to write that the Dismal Swamp was "inhabited almost exclusively by run away negroes, bears, wild cats & wild cattle."[17]

The Great Dismal Swamp was known throughout America as a haven for fugitive slaves. Poets and novelists wrote about it as the sanctuary for escaped slaves. Henry Wadsworth Longfellow wrote a poem that he titled, "The Slave in the Dismal Swamp." Describing what it must have been like for the runaway slave, Longfellow wrote: "In dark fens of the Dismal Swamp The hunted Negro lay; He saw the fire of the midnight camp And heard at times a horse's tramp And a bloodhounds distant bay...."[18] Harriet Beecher Stowe also wrote of the slave in the Dismal Swamp in her 1856 novel, *Dred: The Tale of the Great Dismal Swamp*, in which she described the plight of fugitive slaves there.[19]

Because runaways would "lie out hid...in the Swamps, Woods and other Obscure Places, Killing Cattle and Hogs, and committing other Injuries to the Inhabitants in this Government...," the legislature of North Carolina enacted a law to outlaw what they called "outlying" slaves.[20] Two Justices of the Peace were given the authority to issue a Proclamation demanding the slave to surrender; and the sheriff of the County in which the slave committed depredations was empowered to exhaust all means to apprehend the runaway. The law also directed the sheriff to draft a notice that was to be placed on every church door in the county. If the slave did not return immediately after the notice was issued, it was "lawful for any Person or Persons whatsoever to kill and destroy such Slave or Slaves by such Ways and Means as he or she shall think fit, without accusation or Impeachment of any crime for the same."[21]

If the runaway was killed, the owner of the slave was compensated for the value of the slave.[22]

Although outlawry legislation was initially directed at runaways who fled to the swamps, owners in piedmont North Carolina, and those who lived in areas of the state where the topography was not so hospitable to runaway slaves, outlawed their slaves as well. In an effort to make the public more cognizant of a runaway, and the fact that the slave had been outlawed, some slaveowners had the outlawry proclamation published in the local newspaper. This was not common, but the presence of the notice—sometimes beneath the advertisement for the same runaway—revealed the owner's frustration and anger with his runaway property. James Merritt of Jones County had his slave outlawed only seventeen days after he fled. The proclamation for Merritt's slave, Ellis, was typical:

> Whereas complaint upon oath hath this day
> been made to us, two of the Justices of the
> Peace, by James Merritt...that a certain
> male slave...named Ellis, hath absented
> himself from his master's service, and is
> lurking about in the county, committing
> acts of felony and other misdeeds: These are
> therefore...to command the said slave forthwith
> to surrender himself and return home to his
> master...if the said slave...doth not surrender
> himself and return home immediately...any person
> may kill and destroy the said slave, by such
> means as he or they may think fit, without
> accusation or impeachment of any crime of
> offence for so doing, and without incurring
> any penalty of forfeiture thereby.[23]

The proclamation was signed by R.M. Daniel and C.A. Hatch, two Justices in Jones County.

Because owners were compensated for the death of an outlawed slave, they sometimes offered a greater reward for the slave's head than for apprehending and returning the runaway home or confining the slave in jail. In April 1799, J.W. Bradley of New Hanover County offered ten dollars for the return of

Michael—his outlawed runaway slave—and fifty dollars if he was brought to him dead.[24]

In many cases, slaveowners threatened to outlaw their runaways. Often fugitive slaves simply lurked in their neighborhood, hid in the woods during the day, and at night, visited relatives, friends, and acquaintances. Owners were often aware of these activities, and would sometimes inform their other slaves that the runaway would be outlawed if he or she did not return home within a few days. The owner's hope was that the slave would be frightened into returning. Perkins offers an example of this "cat and mouse" game in reference to the slave Jim who absconded from his owner. Jim was purchased by Dr. Hugh Jones while he was in flight. Jones informed his slaves that Jim had been purchased by him, and that the slaves should inform the fugitive that he should come to work. Within the hour, Jim had joined Jones's other slaves at work.[25] Some advertisements placed by owners also contained the threat of outlawry.[26]

Although slaveholders were compensated for the death of their fugitives, slaves were far more valuable to their owners alive. And for that reason, masters exhausted all avenues to capture their runaways. Only as a last resort did owners actually go before two Justices to have their slaves outlawed. And if advertisements for runaway slaves who were outlawed is an indication of the practice of legally outlawing runaways, then it was an act that occurred infrequently.[27]

The 1741 slave code provided the basis for slave legislation until its demise in 1865. Portions of the 1741 code, however, were repealed, and new laws were adopted when whites in the North Carolina were alarmed by slave conspiracies in the state and abroad, and when there was a demand by slaveowners to strengthen the slave code to check the runaway problem. Twelve years after the passage of the 1741 laws, the General Assembly established a patrol system in North Carolina. The law authorized the Justices of the Peace in each county to divide their counties into districts, and to "appoint three freeholders in each district as searchers." The patrollers were empowered to search slave quarters four times a year for guns, swords, and other weapons. Patrollers who failed to perform their duties had to pay a fine of forty shillings. Patrollers, like sheriffs and jailors were exempt from paying provincial, county, and town taxes. They also did not have to serve as constable, work on the roads, serve in the militia, or as a juror.[28]

The 1753 law did not create a "true" patrol in the sense that it was empowered to retrieve runaways and to search for slaves who were off the plantation without a pass. The law did, however, serve as guide for future patrol legislation.[29] In 1775—the year the American Revolution began—many eastern counties adopted resolutions to create a more rigorous slave patrol system. This action came in response to the fear of slave insurrection. The outbreak of the war created racial tension, and the paranoia among whites that slavery in North Carolina could be undermined by black resistance. Jeffrey Crow wrote in this regard that: "The movement for Independence was unavoidably affecting the institution of slavery and the behavior of the black bondsmen."[30] The patrollers in the eastern counties of Craven, New Hanover, and Pitt were authorized to check slave passes; and in Pitt County, they could shoot slaves who had absented themselves from their owner's plantation, and would not submit to the patrollers.[31]

In 1779, the General Assembly repealed and enacted new legislation concerning the patrol. Legislators felt that the number of times that patrollers were required to search, and the sum of forty shillings for neglect of their duties, were insufficient. As a result, patrollers were required to search slave quarters once a month rather than four times a year. Additionally, patrollers were to be paid by an owner if they apprehended a slave without a pass. The captured slave was to be treated like a runaway, and patrollers were to be paid as if they had returned a runaway slave. The law also required that patrollers pay one hundred pounds if they neglected their duties.[32]

The Haitian Revolution of 1791 and slave unrest in North Carolina during the 1790s forced the General Assembly to enlarge the powers of the county patrol.[33] In 1794, the lawmaking body of the state repealed the 1779 patrol act by authorizing the Justices of the Peace in each county to appoint at least six patrollers in each district. Under the new law, patrollers were required to search for guns and other weapons at least once every two weeks. Additionally, they were empowered "to inflict a punishment, not exceeding fifteen lashes, on all slaves they may find off their owner's plantation, or travelling on the sabbath, or other unreasonable time, without a proper permit or pass."[34]

In 1802—citizens of Bertie, Camden, Currituck, Halifax, Hertford, Washington, Martin, and Warren Counties—were all alarmed by a slave conspiracy. In what appeared to be a well-organized plot, slave ministers used religious gatherings to plan the rebellion. The slaves were inspired by the Haitian Revolution, and by Prosser's Gabriel's slave conspiracy in Virginia in 1800. The conspirators planned the revolt for June 10, 1802. However, while searching slave homes in Bertie County, a patroller discovered a letter bearing the names of fourteen slaves who were possibly involved and information concerning the plot. A number of slaves were arrested, tried and convicted of conspiracy to rebel. Eleven were hanged, some of the conspirators were banished from the state, while others were beaten and their ears cropped.[35]

In November, 1802—in response to the slave conspiracy of the past summer—legislators met in Raleigh and enacted stiff legislation concerning slave conspiracy and rebellion. The lawmakers also amended the patrol act of 1794. Under the new law, each country was given full power and authority to carry out and administer its own patrol system, "...subject to such rules, regulations and restrictions as their respective county courts shall ordain and establish, and under such fines and penalties as the said court shall fix and direct."[36] The law allowed a greater degree of county and municipal autonomy over the patrol. One factor affecting the legislature's decision was the fact the slave and free black populations were concentrated in the Piedmont and eastern sections of the state, therefore greater control of the blacks was needed by county courts in this area. The degree of control varied from county to county in North Carolina, and so did the need for the patrol system.[37]

Between 1802 and 1830, counties and municipalities began enacting their own slave patrol ordinances in response to—in most cases—rumors of slave conspiracies. The most rigorous codes were passed in the eastern counties and towns where the black population was largest.[38] By 1830, North Carolinians were confronted with a number of problems, including, economic recession, which forced many planters and farmers to liquidate their holdings and move southward; they were confronted with the nullification crisis of 1828, and the challenge by abolitionists to end slavery in the United States immediately. So-called seditious literature which denounced slavery, and also urged slaves to rebel against their owners found its way into the South, and more importantly, into the hands of free blacks and literate slaves, causing discontent among slaves, and more worries for whites in their efforts to maintain discipline among their bondsmen.

David Walker, a free black, born in Wilmington on September 28, 1785 was the author of such a "seditious" work of literature. Walker, who had moved to Boston during the 1820s, and had used his literary skills by contributing articles to *Freedom's Journal*, the nation's first black-owned newspaper, published a pamphlet in September, 1829 entitled, *Appeal in Four Articles, Together with a Preamble to the Colored Citizens of the World, But in Particular, and Very Expressly to Those of the United States of America.*[39] The *Appeal*, based to a great extent in Biblical history and Christian ideals, was Walker's way of telling slaves that they were men, and that America belonged to them because..."we have enriched it with our blood and tears." He, therefore denounced the colonization of blacks in Africa, and called for slaves to rebel against their white owners.[40] David Walker's *Appeal* caused alarm throughout the South. Abolitionists and proslavers alike, denounced the pamphlet as militant propaganda designed to incite an all out servile insurrection.

The North Carolina General Assembly enacted legislation in 1830 which banned Walker's *Appeal*, and all other literature that might "excite insurrection, conspiracy or resistance in the slaves or free negroes and persons of color within the state...."[41] The penalty for bringing such literature into the state, or possessing it was imprisonment for at least a year. A second offense brought the penalty of death. The legislature also attempted to destroy the slave's ability to understand and to comprehend literature aimed at freeing him by passing a law which forbade whites and free blacks to teach slaves to read and write. Whites were required to pay a fine, while free blacks faced a fine, a jail term or thirty-nine lashes.[42]

Also in 1830, lawmakers again enlarged the powers of the patrol. They empowered each county court to set up a patrol committee, consisting of three members, to appoint as many patrollers as it deemed necessary. Patrollers still had the authority to inflict punishment upon slaves (giving them no more than thirty-nine lashes) when they caught them without a pass. They also could disperse gatherings of slaves, apprehend runaways in their respective districts, bring thieves to justice, and for the first time, they were clothed with the authority to apprehend whites who traded with slaves. The exemptions granted patrollers under previous acts remained in force, and under the new law, patrollers were to be compensated by the county.[43] In addition to the new patrol act and the law aimed at punishing citizens who taught slaves to read and to write, the North Carolina legislature enacted a number of other laws concerning slaves and free blacks. The new laws were more extensive and rigid, and the penalties for both blacks and whites were more severe.[44]

The panic and the fear of slave rebellion in North Carolina caused by Walker's *Appeal* in 1829 and 1830 were exacerbated in 1831 by Nat Turner's slave insurrection in Southampton County, Virginia. On Sunday night, August 21, 1831, Turner and six other slaves began their rebellion by killing Joseph Travis and his entire family. When the slave insurrection ended thirty-six hours later, fifty-nine whites had been killed by Turner and his comrades. Within hours of the rebellion, news had reached Hertford County, North Carolina situated just across the border from Cross Keys in Southampton County where the insurrection began. Because there was a high concentration of slaves and free blacks in the section closest to the scene of the outbreak of violence, mass trauma and panic among whites ensued in that area of the state. Whites feared that slaves in North Carolina would also rebel.[45]

Authorities in the counties in northeastern North Carolina bordering southern Virginia reacted swiftly to the revolt in Virginia by dispatching their militia, the patrol, and volunteers to aid their northern neighbor in squelching the insurrection and quelling the threat of insurgency in North Carolina. Governor Montfort Stokes of North Carolina received a number of requests from county authorities for additional arms and ammunition. The slave patrol throughout eastern North Carolina, including, the southeastern counties of Duplin, Sampson, and New Hanover also was effective in the state's effort to put down any threat of a black insurrection. Patrollers were given free reign to flog and to arrest suspected blacks. There were accounts of indiscriminate killing of blacks by the patrol and the militia throughout the eastern part of the state.[46]

The Turner revolt greatly altered the relationship between blacks and whites in North Carolina and the South. The most blatant change in the relationship was the treatment of slaves. After 1831—culminating in the North Carolina Constitutional Convention of 1835—the state enacted laws to reduce the threat of slave rebellion; and they sought to neutralize free blacks who were in the vanguard of the abolitionist struggle in the state.[47]

By 1835, the slave patrol in North Carolina had become the symbol of the day to day control and discipline of the slave population. The effectiveness of the patrol varied from community to community and from county to county. In some communities, it was powerful and effective, while in others, it was weak and ineffective. Slaveowners in some counties relied heavily on patrollers to return slaves who left their owner's plantation without a pass. This was especially so when the owner suspected that the runaway had not gone far. In advertising for his runaway slave, Rose, Christopher Dawson of Craven County stated that she could be easily apprehended by the patrollers, because undoubtedly she was lurking about the plantation on which her mother lived.[48] Many owners felt that it was a violation of their privacy for patrollers to enter slave quarters on their plantation and search for contraband. Other slaveholders refused to submit to a patroller's authority to whip their slaves; and for that reason, patrollers were often the target of law suits.[49]

Without a doubt, patrollers did deter or defer potential slave unrest. In many communities, they instilled fear in blacks because of the punishment they inflicted upon slaves—the innocent and the guilty alike. Sarah Augustus who was born a slave in Fayetteville, North Carolina stated that she had seen the "patterollers"—the name given to patrollers by the slaves—hunt runaways and had seen the slaves who had been beaten by them. Blount Baker, an ex-slave born in Wilson County, North

Carolina recalled that he had felt the whip of a patroller. And Hannah Crasson, born in Wake County, remembered that the patrollers came to her house one night while her family was singing and praying. She particularly remembered the ropes that the patrollers wore around their necks.[50]

Slaves often toyed with patrollers, sneaking past them to go to dances on other plantations. Anthony Dawson, an ex-slave, born in North Carolina in 1832 remembered a song that slaves sang about the patrollers. They sang: "Run, nigger,run, De patteroll git you! Run, nigger, run, De patteroll come! Watch, nigger, watch, De patteroll trick you! Watch, nigger, watch, He got a big gun.[51] Although the patrol system in North Carolina played an active role in attempting to control the slave population, it did not completely stymie the ability of slaves to assert their humanity, nor did it crush their desire for freedom, or totally restrict their movement.

In their efforts to secure legislation against runaways, and also against free blacks and whites who dealt with fugitive slaves, slaveowners and the lawmaking body of the state seemed most adamant and persistent in enacting laws directed at people—whether slave, free black, or white—who harbored or concealed runaways. They also fought to pass laws that convicted people who conveyed them out of the state, enticed or persuaded them to abscond, or stole runaways who had fled from their owner. Some of the stiffest legislation enacted in North Carolina regarding the problem of runaways was directed at individuals who committed these crimes. Harboring a slave meant protecting the runaway from would- be apprehenders. Conveyance legislation sought to prosecute those, especially captains of vessels, who aided runaways in leaving North Carolina, while enticement laws were directed at individuals who persuaded a slave to leave their owner. Legislation against theft of slaves received the severest penalties. Harboring runaway slaves was the most common of these crimes. Under the 1741 slave code, persons found guilty of concealing runaway slaves were required to pay a minimum of forty shillings, and five shillings more for each twelve hours the slave was harbored. Persons who refused or were unable to pay the penalty, were to be sold into servitude until the court deemed that the person's time as a servant would pay the harboring penalty.[52]

By the 1790s, it appears that the act of concealing and aiding runaways had reached a crisis in North Carolina. Believing that the penalty for harboring fugitives was not grave enough, the legislature increased the penalty to fifty pounds in 1791.[53] Court action attests to the problem that slaveholders faced with regard to people harboring their slaves. In 1792, Steven Gray of Bertie County filed suit against William Bazemore, also of Bertie County, for harboring his slave, Cato. Gray demanded two-hundred pounds from Bazemore for depriving him of his slave's work.[54] During the 1790s, Catherine Edwards of Chowan County gained a reputation as a harborer of runaway slaves, and was ordered to appear before the court in 1793.[55] In 1806, under an order of the Rockingham County court, Meredith Brown was whipped at the public whipping post for harboring a runaway slave.[56]

Newspaper advertisements for runaway slaves whom owners believed were harbored, also illustrate the problem of concealing and maintaining fugitives. A large number of slaveowners concluded their advertisement by stating that: "...all persons are forewarned from harboring" said slave, or "...whoever harbors him will be prosecuted with the utmost rigour" of the law.[57] Owners' perceptions of who harbored their slaves fell into three categories.

First of all, the slave may have been concealed by other slaves, either on a neighboring plantation, or by relatives in or outside the county. Slaves who had previous owners were believed to have been concealed on one of his or her former owner's plantations by friends, or family members.[58] Secondly, the newspaper advertisements reveal that owners believed that slaves were secreted by free blacks. Free blacks sometimes aided slaves in absconding, and also provided shelter and protection from the slave's owner and law enforcement authorities. There were cases in which the free wife or the free husband gave refuge to their runaway slave spouse—in some instances for years.[59] And finally, slaveowners were aware that slaves were sheltered by whites. They sometimes referred to these individuals as the "lower order," of white people or what Bill Cecil-Fronsman called "common whites." John Buie's notice for Hannah typified the feelings of some owners. Hannah escaped from Buie in the spring of 1838. On April 25, 1838, his advertisement appeared in the *Fayetteville Observer*. He wrote that Hannah had run to Robeson County on a previous departure and had "lived there among the free colored people a considerable time, and she has also lived among, and has been employed and entertained by some of the lower order of white people in that County during the last Winter and Spring."[60]

Owners frowned most on white concealment of their property. Whites who harbored runaways did so for a variety of reasons. Many whites maintained fugitive slaves until they could make their escape on board a northern bound vessel. In other cases, these were people who abhorred slavery, and the aid given to runaways was their way of striking out at the institution. There also were cases in which whites harbored slave runaways for no other reason than to use their service, while some whites allowed fugitives to stay on their plantation because the slave's spouse was there. Still, other whites harbored runaways long enough to sell them.[61]

Coastal towns often provided sanctuary for fugitive slaves. Runaways from the countryside sometimes found refuge among the slaves and the free blacks in town. There was a dramatic increase in the free black and slave populations in towns, such as, Wilmington, New Bern, and Edenton between 1800 and 1840. In 1800, there were 752 blacks in Edenton in a total population of 1,302. These free blacks and slaves made up 57.7% of the population. At the same time Wilmington had a total population of 1,689 of whom 1,144 or 67.7% were free blacks and slaves. In Newbern, there were 1,442 free blacks and slaves in a total population of 2,467. They made up nearly 60% of the population. By 1840, there were 2,816 free blacks and slaves in Wilmington in a total population of 4,744. Blacks comprised 59.3% of the total population. In the same year, blacks in New Bern made up 54.2% of the total population which had grown to 3,690. The presence of large numbers of blacks in these towns afforded runaways the opportunity to blend into the population, and sometimes even find employment.[62] All three towns gained reputations as safe "havens" and "asylums" for slave runaways[63] (see map 4).

When an owner believed his slave was harbored, he usually offered a reward for information leading to the arrest and the

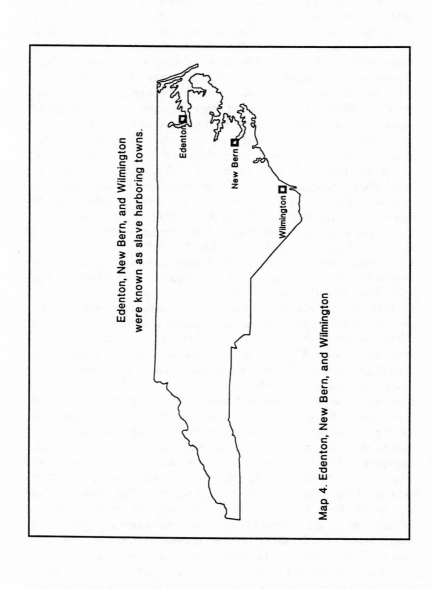

Edenton, New Bern, and Wilmington were known as slave harboring towns.

Map 4. Edenton, New Bern, and Wilmington

conviction of the guilty party. This was in addition to the reward for apprehending the runaway, and the expenses required by law. Some masters offered this reward based on who harbored the slave. Benjamin Smith of New Hanover County, for instance, offered a reward of ten dollars for the apprehension of his runaway slave, Toney. Additionally, he offered fifteen dollars if Toney were harbored by slaves, and twenty dollars if free blacks concealed him.[64] Owners were willing to pay even more if the slave was secreted by whites. T. Cowan, also of New Hanover County, was willing to pay fifty dollars if it could be proved that a white person harbored his slave Randall.[65]

People who harbored slaves—both black and white—made life easier for runaways. They aided them in depriving owners of their labor, and they helped to incur an expense that slaveowners felt was entirely unnecessary. Because the longer the slave was out, the more money the master had to pay to retrieve his valuable property. As a result, owners of slave runaways exhausted all means to prosecute those who harbored their slaves, and the additional reward served as an incentive to citizens to provide information about those who harbored, maintained, and gave aid to fugitives.[66]

Slaveowners who lived in the coastal counties of North Carolina were particularly concerned about their runaway slaves boarding a vessel and then being harbored by the ship's captain, or employees of the vessel. Moreover, they feared that masters of vessels would convey their property out of the state, increasing the chance that the slave would never be apprehended. In 1791, the General Assembly confronted this problem by enacting legislation penalizing persons who harbored slaves on their ship. Slaves were not to board vessels without a pass from their master, mistress, or Justice of the Peace. These restrictions applied to the hours between sunset and sunrise, and on Sunday. Ships that landed in Wilmington, New Bern, Edenton, and other coastal towns were usually commanded by men from other states and foreign countries. They would often give refuge to runaway slaves by employing them, and also carrying them off.[67]

The extent to which owners of slaves and legislators viewed harboring and conveyance by shipowners bound out of the state culminated in the passage of more legislation in 1792. To prevent the "iniquitous" practice—the term used by the General Assembly—of taking fugitive slaves out of the state, lawmakers made it a crime punishable by death, without benefit of clergy.[68] Slaveowners in the eastern part of the state who advertised for their escaped slaves often ended their advertisement with a warning to ship captains not to harbor, employ, or convey their property out of the state. James Lewis's advertisement was typical. He wrote: "Masters of vessels and others are cautioned at their peril, from harboring, employing, or taking off said fellow, as the law in such cases provided will be enforced against them."[69] Samuel Noble of Wilmington warned captains and their crews not to conceal his two male runaways, Jack and Peter, as the law against such a "pernicious" act would be rigidly enforced.[70]

In addition to warning masters of vessels not to conceal and carry off fugitives, some owners pointed out in their notices that their runaways had probably boarded a vessel, or were making their way to one of the seaport towns in the state to conceal themselves on a ship that was leaving the state. Edward B. Dudley, governor of North Carolina from 1836 to 1841, showed his disgust with ship captains who would carry slaves out of the state to freedom. Advertising in a Wilmington newspaper, Dudley wrote that one of his slaves had been taken to Boston by a ship captain.   Outraged, he offered the almost unheard sum of $1,000.00 for the return of the slave and the conviction of the captain.[71] And John Work of Iredell County pointed out that because his slave Frank had often threatened to leave the state by ship, he was certain the runaway was probably headed for Fayetteville or Wilmington to get aboard some ship.[72]

Other owners expressed their disillusion with the practice by ship captains of concealing and carrying off runaways. Stephen McDowell of Bertie County hired a slave catcher, and instructed one of his other slaves to assist the man in apprehending his slave Jim. The runaway's mother lived below Edenton, and McDowell feared that Jim would lurk about the town until he could board a vessel to leave the state.[73] John Gray Blount, the popular planter in eastern North Carolina demanded compensation for his runaway slave who was taken to Boston aboard a ship.[74] Litigation concerning the problem of conveyance by captains never reached the point that it did for harboring by North Carolina citizens, but there are several cases in which persons were sentenced to death for carrying off slaves.[75]

Runaway slaves in North Carolina fled from their owners for a variety of reasons, and in most instances, they ran away of their own volition. However, there were times when slaves were enticed, seduced, or persuaded to abscond by other slaves, by free blacks, and by whites. To discourage this act, the legislature enacted a law in 1741 which imposed a fine of twenty pounds. Persons who were unable to pay the penalty were required to serve the owner of the enticed slave or slaves for five years.[76] Blacks obviously enticed other slaves to run for companionship while in flight, or the fact that the slave was a friend or family member. Whites on the other hand persuaded and seduced slaves to run for the sake of selling them, freeing them, or using them for their own purpose.[77]

Worse than harboring, conveying, or enticing slaves to leave their master, was the act of stealing and selling another man's runaway slave. It was a problem as old as slavery itself in North Carolina. Knowledge that a slave was a runaway, and to take advantage of that situation, infuriated North Carolina slaveowners. There are reports of theft rings that stole, sold, and restole and resold runaway slaves. The law was especially stringent for citizens who committed the act of stealing slaves. Effective April 1, 1779, anyone convicted of stealing a slave was "judged guilty of Felony and shall suffer death without benefit of Clergy."[78]

After 1779, the courts in North Carolina were inundated with lawsuits filed by slaveowners against men who stole and sold runaway slaves. The North Carolina Supreme Court upheld Anson County Superior Court's conviction, and the sentence of death for William May. May was convicted of stealing a slave, and selling him in South Carolina.[79] William P. Moore advertised in the *American Recorder* that his slave, Jack Battle had left him on November 5, 1815. Sometime later, Moore obtained information that Battle had been taken while he was in flight by Benjamin and Samuel Sparrow. Their intention was to sell Battle. Moore filed suit against the two men, and both were eventually found guilty of stealing Battle.[80]

Slaveowners sometimes did not know if their slaves fled on their own, or if they had been stolen. For that reason—in advertising for their slaves—many owners indicated that their slaves had absconded or had been stolen. J. Benton placed an advertisement in the newspaper for four slaves of Edgecombe County whom he believed had been stolen. He wrote: "Stolen or Runaway the 30th of last month Four Negroes belonging to the Estate of Thomas Howerton...Sarah and three children, Sarah, Tilly and Ascension...It is believed the negroes were stolen by a man named Joseph Horn...If stolen $50 will be given for the apprehension and conviction of the thief." In addition, he offered twenty-five dollars for the capture of Sarah and her three children.[81] John Sommerville of Granville County had reason to believe that his three male slaves, Augustine, Little Tom, and Duke were carried off and sold. Sommerville offered a reward of 200 dollars for the conviction of the thief.[82]

Flight by slaves into other colonies before 1787 was a serious concern of slaveowners. After 1775, several northern colonies abolished slavery, or drafted proposals of gradual emancipation. Slaves who ran to Pennsylvania, Rhode Island, and Massachusetts, for example, often found refuge and freedom there. Slaveowners in the South obviously desired legal means by which to obtain their runaway slaves once they had entered free territory. Slaveholders throughout the South received the proverbial "shot in the arm" when delegates representing the thirteen colonies met in Philadelphia in 1787 to draft the Federal Constitution.

Delegates assembled at the Constitutional Convention, which met between May and September, 1787, were confronted with a number of issues involving slavery in the United States, and among these was the problem of fugitive slaves. The North Carolina delegation to the Convention was selected in January 1787. Two of the appointed delegates, however, were replaced by other men because of health or their simple refusal to serve.[83] The delegates who represented North Carolina, William R. Davie, Richard Dobbs Spaight, Alexander Martin, Hugh Williamson, and Richard Blount, like other delegates to the Convention were educated, politically active, and well-to-do financially. All but one man, Hugh Williamson, owned a considerable number of slaves. Spaight led the group in slave ownership with seventy-one.[84] Because of the money tied up in slaves, and the expenses that recapturing fugitive slaves entailed, it is not difficult to understand why North Carolina delegates, and Southern delegates as a whole, sought to secure a fugitive slave clause in the Federal Constitution.

Debate over the issue began in late August 1787 with Pierce Butler of South Carolina introducing a provision to secure the return of fugitive slaves who escaped from one state to another. It mandated that runaway slaves would be delivered, upon claim, to their owner. After little opposition by northern delegates, the proposition was passed unanimously.[85] The final draft which became Article IV, Section 2 in the revised draft of the Constitution read as follows: "No person legally held to service or labor in one state, escaping into another, shall, in consequence of regulations subsisting therein, be discharged from such service or labor, but shall be delivered up, on claim of the party to whom such service or labor may be due."[86] The insertion of this clause in the Federal Constitution was significant for a number of reasons. First, southerners could argue that the United States Constitution recognized the institution of slavery, and that it defended the right of slaveowners to their chattel property. Secondly, it meant that slaveowners could legally track down their runaway slaves to the far corners of the United States—the laws in any state notwithstanding.[87]

Though there was the initial hope among slaveowners that the insertion of the fugitive slave clause in the Federal Constitution would prove effective in the wholesale return of runaway slaves, they soon realized that "the provision of the Constitution remained unexecuted."[88] For that reason, the United States Congress enacted the first Federal Fugitive Slave Law in 1793. Passed in accordance with a "Fugitives Form Justice Law," the Fugitive Slave Law went beyond the stipulations of the fugitive slave clause in the Constitution. It empowered a judge or magistrate in the state or territory to which the slave ran, to give a certificate to the claimant of the slave "for removing the said fugitive from labour, to the state or territory from which he or she fled." In addition, Congress imposed a $500 fine on persons who hindered the arrest of runaways, and who harbored and concealed fugitives.[89]

The law of 1793 served the nation until 1850. Because northern citizens often did not cooperate in aiding slaveowners in capturing their runaway slaves, and sometimes harbored and protected slaves in flight, several attempts were made between 1793 and 1849 by southern Congressmen to strengthen the 1793 law.[90] Proposals for more severe national legislation meant that slaves from North Carolina and throughout the South were finding refuge and freedom in the northern states. Additionally, many whites and free blacks in the North harbored runaway slaves, and provided aid to them in their quest to be free of the shackles of slavery.

By 1840, slaveholders in North Carolina had secured a corpus of state legislation to aid them in the prevention of slave flight. They also were successful in getting legislation to help them apprehend their slaves once they had fled. The task of retrieving their runaway slaves was oftentimes made more difficult because slaves, free blacks, and whites aided slaves while they were in flight. It was because of this that the General Assembly sought to punish individuals who harbored, sheltered, and maintained fugitive slaves. Enticing and stealing runaways also brought stiff penalties. The court dockets in North Carolina were filled with cases that involved the these crimes. The legislature granted exemptions to law enforcement officers in their quest to transport runaway slaves to jail, and to their owners. Slaveowners also were successful in getting outlawry legislation passed to frighten slaves into returning home. Southern Congressmen fought bitterly to secure federal fugitive slave legislation. Although there was a large body of laws in North Carolina to address the problem of flight by slaves, slaveowners "never seemed altogether satisfied with the results of the laws which were enacted at their behest," suggesting that legislation alone would not completely deter or crush the spirit of slaves to escape the horrors of slavery.[91]

Notes

1. See the advertisement in *The Star*, May 31, 1811 by Paul Karriker of Cabarrus County for his runaway slave, Simon. Karriker stated that Simon was his only slave and that he had spent a large sum of money and had gone to a lot of trouble to apprehend his fugitive slave. See chapter I, 9-10 for the average number of slaves held by North Carolina slaveholders and the percentage of slaveholders owning one slave.

2. See for example The *State v. Moses* in Thomas P. Devereux, *Cases Argued and Determined in the Supreme Court of North Carolina From December Term, 1826 To June Term, 1826* (Raleigh: Gales and Son, 4 volumes, 1829), I, 360-63.

3. Governor Henderson Walker to Governor Francis Nicholson, in Saunders, *Colonial Records*, I, 512-15. Also see Attorney General Bartholomew Farlow's letter in which he responded to the governor's letter, 515. A number of scholars have attempted to vindicate North Carolina's reputation as a harborer of runaway slaves, servants, and even people who were fleeing from justice in Virginia and in South Carolina. For that discussion, see Hugo P. Leaming, "Hidden Americans: Maroons of Virginia and the Carolinas" (unpublished doctoral dissertation, 2 volumes, University of Illinois at Chicago Circle, 1979), I, 131-62. See also Gerald Mullin, *Flight and Rebellion: Slave Resistance in Eighteenth-Century Virginia* (New York: Oxford University Press, 1972), 110-12.

4. Ibid., 514.

5. For the Virginia slave code, see William D. Hening, ed., *The Statutes at Large, Being a Collection of All the Laws of Virginia* (Philadelphia: Printed by Thomas DeSilver, 1823). For the South Carolina slave code, see Thomas Cooper and David J. McCord, eds., *The Statutes at Large of South Carolina* (Columbia: Printed by A.S. Johnston, 1840). For a fine discussion on the impact of the Virginia and South Carolina codes, see Katherine Ann McGeachy, "The North Carolina Slave Code" (unpublished Master's thesis, University of North Carolina at Chapel Hill, 1948), 5-6. See also, Benjamin F. Callahan, "The North Carolina Slave Patrol" (unpublished Master's thesis, University of North Carolina at Chapel Hill, 1973), 3, 6; and Elsa V. Goveia, "The West Indian Slave Laws of the Eighteenth

Century'" in Laura Foner and Eugene O. Genovese, eds., *Slavery in the New World: A Reader in Comparative History* (Englewood Cliffs, N.J.: Prentice-Hall, Inc., 1969), 113-37.

6. Clark, *State Records*, XXIII, 63.

7. Ibid., 63-64.

8. One of the best accounts of the Stono Rebellion of 1739 is in Wood, *Black Majority*, 308-26. Wood pointed out that the 1740 Negro Act was means by which South Carolinians attempted to control the black majority population in South Carolina. See especially, 324-25.

9. Clark, *State Records*, XXIII, 197-98.

10. Ibid., 198. See also, Marvin L. Michael Kay and Lorin Lee Cary, "Slave Runaways in Colonial North Carolina, 1748-1775," *North Carolina Historical Review* I (January 1986): 20-22.

11. Clark, *State Records*, XXIII, 198-99.

12. Ibid., 198-99.

13. Ibid., 200.

14. During the colonial era, the Dismal Swamp covered about 2,200 square miles. Drainage over the years has reduced its size to 750 square miles (by 1939). The swamp's northern border lies south of Norfolk, Virginia and is contained by Norfolk and Nansemond Counties in Virginia and Currituck, Camden, Pasquotank, and Gates Counties in North Carolina. George Washington and five other men formed the Dismal Swamp Land Company in 1764 to drain the swamp to dig a canal. The company also cut and sold the fine timbers that the swamp contained. In 1787, the Virginia General Assembly authorized the digging of the canal, and three years later, the legislature of North Carolina authorized the dig on its side. In 1793, black slaves began digging the canal, which lasted through the 1820s. See the *Dismal Swamp Land Papers*, Manuscript Department, Duke University Library, Durham, North Carolina. For excellent descriptions, histories, and general information about the Great Dismal Swamp, see the following: Arthur M. Schlesinger, ed., Frederick Law Olmsted, *The Cotton Kingdom* (New York: Random House, 1984), 121-22; The Federal Writers'Project of the Federal Works Agency: Works Projects Administration, *North Carolina: A Guide to the Old North State* (Chapel Hill: The University of North Carolina Press, 1939), 275-77; Alexander Crosby Brown, *The Dismal Swamp Canal* (Chesapeake, Virginia:

Norfolk County Historical Society, 1970; for a concise description of the origin of the canal and interest in the Dismal Swamp as a profitable venture, see Crosby's article, "The Dismal Swamp Canal," *The American Neptune* IV (July, 1945): 203-21; a romanticized view, but an excellent account of the fauna, flora, wildlife, and seasonal changes can be found in Charles F. Stansbury, *The Lake of the Great Dismal* (New York: Albert and Charles Boni, 1924), 4-5. Scholarly examples are Herbert Aptheker," Maroons Within the Present Limits of the United States," *Journal of Negro History* XXIV (April 1939): 167-84; Mullin, *Flight and Rebellion*; Leaming, "Hidden Maroons"; Crow, *The Black Experience in Revolutionary North Carolina*, 41-42; Marion G. McDougall, *Fugitive Slaves, 1619-1865* (Boston: Published by Ginn and Company, 1891), 57. For a discussion on maroons in the Western Hemisphere, see Richard Price, ed., *Maroon Societies: Rebel Slave Communities in the Americas* (Garden City, New York: Anchor Press/Doubleday, 1973).

15. Robert Arnold, *The Dismal Swamp and Lake Drummond: Early Recollections, With Vivid Portrayals of Amusing Scenes* (Norfolk: Evening Telegram Print, 1888; Murfreesboro, North Carolina: Johnson Publishing Company, 1968), 6.

16. Robert C. McLean, ed., "A Yankee Tutor in the Old South," *North Carolina Historical Review* XLVII (January 1970): 56, n. 22.

17. Ibid., 56.

18. *The Complete Poetical Works of Henry W. Longfellow* (Boston: Houghton Mifflin Company, 1902), 26-27.

19. Harriet Beecher Stowe, *Dred: Tale of the Great Dismal Swamp* (Boston: Phillips, Sampson and Company, 2 volumes, 1856).

20. Clark, *State Records*, XXIII, 201.

21. Ibid,. 202.

22. The amount paid to the owner of the slave varied over the years. During the Colonial days, owners were given the market value of the slave. By the 1790s (at least in some counties) owners were given two-thirds the value of the slave. See Henry Potter and others, eds., *Laws of the State of North Carolina* (Raleigh: Printed by J. Gales, 2 volumes, 1821), II, 828.

23. *New Bern Spectator*, July 10, 1830.

24. *Wilmington Gazette*, April 19, 1799; *Carolina Centinel*, March 18, 1820.

25. McLean, "A Yankee Tutor," 62.

26. See for example the *Wilmington Gazette*, October 2, 1813 for the slave Abram; the notice for Simpson's slave is in the same newspaper, January 13, 1816. Also see the dates October 14, 1801 and January 27, 1807; *People's Press*, September 25, 1835. For examples in which owners outlawed their slave, see the *North Carolina Gazette*, March 24, 1775 for the slaves Jack and Adam, and May 5, 1775 for the slave Jem; *Hall's Wilmington Gazette*, February 9, 1797 and March 8, 1798; *Cape Fear Recorder*, April 5, 1817 and April 14, 1821.

27. McLean, "A Yankee Tutor," 62-63. Perkins maintained that instances of outlawed slaves being killed were rare.

28. John Haywood, *A Revisal of all the Public Acts of the State of North Carolina and of the State of Tennessee* (Nashville: Printed by Thomas Bradford, 1810), 62-63.

29. Callahan, "North Carolina Slave Patrol," 8.

30. Jeffrey J. Crow, "Slave Rebelliousness and Social Conflict in North Carolina, 1775 to 1802," *William and Mary Quarterly* (January 1981): 82. This is an excellent analysis of the racial conflicts generated by the Revolution. Crow also showed that the Insurrection Scare of 1802 was the culmination of these conflicts. For an even more thorough analysis, see Sylvia Frey, *Water from the Rock: Black Resistance in a Revolutionary Age* (Princeton: Princeton University Press, 1991), chapter 2 especially. Also see Robert A. Olwell, "'Domestick Enemies,': Slavery and Political Independence in South Carolina, May 1775-March 1776," *Journal of Southern History* 55 (1989): 21-48.

31. Callahan, "North Carolina Slave Patrol," 9.

32. Clark, *State Records*, XXIV, 276.

33. Crow, "Slave Rebelliousness and Social Conflict"; Herbert Aptheker, *American Negro Slave Revolts* (New York: Columbia University Press, 1943).

34. Potter and others, *Laws of the State of North Carolina*, I, 741-742.

35. See the *Raleigh Register*, June 22, 1802, July 6, 1802, and July 27, 1802. Also see the *Bertie County Slave Papers, 1744-1815*, North Carolina Division of Archives and History, Raleigh, North Carolina; and Johnson, *Antebellum North*

Carolina, 510-13; Crow, "Slave Rebelliousness and Social Conflict," 94-102. One of the latest discussions on the Prosser conspiracy in Virginia is Douglas R. Egerton, "Gabriel's Conspiracy and the Election of 1800," *Journal of Southern History* (May 1990): 191-214.

36. Potter and others, *Laws of the State of North Carolina*, II, 975-976.

37. Callahan, "North Carolina Slave Patrol," 14-15.

38. Ibid,. 15-17.

39. Walker's Appeal was published in three editions. Walker made changes and pledged that the third edition would be his last. Two fine edited versions with introductions are David Walker, *David Walker's Appeal in Four Articles; Together with a Preamble to the Coloured Citizens of the World, But in Particular, and Very Expressly, to Those of the United States of America*, edited by Charles M. Wiltse (New York: Hill and Wang, 1965); and David Walker, *Walker's Appeal: An Address to the Slaves of the United States of America*, edited by William Loren Katz (New York: Arno Press and the New York Times, 1969). For a discussion on the impact of the Appeal, Derris Lea Raper, "The Effects of David Walker's Appeal and Nat Turner's Insurrection on North Carolina" (unpublished Master's thesis, University of North Carolina at Chapel Hill, 1969), 19-43. See also, Clement Eaton, A Dangerous Pamphlet in the Old South," *The Journal of Southern History* (August 1936); and Callahan, "North Carolina Slave Patrol," 26-31.

40. Wiltse, *David Walker's Appeal*, 25.

41. James Iredell and William H. Battle, *The Revised Statutes of the State of North Carolina* (Raleigh: Turner and Hughes, 2 volumes, 1837), I, 194.

42. Ibid,. 209.

43. Ibid., 458-459.

44. Most of the new laws can be found in Iredell and Battle, *Revised Statutes*, I, 571-92.

45. Charles Edward Morris, "Panic and Reprisal: Reaction in North Carolina to the Nat Turner Insurrection, 1831," *North Carolina Historical Review* (May 1985): 30. The information on the Turner Rebellion was drawn from a number of sources. See For example, F. Roy Johnson, *The Nat Turner Story* (Murfreesboro, North Carolina: Johnson Publishing Company,

1970); Herbert Aptheker, *Nat Turner's Slave Rebellion* (New York: Humanities Press, 1966); one of the first accounts is William S. Drewry, *The Southampton Insurrection* (Washington: The Neale Company, 1900; Murfreesboro, North Carolina: Johnson Publishing Company, 1968); Raper, "The Effects of Walker's Appeal and Turner's Insurrection on North Carolina"; and Stephen B. Oates, *The Fires of Jubilee: Nat Turner's Fierce Rebellion* (New York: Harper and Row, 1975; Mentor Books, 1976).

46. The white reaction to Turner's Rebellion is summed up in Morris, "Panic and Reprisal," 41-42. One black was even roasted in Duplin County. No accurate count exists for the number of blacks who were whipped, harassed, and killed due to white fears that blacks in their area were planning a rebellion. See also Raper, "The Effects of Walker's Appeal and Turner's Insurrection on North Carolina," for the white reaction and the indiscriminate killing of blacks.

47. For the slave laws and the legislation affecting free blacks passed after 1831, see Bartholomew F. Moore and Asa Biggs, *Revised Code of North Carolina* (Boston: Little, Brown and Company, 1855), 563-80. In 1835, North Carolina held a Constitutional Convention to study its fifty-nine year-old Constitution, and to make amendments. Meeting in Raleigh in June and July of 1835, Convention members stripped free blacks of the suffrage. For the debate on the amendment to abrogate the voting of free blacks, see *Proceedings and Debates of the Convention of North Carolina, Called to Amend The Constitution of the State, Which Assembled at Raleigh, June 4, 1835* (Raleigh: J. Gales and Son, 1836), 351-58. For a summary of amendments and the readings of the proposed amendment, see *Journal of the Convention, Called By the Freeman of North Carolina, to Amend The Constitution of the State, Which Assembled In the City of Raleigh, on the 4th of June, 1835* (Raleigh: J. Gales and Son, 1835, 73-75. A discussion on the debate to disfranchise free blacks can be found in Harold J. Counihan, "The North Carolina Constitutional Convention of 1835: A Study In Jacksonian Democracy," *North Carolina Historical Review* XLVI (October 1969): 346-48; and Franklin, *The Free Negro in North Carolina*, 109-17.

48. *Carolina Centinel*, June 16, 1821.

49. See for example, the case of *Richardson v. Saltar and others*, 1817 in J.L. Taylor, *Cases Adjudged in the Supreme Court of N. Carolina From July Term 1816, to January Term 1818, inclusive* (Raleigh: J. Gales, 1818), 68-70. Saltar, a patroller and the defendant in this case whipped a slave, whom he said did not have a valid pass. The judge in a lower court found Saltar and the men with him (who were not patrollers) guilty of trespassing. The North Carolina Supreme Court affirmed the lower court's decision, adding that the patrol act of 1794 state that only a majority of patrollers present possessed the power to administer punishment to a slave. See also the 1821 case of *Tate v. O'Neal* in Burke County, in Thomas Ruffin and Francis L. Hawks, *Reports of Cases Argued and Adjudged in The Supreme Court of North Carolina, During the Years 1820 and 1821* (Raleigh: Printed by J. Gales and Son, 1823), 418-20; and James Iredell, *Reports of Cases at Law, Argued and Determined in The Supreme Court of North Carolina, From December Term, 1845, To June Term, 1846, Both* (Raleigh: Published by Weston R. Gales, 6 volumes, 1846), 11-14. See also Helen T. Catterall, ed., *Judicial Cases Concerning American Slavery and the Negro* (Washington: Carnegie Institute of Washington, 4 volumes, 1929), II, 139-41.

50. George P. Rawick, ed., *The American Slave: A Composite Autobiography: North Carolina Narratives* (Westport, Conn.: Greenwood Publishing Company, 19 volumes, 1972), XIV, Part I, 52, 64, and 190.

51. Rawick, *The American Slave*, I, 62. The volume is Rawick's introductory one entitled, *From Sundown to Sunup: The Making of the Black Community*.

52. Clark, *State Records*, XXIII, 196-97.

53. Potter and others, *Laws of the State of North Carolina*, I, 654.

54. *Bertie County Slave Papers, 1744 to 1815*, North Carolina Division of Archives and History, Raleigh, North Carolina.

55. *Chowan County Slave Records, Criminal Action Concerning Slaves, 1767-1829*, North Carolina Division of Archives and History, Raleigh, North Carolina.

56. Anselm Anthony to Robert Menzies, September 10, 1806, in *Robert Menzies Papers*, Manuscript Department, Duke University Library, Durham, North Carolina.

57. See for example the *North Carolina Journal*, January 1, 1794, July 16,1794, and May 1, 1797; *Hall's Wilmington Gazette*, March 23, 1797, and April 20, 1797; *North Carolina Gazette, or Impartial Intelligencer, and Weekly Advertiser*, June 4, 1791 and September 24, 1791; *The Carolina Federal Republican*, April 16, 1810 and January 4, 1812; *Hillsborough Recorder*, May 14, 1828; and *Miner's and Farmer's Journal*, October 18, 1834.

58. See the following newspaper advertisements for runaway slaves who were harbored by other slaves, including, family members: *North Carolina Gazette*, May 5, 1775 and January 16, 1778; *North Carolina Gazette, or Impartial Intelligencer*, August 5, 1797; *Newbern Gazette*, August 15, 1800; *True Republican or American Whig*, June 20, 1809; *Carolina Federal Republican*, August 24 1816; *Cape Fear Recorder*, June 10,1816, and January 30, 1819; *Western Carolinian*, April 29, 1823; *Free Press*, October 16, 1829; *Edenton Gazette*, September 2, 1830; and the advertisement for Harry who was harbored in Perquimans County by his mother and father for a year, *Elizabeth City Star and North Carolina Eastern Intelligencer*, May 27, 1826.

59. For example of runaways who were concealed by free blacks, see *Newbern Gazette*, August 15, 1800; *Raleigh Register*, August 20, 1824; *Free Press*, August 22, 1826 and August 29, 1826.

60. Bill Cecil-Fronsman, *Common Whites: Class and Culture in Antebellum North Carolina* (Lexington: The University Press of Kentucky, 1992), 88-89. The notice for Hannah is in the *Fayetteville Observer*, April 25, 1838. Other examples can be found in the *North Carolina Journal*, September 27, 1837; *North Carolina Standard*, August 19, 1840.

61. The following are newspaper advertisements by slaveowners who believed their slaves were concealed by whites: *Raleigh Register*, February 10, 1801, January 18, 1803, and January 16, 1824; *North Carolina Minerva*, June 16, 1798; *Cape Fear Recorder*, July 31, 1819; *The Star*, April 7, 1815, October 20, 1820 and July 7, 1836; *North Carolina Journal*, June 4, 1810.

62. See *Return of the Whole Number of Persons, 1800*, 73-76. See *Compendium of the Enumeration of the Inhabitants and Statistics of the United States*, 1840, 41-42.

63. In advertising for his runaway slave in 1827, Baker Hoskins stated that Edenton was noted for concealing runaway slaves. He believed that his slave was lurking about Edenton; see the *Edenton Gazette*, May 8, 1827. In an advertisement for his slave Demar, Samuel Ashe commented that Wilmington had become an asylum for runaways; see the *True Republican or American Whig*, May 23, 1809. Hundred of notices for runaways pointed out that slaves were lurking or being protected in these towns.

64. Smith also pledged fifty dollars to the person who proved that Toney was harbored aboard a vessel, see *Hall's Wilmington Gazette*, April 20, 1797.

65. *People's Press*, April 20, 1797.

66. Slaveowners usually were willing to pay more for information leading to the conviction of a harborer, than for the apprehension of the slave. Runaway advertisements are replete with this trend in rewarding persons who helped in the apprehension of individuals who secreted and maintained fugitive slaves. See for example, the *Wilmington Gazette*, June 13, 1799 for the slaves Larry and Jimmy, advertised by Benjamin Smith and William Magill, respectively. Also *Wilmington Gazette*, March 6, 1800, December 10, 1801, and January 8, 1805; *Cape Fear Recorder*, January 30, 1819; *People's Press*, November 12, 1834 and November 26, 1834; *Newbern Gazette*, August 15, 1800; *Hillsborough Recorder*, April 9, 1828, and the *Edenton Gazette*, April 20, 1810.

67. Potter and others, *Laws of the State of North Carolina*, I, 653. Also see, Alan D. Watson, *Wilmington: Port of North Carolina* (Columbia: University of South Carolina Press, 1992), 58-59

68. Ibid., I, 684-85.

69. *True Republican and New Bern Weekly Advertiser*, August 8, 1810.

70. *True Republican or American Whig*, April 18, 1809. For other examples, see *True Republican and New Bern Weekly Advertiser*, October 24, 1810 and November 21, 1810; *New Bern Herald*, May 13, 1809 and April 29, 1810; *Carolina Centinel*,

June 27, 1818, July 25, 1818, September 19, 1818, October 3, 1818, February 27, 1819, and August 5, 1820; *Edenton Gazette*, February 26, 1806, September 17, 1807, and February 10, 1808; and the *Cape Fear Recorder*, December 24, 1828; *The Star and North Carolina Gazette*, January 31, 1838; *Washington Whig*, February 6, 1838; *Roanoke Advocate*, July 29, 1840.

71. Governor Dudley's notice is in the *People's Press and Wilmington Advertiser*, February 2, 1838. Other examples can be found in the following: *Wilmington Centinel and General Advertiser*, June 18, 1788; *People's Press and Wilmington Advertiser*, May 11, 1838, May 18, 1838, May 25, 1838, and October 19, 1838.

72. *North Carolina Chronicle; or Fayetteville Gazette*, November 1, 1790. For other examples, see the *North Carolina Gazette or Impartial Intelligencer*, March 23, 1793 and June 14, 1794 for Mundean who nearly made his escape in a ship, and May 14, 1796 for two slaves, Anthony and John who spoke French and English, and were said to be en route to one of the seaports to board a vessel to the West Indies, from where they, no doubt, were brought. See the *Carolina Federal Republican*, September 6, 1817 for three slaves, Sampson, Joe, and Bill who were making their way to New Bern, Swansboro, or Wilmington to board a vessel to leave the state. Other examples can be found in the *Wilmington Gazette*, May 5, 1803, July 23, 1805, June 19,1810, and April 6, 1816; *American Recorder* (Washington), March 15, 1816; *Carolina Centinel*, July 1, 1820 and July 22, 1820; and the *New Bern Spectator*, June 18, 1831 for Ben who boarded a vessel to get to New York.

73. A letter addressed to some man who was not named by McDowell, February 25, 1806, *Bertie County Slave Papers, 1744-1815*, Division of Archives and History, Raleigh, North Carolina.

74. J. Gilpin to John Gray Blount, August 18, 1802 in William H. Masterson, ed., *The John Gray Blount Papers* (Raleigh: State Department of Archives and History, 4 volumes, 1965), III, 532-33.

75. See the case of *State v. Johnson* in Devereux, *Cases Argued and Determined in The Supreme Court of North Carolina*, I, 360-63.

76. Clark, *State Records*, XXIII, 197.

77. A number of slaveowners believed their slaves were enticed to leave their farm or plantation. See the *Carolina Centinel*, November 7, 1818, August 19,1820, December 30, 1820, May 31, 1833, and May 14, 1834; *Western Carolinian*, September 10, 1832; *New Bern Spectator*, November 21, 1834; *The Star*, April 14, 1815, April 18, 1817, and April 10, 1828 for Dick and Abram who were persuaded by a white man to leave their owner. Other slaves informed their owner Hutson Earp that the man was responsible for the slaves' departure. Earp offered $100 reward for the man, and $50 for each slave; *Raleigh Register*, September 10, 1838; *Carolina Watchman*, February 23, 1839; and *Charlotte Journal*, August 1, 1839 and March 5, 1840.

78. Clark, *State Records*, XXIV, 220.

79. Devereux, *Cases Argued and Determined in the Supreme Court of North Carolina*, IV, 328-40.

80. J.L. Taylor, *Cases Adjudged in the Supreme Court of N. Carolina, From July Term, 1816 to January in The Carolina Law Repository, Containing Biographical Sketches and Eminent Jurists; Opinions and Reports of American and Foreign Jurists; and Reports of Cases Adjudged in the Supreme Court of North Carolina* (Raleigh: Printed by Joseph Gales, 2 volumes, 1816), II, 291-92; and *State v. McRae, Devereux, Cases Argued and Determined in the Supreme Court of North Carolina*, II, 166.

81. *The Star and North Carolina Gazette*, January 1, 1819.

82. *North Carolina Minerva*, September 10, 1799. For other examples of advertisements in which the subscriber believed that his slave had been stolen, see the *Raleigh Register*, September 29, 1806; *The Star*, May 10, 1806 and November 22, 1833; *Western Carolinian*, August 19, 1823; and the *Catawba Journal*, February 7, 1826.

83. Hugh Talmadge Lefler and Albert Ray Newsome, *The History of a Southern State: North Carolina* (Chapel Hill: The University of North Carolina Press, third edition, 1973), 279-80. See also Jonathan Elliot, *The Debates in the Several State Conventions, or the Adoption of the Federal Constitution Together With the Journal of the Federal Convention* (Washington: Published Under the Sanction of Congress, 4 volumes, 1836), I, 133-36.

84. Spaight's ownership of seventy-one slaves was followed by Martin of Rockingham County, who owned forty-seven slaves; Davie of Halifax County who owned thirty-six slaves; and Blount of Pitt County who owned thirty. See Clark, *Names of Heads of Families, 1790 Census*, 410, 1000, 608, and 920, respectively.

85. Latham Windley, "Profile of Runaway Slaves in Virginia and South Carolina from 1730 through 1787" (unpublished doctoral dissertation, University of Iowa, 1974), 228-31. McDougall, *Fugitive Slaves*, 14-15.

86. Elliot, *Debates*, I:304;

87. Windley, "Profile of Runaway Slaves," 228-29; Eddie Marie Ervin, Runaway Slaves in Antebellum North Carolina (unpublished Master's thesis, North Carolina College for Negroes, 1946), 29.

88. McDougall, Fugitive Slaves, 16.

89. Richard Peters, ed., *The Public Statutes at Large of the United States of America* (Boston: Charles C. Little and James Brown, 1850), I, 305. The wording of the law and its interpretation can be found on pp. 302-05. Also see, *Annals of Congress: The Debates and Proceedings in the Congress of the United States, Second Congress, October 24, 1791 to March 2, 1793* (Washington: Gales and Seaton, 1849), 861. Also see Paul Finkelman, "The Kidnapping of John Davis and the Adoption of the Fugitive Slave Law," *Journal of Southern History* LVI (August 1990): 397-422.

90. A number of efforts were made to amend the 1793 law, primarily, by making the penalties for harboring runaways more severe. The 1850 Fugitive Slave Law which was a part of the Compromise of 1850 gave much comfort to the planter class in the South. For a fine discussion on proposed amendments to the 1793 Fugitive Slave Law, see McDougall, *Fugitive Slaves*, 21-33.

91. Ervin, "Runaway Slaves," 37.

CHAPTER THREE

Runaway Slaves: A Physical Portrait

Hundreds of North Carolina slaveowners used the state newspapers to advertise for their runaway slaves between 1775 and 1840. Their primary concern was to recover their absconded property. For that reason, they included as much information as possible about their slaves in a ten to thirty line advertisement. Because owners wanted the public to know what distinguished their slaves, they provided in many instances, minute, detailed information about their fugitive slave. Many slaveowners included such information as the runaway's name, approximate age, gender (in every case), complexion, height, weight, scars, diseases, the condition of the fugitives' teeth and gums, cuts, scarification—which meant that the slave was African born, clothing worn and taken, and a number of other features of the slave's physical being. This chapter analyzes more than 2,200 newspaper advertisements for 2,771 runaway slaves for the years 1775 to 1840. This number includes 110 infants and young children ranging in age from a few months to ten years of age who were taken along by family and friends.

Slaveowners were careful to provide the name of their fugitives in their runaway notices. In a few cases, they listed the names of children who left with their parents. Ninety-eight percent (98%) of the slaves who fled were identified by name. Though it was not customary for slaves to have a surname, many runaways used the last name of a present or a previous owner. Masters often pointed out that slaves gave themselves their last name. Thus, in advertising for his runaway slave, Allen, Daniel Dickinson wrote that the fugitive "...calls himself Allen Woodard."

Bacchus, a slave who belonged to Abner Pasteur of Craven County, referred to himself as Bacchus Hill.[1] No definitive patterns existed among slaves who decided to take on a surname, though a number of the fugitives were skilled artisans. Skilled slaves were mobile, and their contact with people beyond the farm and the plantation—primarily in and around the towns of North Carolina, and their association with free blacks, especially—no doubt, proved instrumental in their using a last name.

Slaveowners could not always be sure that their fugitive would give their real name. To avoid capture, runaways sometimes changed their names, and in some cases, used several different names. Some owners believed that if their slaves were apprehended, they would not only change or refuse to provide their master's name, but would also alter their own name. This, coupled with the slave's refusal to give an area of residence made it difficult for the sheriff or jailor to provide specific information in their take-up notices.

In an attempt to aid citizens in identifying their fugitives, a number of masters included the many aliases their slaves would use while in flight. For example, W.H. Hill of Wilmington began his notice for his runaway slave, John, by writing that the fugitive was sometimes called "Johnson," and at times he called himself "John Hill." Peter and his wife Nan fled from their Montgomery County owner, William Harris, on December 30, 1833. On February 15, 1834, Harris's notice for the two slaves appeared in the *Western Carolinian*, a Salisbury newspaper. Harris pointed out that the slaves had "...been heard of in Randolph County, under false names: Peter called himself Walter, and Nan took the name Polly."[2]

Slaves who attempted to pass as free, possessing free papers, and those who possessed a pass—given to them by their owner, written by the slave, or stolen—often used different names. The fugitive Sam, for instance, who called himself "Samuel Knox" possessed a false certificate with the latter name on it. His owner feared that if the fugitive secured another pass, he "would give himself some other name." John Headen of Chatham County believed that his slave Peter, would attempt to escape to Indiana "...as he obtained a free negro Pass in the name of James Weaver, dated some four or five years ago. No doubt he will call his name Weaver." Johnston, a slave who belonged to George L. Moore of Granville County, very shrewdly procured the free pass of a Jeremiah Mayho—granted to him by the General Assembly of North Carolina. Johnston, a blacksmith, who had fled on two previous occasions, made his third escape on December 27, 1817, and used Mayho's papers to pass as a free man.[3] Names then were a vital part of the runaway slave notices. The slave's name, coupled with bits of information about his physical makeup provided key ingredients in the owner's quest to recover his property.

The newspaper advertisements clearly indicate that runaway slaves in North Carolina after 1775 were creole, or country-born. Of the 2,771 slaves who fled, and for whom birthplaces were given, only forty-five, or 1.6 percent were born outside the United States. Thirty-five were African-born, while ten were born in the West Indies.[4] These findings are not dramatically different than those for runaways in Virginia after 1775. Lathan Windley found that 6 percent of the fugitives in Virginia after 1775 were African born, whereas 15.1 percent of runaways were African born before 1775. Percentages for South Carolina, however, were different. About 12 percent of the slaves who fled after 1775 were foreign-born, while 24.3 percent of those who fled before 1775 were born outside of colonial America.[5]

This contrast between the high incidence of African-born flight before 1775 and lower incidence of flight by Africans after 1775 has been revealed by a number of other studies for Virginia, South Carolina, and North Carolina. In their study of runaways in colonial North Carolina, 1748-1775, Kay and Cary found that 54.1 percent of North Carolina's 134 runaways were Africans. Philip Morgan estimated that 45.5 percent of South Carolina's slaves who fled between 1732 and 1782—for whom the birthplaces were indicated—were African-born.[6]

A number of factors contributed to the small number of foreign-born slaves in North Carolina, and their representation in the runaway population. For instance, the non-importation, non-consumption, and non-exportation agreement invoked by the Continental Congress in 1774 against England cut off the slave trade to the United States until after the Treaty of Paris was signed in September 1783. Though North Carolina was not a major importer of slaves directly from Africa and the West

Indies, the reduction in the number of African-born slaves transshipped to the colony from Virginia and South Carolina decreased after 1775.[7] Secondly, in January 1787, the General Assembly of North Carolina imposed a tax of fifty shillings on slaves below the age of seven and above the age of forty; a tax of five pounds on slaves between seven and twelve, and thirty and forty years, and a duty of ten pounds on slaves between twelve and thirty years of age. A head tax of five pounds was also imposed on slaves shipped directly from Africa.[8] The 1787 tariff was repealed in 1790, but due to the increase in the number of blacks in the state during the 1790s, and the fear that Haitian refugees migrating to North Carolina would inspire slaves to rebel, the legislature passed a law which completely abolished the slave trade to the state. Effective May 1, 1795, it was illegal to bring "slaves and indented servants of color" into the state by land or by water.[9]

From the 1790s to the end of the slave trade to the United States in 1808, the General Assembly enacted a series of laws which barred the importation and the settlement of Africans and West Indians in North Carolina.[10] These measures, coupled with the state's negligible role in the external slave trade, historically, kept the African-born and the West Indian-born presence in North Carolina at a minimum.

All of the African-born and West Indian-born runaway slaves had come to North Carolina before the slave trade ended in 1808. A number of these runaways possessed certain physical characteristics that readily distinguished them from creole slaves. Grinning or smiling would have instantly exposed some African-born slaves because several had filed teeth. Henry Young of New Hanover County described his runaway slave Quamino as having "filed teeth". Dublin, an African-born fugitive who left his owner in Craven County in 1777 had "sharp filed teeth."[11]

The face and arms of slaves also revealed their place of birth. Several masters pointed out that their slaves bore the marks of their African nation. Dick was "very much marked with his Country Marks over his Face and Body...." Ben, an African-born slave who absconded from his owner in Martin County was "marked on each arm with his country marks...."[12] Toby, a slave imported into South Carolina in 1786, and who had only been in Montgomery County, North Carolina for about two or three years, had the marks of his country on both sides of his face. And J. Lanier advertised for four African-born slaves who fled together. The four fugitives—Jack, Aka, Sam, and Botswain—were scarred on the body, or the body and the face with their country marks.[13] Ethnic markings were the most distinctive physical traits that owners used to describe their African-born fugitive slaves.[14]

West Indian-born slaves were described by their owners along the same lines as creole runaway slaves. Their physical description of West Indian slaves most often included brands that the fugitive received while in the West Indies. Thus, George McKenzie of Plymouth, Washington County advertised that his fourteen year-old slave runaway was "branded on the shoulder in the West Indies with the letters G.M.K." Joe, a West Indian slave was branded on the cheeks by a former owner.[15]

The most common description of West Indian slave runaways was their facility in English and their ability to speak several languages. Such was the case of the slave, Joe, who spoke broken English. John, who was raised in St. Croix, the West Indies, and who had only been in the United States a few years prior to 1809, spoke Spanish. John Manning placed a runaway notice in the *Edenton Gazette* for his fugitive slave, Frank, who was born on the Island of Guadeloupe. Manning pointed out that Frank could speak French.[16] Slaveowners, then, were quick to describe the physical traits of African and West Indian-born slaves in an effort to make the public cognizant of the differences which existed between country-born and foreign-born black slaves.

The overwhelming majority of slave runaways in North Carolina between 1775 and 1840 were male. A total of 2,179 male slaves fled, while 482 females left their owners during these years (see figure 1). Similar percentages existed for Virginia and South Carolina slave runaways.[17] The 110 children who fled with their parents most often were not identified by gender, and except for a few cases, very little information was given about young children. Descriptions were provided for the 2,661 male and female runaways.[18]

A number of factors explain why male slaves ran away at a rate of more than four and a half times that of female slaves. Female slaves in North Carolina and throughout the South began

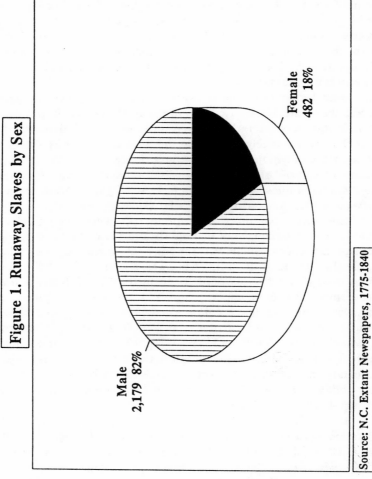

Figure 1. Runaway Slaves by Sex

Female
482 18%

Male
2,179 82%

Source: N.C. Extant Newspapers, 1775-1840

bearing children during their mid-to-late teens in order to replenish their master's farms and plantations with laborers. Being the primary caregivers to their children, female slaves no doubt thought long and hard about the risks and the dangers that flight entailed fleeing alone, much less, with children. And though they desired freedom as much as men, the task of uprooting and taking a child or children in flight was onerous, time-consuming, and exhaustive. Slave mothers were central to the slave family, and "...the slave family was made viable because women secured their family's tenure on a given plantation once they had children."[19] It was because of their family ties—especially to their children—that female slaves were more reluctant to run away.[20]

A few female slaves, however, did escape taking their child or children with them. Consider for instance, Poll, a seventeen year-old slave who belonged to James Wells of Jones County. She fled with her fourteen month-old son, Hardy, on October 3, 1793. Henry Potter of Raleigh placed a runaway notice in the *Raleigh Register* for Sooky and her four year old daughter, named Olive. Sooky fled with her child just two days after she was purchased by Potter at a Wake County sheriff's sale. In a daring move, Peggy escaped from her owner in New Hanover County, taking her three children, ranging in age from two months to six years.[21] Another factor which contributed to a lower incidence of flight by female slaves was the fact that women were tied to the farms and plantations in North Carolina moreso than men. Additionally, male slaves were more likely issued a pass to visit their loved-ones, and to generally go on errands for their masters. Men were more familiar with areas in and outside the county in which they lived, primarily because they were hired out more frequently than females. Many male slaves' occupational skills carried them outside the realm of farm labor, and into the towns, waterways, and other ares of North Carolina. Male slaves often fled from the individuals to whom they were hired.

Hirers of slaves who absconded from them were required by law to advertise for the runaway. Abel, a seventeen year-old male slave, for instance, was hired for a year by John Alderson of Hyde County. Within a few days of his hire, Abel and another slave, named Isaac, ran away. Alderson believed that the men would attempt to leave the state by boarding a vessel. Stephen, known in Wake County as "Goodwin's Stephen," and who was hired out to Albert Utley in January 1817, left the hirer eleven months later and lurked about the city of Raleigh. J.M. Jelks's slave, Tom, only fifteen years of age, escaped from his Wake County hirer and made his way to Chapel Hill. While there, the slave had the ingenuity to pass as free, and to hire himself out at the University of North Carolina as a wood cutter. Tom was apprehended, but he was able to escape from his captor.[22]

Female slaves could not move about alone through the countryside and towns without raising some suspicion among whites. And finally, female slaves faced more difficulty than male slaves passing as free.[23] Because of this, it was common for female slaves to runaway in mixed groups (consisting of men and women), with their husband, and husband and children. Rarely did a group of women (two or more) runaway without the presence of a man.[24] As Kay and Cary put it: "The possibilities, therefore, either prompted or favored male runaways in what was at best an extremely risky enterprise."[25]

Although women fled less frequently than their male counterparts, their proportion in the overall slave population in North Carolina was almost equal to that of men. By 1820, for instance, there were 106,551 male slaves and 98,466 female slaves in North Carolina. According to the 1830 Census, the number of male slaves grew by 17,762, an increase of 16.6 percent since 1820. The number of female slaves increased by 22,822, or 23.1 percent between 1820 and 1830—making women 49.4 percent of the slave population in North Carolina. This gap between male and female slaves closed even more by 1840, with female slaves comprising 49.7 percent of the total slave population in the state.[26]

In attempting to recover their fugitive slaves, many slaveowners indicated the age or approximate age of their property. Advertisers provided the age for 2,079 (78.1 percent) of the 2,661 runaway slaves. This is slightly higher than the findings for other states. The large African-born presence in those states, especially South Carolina, no doubt contributed to owners being less sure of their runaways' age.[27] However, there were fewer African-born slaves in the North Carolina slave population. Country-born, or creole slave runaways, most of whom were born in North Carolina, were better known by their owners; therefore, the age, and even more detailed information could be reported by masters.

Owners listed the ages of 1,739 or 79.8 percent of the male fugitives and 340 or 71 percent of the 482 female runaways. Slaves between 20 and 29 years comprised 49.4 percent of all runaways. This high percentage for the age category 20 to 29 years was consistent for males and females. Almost 900 or 51 percent of the male runaways, and 137 or 41 percent of the female fugitives fell within this age range. Runaways between 30 and 39 years of age comprised the second largest age category. Almost 25 percent of the fugitives were in this age group. The number of male and female runaways in the 30 to 39 years age range was 24 percent and 27 percent, respectively. Both male and female runaways, between 20 and 39 years of age, comprised nearly 75 percent of all runaways for whom the ages were given (see Figure 2).

The frequency of flight by slaves aged 20 to 39, by no means, reflected their percentage in the overall slave population in North Carolina. In 1820, slaves 20 to 39 years of age made up about 31 percent of the total slave population. At the same time, slaves under 13 years constituted about 46 percent of the North Carolina slave population. By 1840, North Carolina slaves 20 to 39 years old made up an even smaller share of the total slave population—about 20 percent—while very young slaves comprised almost 52 percent of the total slave population. Runaways 10 to 19 years of age constituted a much smaller percentage than their age group in the overall slave population. Runaway slaves 40 years and older more closely represented their age category in the overall slave population. In 1820, slaves 40 years of age and older represented about 9.5 percent of the total slave population, while in 1840 they were about 14 percent of that population.[28]

What factors then accounted for the high frequency of flight by slaves between 20 and 39 years of age, and less frequency by younger and older slaves? One possible explanation is that a sizeable number of these men and women had been owned by several masters. About 60 percent of the fugitives, for whom age and the number of previous owners were given, fell within the 20 to 39 year old age range. These runaways were familiar with

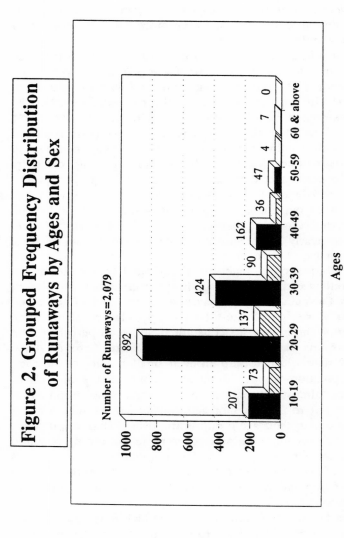

Figure 2. Grouped Frequency Distribution of Runaways by Ages and Sex

N.C. Extant Newspapers, 1775-1840

different areas of the state, and more importantly, many of them had been separated from wives, husbands, friends, and acquaintances. And in many cases, they escaped slavery to be reunited with loved ones. Many, of course, fled simply to find freedom.

Owners often included information in their notices about their runaway's former owners, thus providing a clue about the slave's motivation for running away. William Wilkinson of New Hanover County wrote that his slave, Ben, a 22 year old runaway could probably be apprehended on any one of three former plantations on which he had been in bondage. Clary, a 30 year-old slave, born the property of Samuel Johnston, governor of North Carolina from 1787 to 1789, ran away from her second owner, Thomas Routledge, on December 26, 1787. She was accompanied by a male slave, named Dick, 35 years old, who was born in Virginia. Routledge believed that the two fugitives were headed "northwardly". H. Murfree of Hertford County advertised for his 24 year-old slave George who had undoubtedly been separated from his mother and other relatives in Pasquotank County. Murfree speculated that George was headed to Pasquotank County, at least fifty miles away. Allmand Hall of New Hanover County did not know exactly where his 21 year old male slave, Jupiter, was headed because he had two previous owners. Hall anticipated, though, that the fugitive would either make his way near New Bern where his mother lived, or to the New River area of Onslow County where his wife and sister resided on a plantation. Writing in a tone of desperation, Henry Cotten of Edgecombe County advertised that his 30 year old fugitive Jack, had been sold five times, but had always found his way back to Norfolk, Virginia. Jack was, no doubt, very familiar with many parts of Virginia and North Carolina. This time Jack fled with his 22 year old wife, who herself had at least one owner prior to Cotten.[29]

Slave runaways in this age category, both male and female, were better able to withstand the hazards that they encountered while in flight. Additionally, a slave in his or her twenties or thirties was more likely to be hired out by an owner. This increased their awareness of their environment, brought them into contact with free blacks in the towns of North Carolina spawning their desire for freedom. Young slaves, especially those

under 15 years of age, were unfamiliar with the world outside
the farm or plantation. It was the element of the unknown, fear,
and attachments to their parents that dissuaded young slaves
from running away.

Older slaves, on the other hand, probably did not abscond
as often because of the physical strain that flight entailed.
Though slave runaways 40 to 49 years of age represented 9.4
percent of the fugitives whose age was given, slaves 50 years
and older represented a tiny fraction. All but two of the slaves
in this age category were men. It could also be that slaveowners
did not advertise for fifty and sixty year old slaves as readily as
they did for strong, healthy, much younger slaves. Their market
value was less than younger, preferred slaves. The rewards
offered by owners for older fugitives—on an average—were less
than those offered for younger runaways.[30] Older slaves, too,
were more settled; they had families, and though they desired
freedom, they no doubt, resolved that fleeing at an old age
would present as many problems as they encountered on the
farms and plantations.

The average age of runaway slaves in North Carolina was
27.6 years. The average for male and female fugitives was 26.8
and 27.5 years of age, respectively[31]. Table 5 shows the
frequency distribution of age between ten and sixty-one. The age
25 occurred more frequently for both male and female
runaways, than any other single age. The age 30 was the second
most common age listed for fugitives. Twenty-two percent of all
slaves were listed as 25 or 30 thirty years of age. This was
probably the case because owners often guessed the age of their
slaves, and merely reported ages in convenient multiples of five.
However, this does not mean that subscribers exaggerated or
reduced their slaves ages significantly. Their approximations
were probably close to the runaway's actual age.

Although owners did not indicate the age for about 22
percent of the fugitives, they sometimes provided other pieces
of information that indicated age. Many of these descriptions
were explicit, and would-be captors would face little difficulty in
ascertaining the slave's identity based on age. The subscriber
William Bourden described Nan as being "pretty old". Jem, who
left his owner, Thomas Pugh, Senior in December 1788 was
reported as being "an old negro fellow". Cornelius Harnett, the

Table 5

Frequency Distribution of Runaways
By Age and Sex

Age	Number of Males	Number of Females	Total
10	3	1	4
11	2	0	2
12	4	3	7
13	5	2	7
14	7	1	8
15	8	9	17
16	24	15	39
17	29	10	39
18	73	21	94
19	52	17	69
20	133	26	159
21	87	10	97
22	112	9	121
23	74	14	88
24	76	8	84
25	201	38	239
26	66	10	76
27	74	10	84
28	61	11	72
29	8	1	9
30	187	32	219
31	6	5	11

Table 5 (cont'd)

Age	Number of Males	Number of Females	Total
32	28	5	33
33	20	2	22
34	16	4	20
35	121	30	151
36	16	6	22
37	14	1	15
38	16	3	19
39	0	2	2
40	100	25	125
41	1	0	1
42	7	0	7
43	4	0	4
44	2	0	2
45	46	10	56
47	1	1	2
49	1	0	1
50	35	3	38
52	2	0	2
55	8	1	9
60	6	0	6
61	1	0	1

Source: North Carolina extant newspapers, 1775-1840

Revolutionary patriot, one of North Carolina's delegates to the Continental Congress, and the man for whom Harnett County was named—advertised in August 1775 that his "old negro man" Cuffee fled in July 1775. Nancy was described by her owner, Benjamin Sith of New Hanover County, as a "young black slave girl".[32]

Complexion or color was one feature of the runaway slave's physical makeup that readily could be observed and described by North Carolina citizens. And for that reason, slaveowners were careful to include this characteristic in their notices. Complexion was indicated for 1,876 runaways, about 70.5 percent of the 2,661 slaves for whom descriptions were given. Two basic color categories can be discerned from the runaway notices. The first category is comprised of those runaways who were distinguishably "Negro". The second group is made up of fugitives who were described as yellow, light, bright, and mulatto. Owners described 983 slaves (52.3 percent) of the 1,876 fugitives as being "black", "dark", and "brown". About 31.5 percent of all runaways were said to be black complexioned. Masters often used terms to distinguish their slaves' degree of blackness. Thus, James Coffield wrote that his "Negro Fellow" Hause was "pretty black," while Moses was described as "very black". Sign and Jesse, two runaways who fled from their owners in New Bern and Washington, North Carolina, respectively were said to be "quite black". Nance, a 16 year-old slave girl who belonged to Lemuel Brinson of Craven County was portrayed as being a "light black complexion". And Claton Lea of Wake County described his fugitive Ben as "a very slick black" man. Generally, however, subscribers stated only that the runaway was of a black complexion.[33]

Dark complexioned slaves constituted about 18.2 percent of the fugitives whose color was described. Some 342 such slaves were described in this manner. It is quite possible that owners used the terms "black" and "dark" interchangeably in describing runaways, except in instances where slaves were exceedingly black. Brown colored fugitives comprised the remainder of the runaways in this category. These slaves totaled 49, making up 2.6 percent.

Of the slaves in the second category, 495 were described as being "yellow" or "yellowish." These slaves made up 26.4 percent of the fugitives—who in many instances—were so "light" that owners feared their escape meant their blending into the white population. Owners reported that 289 fugitives were mulattoes, the offspring of black and white parents. Figure 3 shows that 92 runaways were light, while 17 were said to be of a bright complexion. It is likely that a number of yellow-complexioned slaves were mulattoes, and some fugitives who were described as mulatto, although very light, were several generations removed from a white parent. Many owners, no doubt, used the terms "yellow" and "mulatto" interchangeably, as did owners who described their slaves as "black" and "dark".[34]

Mulatto slaves, those runaways who were described as "yellow," and fair-complexioned clearly illustrate the degree of miscegenation in North Carolina. Race mixing began very early throughout colonial America, and North Carolina was no exception. As early as 1715, the North Carolina General Assembly enacted legislation concerning sex and intermarriage between blacks and whites. The law—which was concerned with the offspring of blacks and whites—placed a penalty of six pounds on "any White woman whether Bond or Free [who] shall have a Bastard child by a Negro, Mulatto of Indyan." The law also banned intermarriage between the races "under the penalty of Fifty Pounds for each White man or woman." Clergymen and Justices of the Peace who performed marriage ceremonies between blacks and whites also were subject to a fine of fifty pounds.[35] Technically then, the law did not ban sex between blacks and whites, rather the legislation was designed to curtail the growing number of mulattoes and yellow slaves, and marriages in North Carolina.

Despite the law, masters copulated with their female slaves; white women had sex with black slave men, and blacks and whites intermarried.[36] The result was a steady increase in the number of mulattoes, slave and free. In their interviews and in their narratives, ex-slaves left valuable information concerning race-mixing in North Carolina. For example, James Curry, who was born in Person County, North Carolina, wrote that his mother "was the daughter of a white man and a slave woman." Sarah Ann Green noted that her father, Anderson Watson had blue eyes because he was the son of his owner, Master Billy.[37]

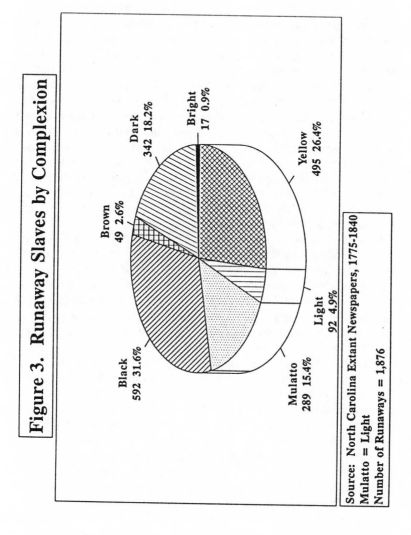

Figure 3. Runaway Slaves by Complexion

Source: North Carolina Extant Newspapers, 1775-1840
Mulatto = Light
Number of Runaways = 1,876

Newspaper notices for runaway slaves also shed some light on miscegenation in North Carolina. In addition to stating that their runaways were mulattoes, many owners provided specific information about the fugitive as related to his "mulattoness." In advertising for his mulatto slave Sam, David Day of Halifax County pointed out that the slave had a white father in Gates County. Richard Hines, an Edgecombe County farmer, wrote that his runaway slave "Harry is a bright mulatto (half white) with large freckles...." Crawford, an 18 year-old fugitive was depicted as being almost white, with straight hair. Mary, a mulatto slave, absconded from her Cumberland County owner on May 12, 1808. She carried her baby boy "Duncan, almost white, with straight hair." And H. Y. Waddell placed an advertisement in the *People's Press*, a Wilmington newspaper, which pointed out that his mulatto slave, Jo, was "two-thirds white".[38]

According to many runaway notices, slaves continued the tradition of race-mixing in North Carolina. Several slaves escaped from their owners, and violated the taboo of Southern society, by taking a white woman with them. Ned, for instance, a yellow slave who belonged to Benjamin Rowe of Craven County, left his owner in early 1820 accompanied by a white woman. George, a 28 year-old slave left Salisbury, North Carolina on April 4, 1823, and "took with him a white girl, 18 or 20 years of age, sandy hair, rather inclined to be red, large and full breasted." In a lengthy notice for his runaway slave, Atta, Neil Brown of Robeson County illustrated the technique that his fugitive and a white girl would use to secure Atta's freedom so that the two could find "some place where they may live in the habits of the relationship of man and wife unmolested." Brown believed that Atta, a "smooth" black complexioned slave would either secure a pass, or pose as a servant of the girl. Brown added that: "Any information respecting the above persons...will confer a great favor on the subscriber, as also oblige the respectable friends of the unfortunate girl." Joel Harris of Halifax County sold his slave, Austin, because the "bright mulatto" had been intimate "with a white woman, named Sally Doile, and with whom he tempted to run off, but was pursued and separated from this said Sally Doile, and got as far as Fluvanna, Virginia before he was apprehended." Fourteen months after he was sold to Peter Epps of Warren County, Austin fled again in

April 1826. Epps described the runaway slave as "one of the shrewdest negroes" he had ever seen, believing that Austin would "invent many plausible tales to prevent his being apprehended." He also felt that Austin would forge himself a free pass.[39]

What then was the significance of color in the runaway's ability to move about in and out of North Carolina? Yellow slaves, mulattoes, and other light-colored fugitives often used their complexion to their advantage. These runaways could pass as white, or as free, and because of their complexion, many of them found the acquisition of a "ticket" or pass, and of forged free papers an easier task. Together these slaves constituted 47.6 percent of all runaways for whom complexion was indicated. Mulattoes alone made up 15.4 percent of the 1,876 runaways whose color was described.[40]

The number of fugitives who passed as free and those whom owners believed had obtained free papers and a pass of some kind, illustrate the significance of a runaway's color. Of the 361 slaves whom subscribers identified by complexion, and whom they believed would pass as free, 246 or 68.1 percent were yellow, mulatto, and in general, very light complexioned. On the other hand, black and dark-skinned slaves passed as free less frequently. Slightly less than 32 percent of the black and dark-skinned slaves were reported to be passing as free (see figure 4). An additional 73 slaves passed as free, but owners provided no indication of color.

Light-complexioned slaves were often ingenious in using their color to pass as free, and to pass for white. One of the most remarkable examples is that of the slave Piety. Nathaniel Hunt, executor of the estate of John Hunt advertised in the *Raleigh Register* in 1808 that the "bright mulatto woman" ran away from Franklin County on June 22, 1808. Hunt wrote that Piety, 16 years of age at the time, would pass as free. For sixteen years, Piety passed as a free woman—living in Halifax town and in Plymouth, Washington County, North Carolina. Changing her name to Patsey Young, the runaway worked as a seamstress, baker, and brewer, primarily in the town of Halifax. In the summer of 1823, she married a free black man, named Aehrael Johnson of Plymouth. Later Johnson leased a farm in the

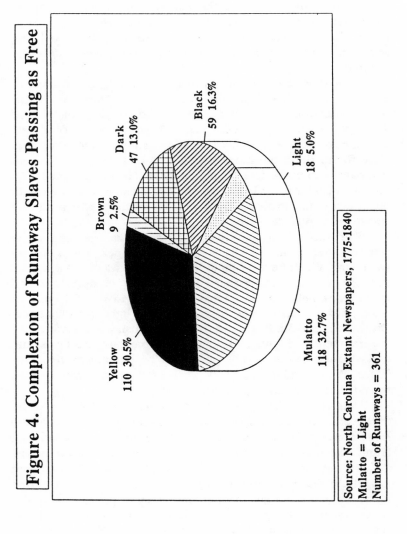

Figure 4. Complexion of Runaway Slaves Passing as Free

Black
59 16.3%

Dark
47 13.0%

Brown
9 2.5%

Yellow
110 30.5%

Light
18 5.0%

Mulatto
118 32.7%

Source: North Carolina Extant Newspapers, 1775-1840
Mulatto = Light
Number of Runaways = 361

town of Scotland Neck, Halifax County where he, Piety, and her four year-old daughter, Eliza lived. In June, 1824, sixteen years after she left Hunt, Piety and Eliza were apprehended by him. She and her daughter remained with Nathaniel Hunt until they fled on August 8, 1824. Hunt was convinced that Johnson had aided Piety and her daughter in their escape, and believed that the free black man would get them out of the state and aid them in passing as free persons. During the sixteen years that Piety was a free woman, she gained the friendship of a number of people—probably slaves, free blacks, and whites—in Halifax and Plymouth. And because of the acquaintances made by the slave, and the fact that she was married to a free black man, Piety no doubt, met with similar success in her second flight from bondage.[41]

Other mulatto and yellow-complexioned slaves used their color to secure their freedom, and that of their children. The female slave Bess, described as yellow-complexioned, with straight hair, eluded her captors for more than eight years. She left her New Hanover County owner Joseph Green in 1827 or 1828 and passed as free. Her three children accompanied her while she was in flight. Bess's success was owed to many people, including a white woman named Priscilla, who harbored her and the children. She made a living as a "first rate seamstress" in New Hanover County until she moved to Fayetteville in 1833. It was there that her new owner Arch'd McRae believed that she was passing as free, using the name Sarah, or Betsey.[42]

Both female and male slaves used their complexion to manipulate their hostile environment. For instance, George, a slave who absconded from Murfreesboro, North Carolina "being a pretty bright mulatto" attempted to pass as a free man. In addition, the slave's owner, H. Murfree believed that George would lurk about the Pasquotank County plantation on which his mother and other relatives lived. Wiley Mobley of Sampson County described his runaway slave, Simon, as having blue eyes and sandy colored hair; and because his complexion was "nearly white", he believed that the slave would pass as a free man. One of the best examples of a fugitive who attempted not only to pass as a white person, but to live among them, was the slave Cullen, the property of William Rouse of Springhill, Lenoir

County, North Carolina. Rouse averred that his fugitive would "alter his name, and attempt to pass among the lower class of white people as a free man." Describing the fugitive as a gray-eyed kinky haired mulatto, Rouse maintained that Cullen would probably go to Wilmington, Fayetteville, or New Bern to live among the poor whites.[43]

Several slaveowners reported that their fugitives had obtained a pass. Those slaves who passed as free, in most instances, had in their possession forged free papers. Fugitives who did not pass as free were said to have obtained a ticket illegally, or had been given a pass by their owners or some member of their master's family to go on an errand or to visit relatives, but they failed to return. Of the 157 runaways who possessed a pass or free papers, and of those whose color was given, 56.7 percent were yellow, mulatto, and light, whereas 43.3 percent were described as black, dark, and brown (see figure 5). Another 33 runaways were said to have a pass, but owners failed to provide the complexion.

Before 1850, it is difficult to say how many mulattoes there were in North Carolina. Census forms only had columns for denoting blacks, slave and free, including ages and the number of males and females. In 1850, however, enumerators wrote "B" or "M" which indicated that the person of color was black or mulatto. Census takers used their own judgement to determine the degree of African blood in an individual. In 1850, enumerators counted 3,638,808 blacks in the United States, of whom 405,751, or 11.2 percent were mulattoes. In North Carolina, there were 34,020 mulattoes, who constituted 10.8 percent of the black population in the state. A little more than half (50.5 percent) of the mulattoes in North Carolina were free, while the remainder—49.5 percent—were in bondage.[44]

Between 1775 and 1840, mulatto runaways in North Carolina fled at a rate almost three times their proportion in the slave population. For example in 1850, mulatto slaves made up 5.3 percent of the slave population in North Carolina, while constituting 15.4 percent of the runaway population during the years 1775 to 1840. Their ability—like other fair-skinned slaves, to use their complexion to obtain their objectives, whether it was to visit relatives and friends, seek passage aboard an outgoing vessel, pass as white, or find freedom—gave these slaves

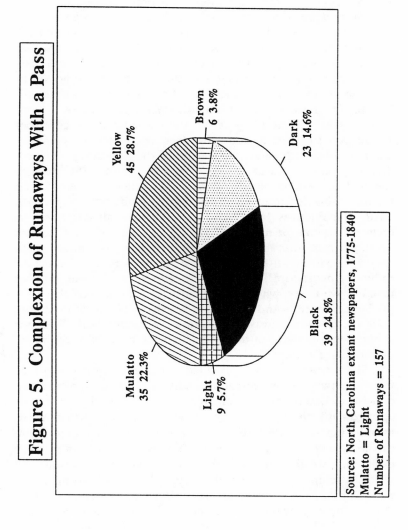

Figure 5. Complexion of Runaways With a Pass

Yellow
45 28.7%

Brown
6 3.8%

Dark
23 14.6%

Mulatto
35 22.3%

Light
9 5.7%

Black
39 24.8%

Source: North Carolina extant newspapers, 1775-1840
Mulatto = Light
Number of Runaways = 157

an advantage over their darker-skinned brethren in slavery.

Physical descriptions consumed a large part of the runaway slave notice. Hundreds of slaveowners, for example indicated the approximate height and weight of their fugitives. And when that information was not given, many subscribers described their slave's body build. Male runaways, as a whole, were reported to be between five feet five inches and five feet nine inches tall. The range, however, was from four feet eight inches to well over six feet. Female fugitives, on the other hand, ranged from a little over four feet to about five feet six inches. Many owners did not specifically state the height of their runaway. Instead, they gave some indication of the slave's stature. Thus Joseph Hatch described his slave Amy as a tall, yellow-colored "Negro Woman" who fled from his Jones County plantation on July 18, 1818. The fugitives Jack, Ben, and Bill were all described by their owners as being "quite tall." J.A. Cameron of Chatham County wrote that his fugitive George was "of rather small stature." London, an African-born 50 year-old runaway was said to be of "low stature." James Jackson reported, likewise, that his female slave Lusey, who fled with another slave named Natt, was of "low stature." And Jeremiah Norman of Bladen County referred to his runaway Joe as "low and stout built."[45] Other subscribers pointed out that their fugitives were of a "common" or "middling" height.

Slaveowners seldom provided specific information about their runaway's approximate weight. It was evidently more difficult to determine how much a slave weighed than it was to approximate his or her height. However, they provided more information for male slaves. Only a few references were made to the specific weight of females. If owners found difficulty in estimating weight for men, then their task was compounded when attempting to appraise the weight of women. In advertising for his slave Peter, James Biggs of Fayetteville, wrote that the thirty year old fugitive "has the Appearance of weighing 180 or 190 wt...." Armistead Abbott of Stokes County experienced more difficulty in attempting to describe the weight of his slave Sam. He placed the runaway's weight between 150 and 180 pounds. Harry, a twenty-two year old house servant who fled from his Raleigh owner in April 1823 and again in July 1824 weighed between 115 and 122 pounds.[46]

Most owners who attempted to describe the size of their runaway slaves used such terms as "pretty stout", "fat", "fleshy", "slim", "corpulent," and "slender". The overall picture revealed by the notices is that fugitive slaves were rather stout. Hundreds of advertisements exist for slaves who were described in this manner. This in no way suggests obesity. Many owners, for instance, added that their slaves were stout and well built. Others wrote that their fugitives were set and well made. These, of course, were references to male slaves. When references to female slaves were made in this regard, the term stout was used most often without any other descriptions about the slave's weight. Thomas Holton of Salisbury, for example, noted in his advertisement for the slave George that he was "about five feet four inches high, full faced, very black, and very stout made." Harry was described by Samuel W. Burns of Cabarrus County as a twenty-five year old "stout made", very black complexion, "handsome fugitive." And in 1827, Thomas G. Polk, also of Salisbury, advertised for a bright mulatto slave, six feet high, who was "stout, and well made."[47]

In addition to providing information about the most visible physical traits of their fugitives, scores of advertisers gave information that required closer examination by citizens. These included scars, burn marks, cuts, bruises, and missing fingers. These and other impairments were usually associated with the occupational hazards that plantation and farm labor entailed. The use of the axe for cutting wood and the scythe for cutting grass and weeds took their toll on many slaves. And some owners were careful to include these horrible injuries in their notices. Charles Smallwood of Beaufort County reported that his slave Shade had four fingers cut off his right hand by an axe. Cato, described by his owner as a handsome black man, walked lame as a result of one of his ankles being cut by an axe. The runaway Abram, who left his owner no less than two times, was cut on the knee by an axe. And the slave Bob of Orange County had several cuts on his hands caused by an axe and scythe blade.[48]

Owners indicated that a number of slaves had suffered burns, most often when they were children. This seems to have been a common childhood problem. Most of these accidents occurred during winter when children gathered around fireplaces and cook stoves. These burn marks and the afflictions they sometimes brought on lasted right through adulthood. John Dickson of Cumberland County, for instance, informed newspaper readers that his eighteen year-old runaway March, was burned when an infant, losing most of the fingers on his left hand. Primus became lame in one of his hips due to a burn. John Manning of Martin County wrote that his slave Peter could be easily recognized because of a burn on the back of his head. And Harry, a slave who lived in Mecklenburg County, nearly burned off the little finger of his left hand.[49]

Slaves suffered a number of other injuries on and off the farms and plantations of North Carolina. The significance of these reportings by owners reveals that slaves had many accidents and suffered a number of physical problems as a result. The daily toil of slave labor produced cases in which slaves were kicked in the face and head by horses or wounded by the cotton gin; and some slaves even received percussions that sometimes resulted in blindness.[50]

Slaves in flight were always at risk of being wounded or killed by whites and other slaves. At least five owners reported that their runaways had been shot, either while on a previous departure, or while in flight after leaving the subscriber. In May 1828 two male slaves, Carolina and Daniel left their owner Robert Powell in Richmond County. Shortly thereafter, Carolina was apprehended and placed in the Stokes County jail. He told his owner that he departed with Daniel in Stokes County, and that Daniel had been shot in his right arm. Anyone who examined James Tigor's fugitive slave Dave, would have found perceptible gunshot wounds on the calf of one of his legs. Hannibal, a slave who ran from his Mecklenburg County owner on at least two occasions, and who was in the habit of changing his name and his owner's name, had "...a scar on his cheek bone, occasioned by a bullet shot at him near Jonesborough, Tennessee...."[51] In addition to gunshot wounds, runaway slaves had to face inclement weather conditions. Obviously, the worst time of year was during the winter. The most common physical ailment associated with weather was the loss of toes caused by frostbite.[52]

The injuries suffered by runaway slaves were a reflection of the physical impairments that North Carolina slaves suffered in general. The kinds of injuries and the number of runaways who fell victim to the plow, a horse's kick, or to an axe corresponded to the misfortune that slaves experienced in other southern states. Windley, for instance, found that 101 Virginia runaways and 85 South Carolina fugitives were blinded by some means, burned, lost phalanges due to cuts, and suffered other physical defects.[53] In his study on the health of slaves on southern plantations, William Postell noted similar findings. Looking at the physical impairment of thousands of slaves in several parishes and counties in Louisiana, Mississippi, Alabama, and Georgia, Postell found that 4.1 to 9.6 percent of the slaves had been injured or infirmed in some manner.[54]

Many of the marks and scars on the bodies of fugitives were made by the owners themselves. Some owners pointed out that their slaves had been whipped. No less than 60 slaves showed the signs of a flogging. Not only could the slave Frank be identified by an iron on one of his legs, but he also bore the scars of a whipping which he received for committing a felony. One of the most vivid descriptions of the runaway Jerry—a slave who lived in Edgecombe County—was that "...he is marked on the back with the whip, occasioned by his breaking open a store" in Tarboro. In addition to the loss of two toes and deformed appendages, Abram's back was "very much scarred by [a] whipping."[55]

As early as 1741, the North Carolina General Assembly legalized the whipping of slaves, and the inhumane act of cropping, or cutting off slaves ears. Some of the runaways who were advertised as being marked by the whip, no doubt, were beaten at the pillory—the whipping post located in each county. Slaves who committed crimes stood the risk of having a portion of, or one or both ears completely severed. The 1741 law specifically stated that offenders were to "...have one Ear nailed to the Pillory, and there stand for the space of One Hour, and the said Ear to be cut off, and thereafter the other Ear nailed in like manner, and cut off, at the Expiration of one other Hour..."[56]

A few owners advertised for slaves who had met with this barbaric act. James Smith of Bladen County described his fugitive slave, Bob, as a twenty-five year old, very black slave who had one of his ears cropped, and the other ear had a scar on it which looked as if it had been nailed to a post. Murdo McQueen's slave, Jim, had both of his ears cropped, while only the lower part of one of Cato's ears, a Craven County slave, had been cropped off. Although James Jordan's slave lost a portion of his ear to the bite of a horse, both ears had been slit about one half inch because of his bad conduct.[57]

Similar to the whipping and the severing of slaves' ears was the cruel and dehumanizing act of branding slaves. The branding of Africans headed for the New World as slaves was fairly common. Slave traders burned their initials, or those of their trading company into the flesh of Africans, primarily for identification purposes. Slaves who entered Virginia and South Carolina directly from Africa and the West Indies were likely to have been branded. In the North Carolina runaway population, it appears that fugitives were usually branded by their owner, as evidenced by the initials and the advertiser's name.[58] Thus was the case of the slave Isaac who was branded on each cheek with the letter "A" which represented his owner's last name, Alderson. Prince, an African born slave, was burned with the letters W.G., the initials of his owner, William Grimes. Hopton Coor of Wayne County averred that the letters "H" on Tom's right cheek and "C" on his left cheek could be seen upon close examination. And finally, the letter "M" that was burned onto Betty's face by her owner Micajah Ricks in 1838, precipitated her flight with her two sons, Burrel and Gray, aged seven and five.[59]

Not only did slaveowners scar their slaves for the sake of identification, but they also branded them as a form of punishment. George Mackenzie of Washington County, for example, branded his slave Sip with the initials, GMK as punishment for frequently running away. Because Johnston, a Granville County slave had runaway on two previous occasions, George L. Moore branded the fugitive with the letter "R" for "Runaway." The female slave Nance, who belonged to Lemuel C. Brinson of Craven County also had the letter "R" on her right cheek.[60]

Edmund Hatch of Jones County was one of the most notorious slaveholders in the eastern section of North Carolina. He was known for branding his slaves and treating them exceedingly cruel.[61] Samuel Perkins, the tutor for Hugh Jones's children in Hyde County made an entry in his journal on

November 19, 1817, stating that Edmund Hatch's "...cornfields are literally fattened with the blood of his negroes. Every night at eight o'clock he has a horn blown for them to assemble: they are then counted and turned into a building...[and] locked up until light the next morning. I have seen some of them described in advertisements as having E.H. branded on each cheek."[62]

At least five of the nearly two dozen slaves for whom Hatch and Edmund Hatch, Junior advertised were branded with the initials "E.H." Several of their slaves were repeated runaways, and sometimes the slaves even ran off in groups. In June 1818 Hatch advertised for five male slaves who fled. One of those slaves, John, was branded with Hatch's initials. Almost a month later, he placed a notice in the *Carolina Centinel* for three other slaves, including a tall, twenty-one year old female, all of whom fled together.[63] In all, slaveowners indicated that 293 fugitives, or nearly 12 percent had been either branded, burned, shot, cut, or otherwise injured in some manner (see table 6).

In addition to the scars, burns, whip marks, and brands, many owners were careful to point out natural physical attributes that slaves possessed. Owners obviously felt that descriptions of these characteristics were essential to the identification, and the ultimate return of their property. Bad teeth and missing teeth, deformed fingers and toes, head size, facial features, and other anatomical traits were described by masters. From descriptions of teeth, it appears that slaves suffered from poor oral hygiene. William Beadles of Milton, Caswell County wrote that his absconded slave Jack had lost one or two of his eye teeth, and the other teeth were, generally, defective. Lydia's teeth were in poor condition, and she had lost part of her molars—visible when she laughed. Piety, the female slave who eluded captors for sixteen years, also was described as having decayed teeth. In addition to facial scars, Bess had "one or two of her upper teeth somewhat decayed, which may be gone by this time." Hundreds of other fugitives could be identified by decayed and missing teeth.[64]

It is remarkable that owners were so keenly aware of so many parts of their slave's anatomy. A number of owners, for instance, took time to write about their slave's toes in hopes that this would help readers identify their fugitives. Joseph and

Table 6

Description of Slave Runaways Based on Scars

Condition	Number of Fugitives	Percent of All Fugitives
Burns	21	0.8
Cuts	109	4.0
Eye Injuries	13	0.5
Frost Bitten	10	0.4
Broken Limbs	6	0.2
Shot	5	0.9
Whipped	70	2.6
Cropped Ears	17	0.6
Branded	42	1.6
Total	293	11.6

Source: North Carolina extant newspapers, 1775-1840

Henderson Stanfield of Caswell County pointed out that their runaway slave, Sandy, could "...easily be distinguishable by the union of the second and third toes on each of his feet." Jo Grange, a mulatto slave also had a "strange peculiarity about his feet," in which "the two toes next adjoining the great toe, on each foot, are connected together, one half their length, or to the middle joint of each."[65] Owners reported that slaves were bowlegged, and knock-kneed; they possessed kinky hair, straight hair, whiskers, and no hair at all. Fugitives' lip size, foot size, and head size can all be found in the runaway notices.[66]

These descriptions were crucial—at least slaveowners believed so—in making citizens cognizant, that indeed, the slave with whom they came in contact on the road, on the river, or even lurking about area plantations was a fugitive, and that he or she belonged to the subscriber. An awareness of minute scars, bruises, and marks of all kinds in obscure places on their slave's body, reflected a desire that they be able to recognize their property if they ran away or were stolen. Economics also dictated that planters and farmers be aware of their slave's physical problems. Slave injuries and accidents, and inherent afflictions, obviously, could have stood in the way of their labor. And that, of course, was not economically profitable.[67]

Descriptions of slaves in the runaway notices reveal a lot about the slave, but more than that, they provide a window through which scholars are able to view race relations, slave culture, and the problems that both blacks and whites faced in the "Tarheel State." One such problem was that of diseases. North Carolina was hit by a number of serious epidemics between 1775 and 1840, and the fugitive slave advertisements clearly illustrate that slaves were also affected. Yellow fever, cholera, malaria, pellagra, smallpox, and other diseases took their toll on North Carolina's population, both black and white.[68]

The Pettigrew family of Lake Phelps, Tyrrell County often wrote about the impact of diseases on their family members, associates, and friends. While a student at The University of North Carolina at Chapel Hill, John Pettigrew wrote to his father, Charles Pettigrew, exclaiming that the mumps and smallpox were prevalent in Chapel Hill in 1797. In regard to smallpox, the young Pettigrew wrote: "...great care will be taken to prevent its spreading...as the people here are very much afraid of that disease & will use great precaution to prevent its spreading, but if it should get into College it certainly would be very destructive to this institution, as I make no doubt it would kill one half that it infected..." Thomas Trotter of Washington, Beaufort County wrote his friend Ebenezer Pettigrew complaining of having "ague and fever," and that all of his slaves were well except Tom.[69]

Twenty-five Dollars
REWARD.

RANAWAY from the Subscriber, on Saturday night last, a bright complexioned negro man, named

AUSTIN,

About six feet in height, well built, hair inclined to being bushy, and about thirty-five years old; the thumb of his right hand is at present sore, affected by whitlow; one of his hands, wrist, and one side of his face is scarred in consequence of being burnt when young; he can read and write tolerable well and has some knowledge of figures; he talks much through his nose; he is a good rough carpenter and an excellent field hand. Said negro had on when he ranaway, a suit of brown homespun; and took with him a considerable quantity of other clothing; he is a cunning, artful fellow and will probably attempt to pass as a free man; it is probable he will be accompanied by a white woman with whom he was intimate, and who has left the neighborhood. The above reward will be paid for his delivery to me, or secured in any jail so that I can get him again.

Joel Harris.

Halifax co. Feb. 16, 1825. 48-tf

Free Press (Halifax), February 18, 1825

$25 Reward.

RAN AWAY from the Subscriber, on the 14th May last, negro JOHN, his wife CINDERILLA, and their child FRANK, about two years old—John is about 30 years old, 5 feet 7 or 8 inches high, dark complexion, thin visage, and high cheek bones. Cinderilla is a likely negro, about 30 years old, tall, well made, and dark complexion. John belongs to the heirs of Danl. Redmond, but is hired to me for the present year. Cinderilla and her child were purchased by me in January last, at the sale of Bell & Joyner's property in Edgecombe county—said negroes are supposed to be lurking in the neighborhood between Tarborough and Teat's bridge. A reward of $25, will be given for the apprehension of the above negroes, if delivered to me or secured in any jail so that I get them again; or, ten dollars for either of the grown negroes, and five dollars for the child.

ROBT. JELKS.

Halifax County, July, 1829.   48-3

Free Press (Tarboro), July 17, 1829

$75 REWARD.

A REWARD of seventy-five dollars will be paid for apprehending and delivering to me, at Weldon, negroes Daniel, (commonly called Daniel Toles,) Harry (Skinner,) and Ben (M'Alister,) or twenty-five dollars for either of them. They belong to the Roanoke Navigation Company, and are probably in the neighborhood of Rock Landing.

W. H. EDWARDS, Overseer
Roanoke Nav. Company.
March 10th, 1830.   5—4w

Roanoke Advocate (Halifax), April 1, 1830

$10 REWARD
FOR ELAN.

 RANAWAY, on the 28th ultimo, from my plantation on Stone House Creek, about three miles South of Mr. William Eaton's Ferry, negro ELAN, formerly the property of Doct. John T. Clanton, of Halifax county, N. C. *He* is about 5 feet 10 inches high, no particular marks recollected, and is between 19 and 21 years of age. I purchased him at public sale, in the town of Halifax, at last November Court, and have no doubt he is lurking about Dr. Clanton's plantation or neighborhood.—I will give the above reward, if delivered to my overseer at the above mentioned plantation or at my plantation Reedy Creek; or five dollars if lodged in any jail so that I get him again.

PETER MITCHELL.

Warrenton June 11. 16—tf

Roanoke Advocate (Halifax), June 14, 1832

$25 Reward.

LEFT my camp in Nash county, my negro boy

DECATUR,

About 18 or 19 years old, about six feet high, strait and slender, and yellow complected, and one of his fore fingers is stiff, caused from a cut through the joint. This boy I purchased of Lewis Wilson, Pitt county, and where he will probably make his way back where he was brought from. All persons are forewarned from harboring said boy, and all masters of vessels, under the severest penalty of the law, as I intend to have him. His mother lives with said Wilson, and his father with his brother, as I am informed. Any person who will apprehend said boy and commit him to jail, so that I get him again, shall receive the above reward—and let me know at Warrenton, North Carolina.

JOHN G. YANCEY.
Sept. 18. 1835.   39

Free Press (Tarboro), September 26, 1835

Runaway.

FROM the subscriber in this county on the 7th inst., a negro man by the name of Wilie. Said Wilie is of a light yellow complexion, about 5 feet 6 inches high, and about twenty six years of age, had on when he went away a wollen round about, cotton pantalloons and a white fur hat. Said negro man is supposed to be lurking about the lower end of this county, on the east side of Cape Fear River, and also occasionally about the Town of Fayetteville. I will give a reward of Twenty Dollars for delivering him to me.

M. EDWARDS.

September 27.   30—aw.

Runaway,

FROM the subscriber in Cumberland co. on the 10th of March last, a negro girl by the name of Clary, she is about 19 years of age, of a dark complexion, and has a very large mouth; she is about 5 feet high. She is supposed to be lurking about Doct. Maxwell's late residence in this county. I will give a reward of thirty dollars to any person for taking up said negro, and I will give a further reward of $10 to any person who will give me such information as will enable me to convict any white person of harboring said slave.

M. EDWARDS.

September 27.   30—2w

North Carolina Journal (Fayetteville), September 27, 1837

Smallpox was one of the most dreaded diseases in America. And it was the smallpox pustule bumps that slaveowners referred to in their notices for fugitive slaves. Smallpox left scars over the face and body that were visible for the remainder of the person's life. First appearing in the mouth and throat, the pox sores moved to the face, arms, body, and legs. High fever, chills, delirium, and sometimes even coma were all associated with the disease. "At its height, smallpox was one of the leading causes of blindness in the world."[70]

Lazareth Smith of Pitt County pointed out in 1811 that his slave Press, who fled in 1809 "cannot see but very little if any out of one of his eyes, and the other somewhat blinded with the small pox." Argyll, a slave who worked in the lumber mills near Lumberton was "very much pitted with the small-pox, by which he lost one eye." Argyll's wife Brunetta—who was advertised as a runaway by her Fayetteville owner, M. Molton in October 1800, and again by her new owner, William Norment in January 1805—also was marked by smallpox scars.[71]

The runaway notices reveal that slaves across North Carolina fell victim to the ravages of smallpox.[72] Additionally, the disease continued to kill its victims in epidemics down to the end of the antebellum period. One reason is that there was enormous opposition to Edward Jenner's vaccine for smallpox. The variolation which was discovered in 1798 was rejected by the people of North Carolina until about the 1820s. However, years of education and epidemics were the two most important factors which brought about the desire by Carolinians to inoculate themselves against the disease. C. Kirk of Cumberland County, in advertising for his fugitive slave Willis, provide some indication that not only were whites given the vaccination, but slaves as well. Willis had bumps on his face which resembled the smallpox. According to Kirk, the pimples were caused by the smallpox vaccination.[73] Although slaves suffered more during epidemics and were generally in a poorer state of health than whites, slaveowners and health officials tried to maintain some semblance of health care for their property. Todd Savitt insisted that "...Fortunately for slaves and free blacks, their health counted, too, in terms of maintaining a cheap, menial labor force and restricting contagion from others. Blacks counted heavily in all public health actions of city and county government during times of threatened or actual epidemics...."[74]

Slaveowners also pointed out in their runaway notices that slaves were afflicted with common maladies. Colds, venereal disease, warts, rheumatism, and ruptures or hernias were mentioned by slaveowners in their quest to bring about an awareness among citizens as to who their slaves were. Only one slave was said to have had a venereal disease. Jacob Gaster of Moore County advertised in the *Fayetteville Gazette* that a runaway slave, named Charles, who belonged to William Ross of Washington County was brought to his plantation in June 1792. The slave "was effected with the Venereal disease," and through humanity, Gastor said he "employed a physician to cure him which cost six pounds."[75]

At least six slaves were said to have been suffering from rheumatoid arthritis, a disease characterized by inflammation of the joints. Dempsey, a twenty-six year old slave who left his owner in Caswell County, walked lame in one leg, and one of his hips was sunken as a result of arthritis. Alexander Boyd, Junior's slave, Penny, whom he purchased in Raleigh, had "rheumatism in her ancles which causes her to limp a little when she walks." Other slaves suffered from ruptures, no doubt caused by heavy labor. As a result they wore an iron truss. Two such slaves were Isham and Kit. Isham had a swollen testacle; and both men wore an iron truss.[76] Other slaves who escaped had sores on their head, legs, arms, and feet, that would not heal. Scholars have attributed these afflictions to pellagra, intestinal worms, and a number of other viral and parasitic organism related diseases.[77] (see table 7)

The diseases from which slaves suffered were common in late eighteenth- and early nineteenth-century America. Their impact on slaves, however, was more devastating. Nutritional deficiencies among slaves coupled with exposure to the elements, inadequate medical care, and constant labor were prime ingredients in the slave's susceptibility to diseases and other illnesses.[78] Notices for runaways, however, indicate that as a whole, fugitive slaves were relatively healthy. Flight entailed being healthy. Maimed, crippled, and sick slaves in most cases could not have endured the rigors of eluding would-be captors. A few, however, did flee, but in the main the act of running

Table 7

Diseases and Maladies from which Slaves Suffered

Malady	Number	Percentage of All fugitives
Smallpox	27	1.0
Venereal	1	0.03
Rheumatism	9	0.3
Warts	4	0.15
Cancer	5	0.19
Ruptures	8	0.30
Tuberculosis	1	0.03
Total	55	2.0

Source: North Carolina extant newspapers, 1775-1840

away was employed most by those slaves who were more physically fit to endure the hardships of flight.

Despite the hardships of running away, and the great odds against them, a few pregnant female slaves fled. Runaway notices exist for at least eighteen pregnant slaves who absconded from their owners. Most of the fugitives were in their second and third trimester of pregnancy. Henry Lucas discussed in detail the absconsion of his slave Hannah. He wrote that she fled in the summer of 1808 and that she was seven to eight months pregnant. In attempting to draw attention to their fugitives, Peggy and Jane, their owners reported that the women were "advanced in pregnancy."[79] Slaveowners were, no doubt, completely surprised when their expectant slaves absconded. Thomas Palmer's astonishment was evident in his notice for Hasty, who was advanced in pregnancy, "...and owing to the situation, it is presumed she must have been conveyed away by some person, as she could not undergo the fatigue of travelling."[80] What factors then motivated these women to leave their farms and plantations? Possible explanations are that they ran because they desired freedom, or they did not want their children to bare the hardships and cruelties of slavery. And some women were headed for the neighborhoods of previous owners to obviously visit family members from whom they had been separated. At least two of the pregnant fugitives were said to be destined for other slaveholding states. The slave Jin, who was four to five months pregnant fled in 1819 with a mulatto male slave. According to her owner, Frederick Heck, she was headed for a free state to live as a free woman.[81]

Pregnant runaways were aware of the dangers that flight entailed; and for that reason, they chose to flee in groups. Eleven of the eighteen women fled in groups. Fan, Bet, Jin, Fereby, Jane, and Jenny all left with their spouse. An African born pregnant female slave, who spoke no English, fled from William Baxter of Rutherford County in September 1806 with three other African-born slaves. Facing incredible odds, four of the pregnant runaways left with their children. Two women were accompanied by only their children. One such fugitive was Cloe. She absconded from Josiah Corrie of Wayne County in January 1819—taking her one year old son and her daughter, aged five.[82]

By far, one of the most elaborate and detailed descriptions that owners used to pinpoint their runaway slaves were the clothing and the shoes worn by their fugitives. These descriptions were central to the advertisements. In many instances, these delineations consumed most of the notice for the fugitives. Eighteenth- and nineteenth- century clothing often defined status, and it is clear that slave clothing was very different than clothing worn by free people.

As in general portraits of runaways, owners—who were primarily male—described the clothing of male slaves with more precision and detail. Their descriptions of female apparel were most often brief and sketchy. Additionally, a higher percentage of male raiment was described. An obvious explanation for this underdescription of female attire is that men knew less about female clothing. These cursory descriptions of female runaways also could have meant that owners felt more confident in speedily capturing female runaways, and therefore were less graphic in their descriptions for them. And this was late eighteenth- and early nineteenth-century southern America where even white women were regarded as inferior beings. So, it is not surprising that black female slaves would receive only a glancing description. Advertisements, in general, were longer for men.[83] Subscribers meticulously described the attire of about 71 percent of the 2,661 fugitives.

Slaves were issued clothing by their owners, usually twice a year, in the spring and in the fall. The issue in the spring for men consisted of one or two pair of pants, two shirts, and occasionally a straw hat. The women and girls received a calico dress, or fabric to make their dresses. Handkerchiefs and sunbonnets were also given to the women. The winter issue of clothing for men usually consisted of a pair of shoes known as "Negro brogans," a jacket, trowsers, and a shirt. Slave women were allotted shoes, chemise, a petticoat, and a dress. Clothing allotments obviously varied from farm to farm and plantation to plantation, depending on size, number of slaves, the economic standing of the owner, and his generosity.[84]

Slaves—both male and female—usually went without shoes in the summertime. Occasionally, as a part of their winter ration of clothes, men were given woollen hats, and both men and women were provided overcoats; in some cases, blankets were provided. One could readily identify slave clothing, and so the phrase "Negro clothing" was often used in reference to their garb. The material used in "Negro clothing," which was either bought or made by the mistress or slave seamstresses on the plantation, was usually made of cotton, wool, and osnaburg—a rather durable, rough (uncomfortable) fabric, imported from Germany.[85]

Runaway slave advertisements provide the richest source of information on the clothing worn by slaves. We have some idea about the fabrics used in clothing construction for the bondsmen and bondswomen. The notices also tell us something about the colors of clothing; and we are able to glimpse their manner of dress, that is what they wore when they escaped. But again, for the most part, the descriptions of clothing worn by men were more specific and longer. Notices shed some light on how poorly clad, how adequately, and how well-dressed runaways were.

The following delineations are examples of the manner in which owners depicted both male and female attire. In advertising for five newly imported African born slaves in February 1775, Edward Batchelor wrote that the four men "were uniformly clad in coarse green Cloth Jackets, brown Cloth Trowser, a Blanket, and red Cloth Cap; and Wench had on an emboss'd Flannel Petticoat and brown Cloth Cloak." When Daniel left his owner on March 11, 1791, he was clad in an oznaburg shirt, "Negro cotton" jacket and breeches, a velvet waistcoat, and a raccoon skin cap. The runaway Boman had on a shirt, overalls, and a felt hat when he absconded from his owner in August 1812. Fanny left just a week before Christmas 1825, and according to her owner she was dressed for cold weather. She had on a homespun wool overcoat, a sunbonnet, and carried "a black bombazette [wool] and white sprig muslin frock."[86] Slave clothing changed very little over the years. The fabric and colors (primarily dyed brown and blue) that were described in 1775 were likewise described in the late 1830s.[87]

Equally important in their descriptions of the clothes worn by fugitives were reports of the clothing taken by runaways. The fact that slaves took additional clothing when they absconded, presented a problem for their masters in their attempts to get citizens to identify their property. Some slaveowners wrote that it was useless to describe the clothing that their fugitives had on when they absconded because they took other clothing and would change—in some cases—several times.[88] The quantity of clothing taken by some runaways attests to the difficulty that owners faced in describing their slave's attire.

Nearly one-third of Joseph Hawkins's advertisement for his fugitive slave Harry was devoted to describing the clothing taken by the runaway. Harry, described as a "keen artful fellow," and who had run away before, carried with him on his second escape from Hawkins, "a blue broad cloth coat, a black crape frock or surtoat coat lined with silk, a pair of brown cassimere pantaloons patched in the seat, a spencer and pair of pantaloons of common homespun cloth dyed in part with copperas, a pretty good hat and bootees...."[89] On June 18, 1828, Cory escaped with his wife, three children, and a twenty-one year old female slave named Adaline. They absconded from their Halifax County owner, Ricks Fort. Fort wrote in his notice that: "The whole of these negroes carried off a variety of clothes, even their bed and furniture." Adaline had a variety of good clothes because a few days before she and the others ran off, she broke into "her mistress's trunk and took with her sundries of wearing apparel, she also had a black fur hat." Elijah Canaday of Beaufort, Carteret County, advertised for Alford in November 1837. Canaday reveals the problem that owners faced in attempting to identify their runaway's clothing. Alford had on a "blue cloth coat and a slick hat," but he "carried with him a bombazet frock coat and many other things, and will probably appear quite respectably clad." Alford's bombazet frock coat, which was made of wool, indeed helped provide some protection from the elements.[90]

A total of 405 runaways, or a little more than 15 percent of the fugitives, took additional clothing with them. Slaves who took clothing, it must be said, were serious about leaving their owners permanently. They did not abscond because of a flogging, or just to visit relatives or friends, nor did they "fly to the woods" to hide out temporarily. These were men and women who desired freedom, and additional clothing and blankets (from which some slaves would reportedly make more clothes) provided a camouflage, protection from the elements, and bargaining power. Owners pointed out in several instances that slaves would sell their additional clothing.

North Carolina slaveowners utilized the state's press as one means of aiding them in recovering their fugitive slaves. Physical descriptions of their slaves provided the nucleus of the runaway notice. Owners were concerned with providing as much detail as possible about just how their slaves looked—pointing out facial scars, burn marks, cuts, brands, and other aspects of the slaves' physical makeup. Complexion, a characteristic that could be identified at some distance, was a significant aspect of the advertisement. Mulatto slaves and other light-complexioned runaways were at an advantage in that they could use their complexion to pass as free, and to also pass for white. Only a few foreign-born slaves were in the runaway population. The number of African-born and West Indian-born slaves was relatively small in North Carolina after 1775. Male slaves were more likely to run than were females. The ratio of male to female flight was more than four to one. Slaves, male and female, between the ages of 20 and 39 years comprised nearly 50 percent of all runaways for whom age was given. In addition to providing detail about their fugitives' physical characteristics, slaveowners sought to describe their slaves' clothing. The runaway notices resurrect faceless, nameless slaves and bring them to life, providing a picture of individuals who were black, yellow, and every shade in between; men and women who were tall, short, fat, and slender, but most of all, the advertisements paint a portrait of human beings who sought freedom.

Notes

1. See the *Carolina Centinel*, May 18, 1822 for the slave Allen and June 15, 1822 for Bacchus. For other examples of slaves who carried a surname, see the *Carolina Centinel*, December 8, 1821, December 22, 1821, May 25, 1822, September 14, 1822; *Cape Fear Recorder*, June 10, 1816; *Raleigh Register*, November 30, 1802; *Carolina Federal Republican*, March 28, 1818; *People's Press*, May 15, 1833, February 12, 1834, and July 23, 1834; *Herald of the Times*, April 30, 1836; *Newbern Spectator*, October 11, 1839, August 8, 1840; *North Carolina Sentinel*, February 24, 1836.

2. *Wilmington Gazette*, May 13, 1802; *Western Carolinian*, February 15, 1834. According to owners, dozens of slaves would change their names. See the following examples in the *North Carolina Gazette*, July 4, 1777: *North Carolina Minerva*, March 23, 1799; *Wilmington Gazette*, June 26, 1800, June 3, 1802; *The Star*, June 12, 1812, October 16, 1818, January 22, 1819, September 3, 1819; *Carolina Federal Republican*, February 14, 1818; *Raleigh Register*, October 30, 1827; *Miner's and Farmer's Journal*, May 5, 1831, April 17, 1832; *Carolina Centinel*, November 14, 1835; *Wilmington Advertiser*, August 17, 1838, October 5, 1838.

3. *Western Carolinian*, June 24, 1823; *Raleigh Register*, October 21, 1834 and January 9, 1818 for Johnston. A number of other examples of runaways with free papers were found. See the *Elizabeth City Star and North Carolina Eastern Intelligencer*, August 10, 1833 for the female slave Eve who had a free pass bearing the name Mary; *Carolina Federal Republican*, March 19, 1814 for the slave, March, who passed as free with a free pass under the name John Codett; *Raleigh Register*, February 3, 1824, February 13, 1824, March 9, 1824, June 6, 1826. For examples of slaves who possessed a ticket with an altered name, see the *Raleigh Register*, December 5, 1803 and October 30, 1827; *North Carolina Standard*, June 30, 1836, September 4, 1839; *Western Carolinian*, September 13, 1838; *Raleigh Register*, June 22, 1839; *Newbern Spectator*, December 30, 1836.

4. I am aware that this number for foreign-born runaway slaves may be somewhat conservative. Slaveowners did not always indicate birthplaces for their runaways. Many did not do so because African-born slaves had been in the country long enough to have become acculturated, therefore masters employed the same descriptions used to identify country-born slaves. In other words, African-born slaves "were becoming culturally unidentifiable" by the 1820s and the 1830s. See Michael P. Johnson, "Runaway Slaves and the Slave Communities in South Carolina, 1799 to 1830," *William and Mary Quarterly* 38 (July 1981): 438.

5. Windley, "Profile of Runaway Slaves," 67-68.

6. Kay and Cary, "Slave Runaways in Colonial North Carolina," 20; Philip Morgan, "Colonial South Carolina Runaways: Their Significance for Slave Culture," *Slavery and Abolition*, VI (December 1985): 59-60, and Littlefield, *Rice and Slaves*, 124-125 who calculated that African-born slaves made up at least 75 percent of the total number of runaways in South Carolina between 1732 and 1775.

7. Worthington Chauncey Ford, ed., *Journals of the Continental Congress, 1774-1789* (Washington: Government Printing Office, 1904), 76-77. It appears that North Carolina officials enforced the agreement, initially at least, as evidenced by the reshipment of slaves back to the West Indies on at least one occasion. The Safety Committee of Wilmington, meeting December 17, 1774, ordered that Arthur Mabron reship his slaves back to the West Indies. See Saunders, *Colonial Records*, IX, 1098-99.

8. James Iredell, *Laws of the State of North Carolina* (Edenton: Printed by Hodge and Willis, 1791), 577-578; Johnson, *Antebellum North Carolina*, 471; Taylor, *Slaveholding in North Carolina*, 23.

9. For a discussion on why the 1787 law was repealed, see Taylor, *Slaveholding in North Carolina*, 24-25. For the wording of the law, see Frances-Xavier Martin, *The Public Acts of the General Assembly of North Carolina* (Newbern: Martin and Ogden, 2 volumes, 1804), II, 53-54.

10. Potter and others, *Laws of the State of North Carolina*, II, 786-787; Taylor, *Slaveholding in North Carolina*, 25; Rosser H. Taylor, "Slave Conspiracies in North Carolina," *North Carolina*

Historical Review V (1928): 25. The panic and the concern of North Carolinians were taken before the House of Representatives by Robert Williams in January, 1803. Congressman Williams presented a memorial on the behalf of the citizens of Wilmington in reference to the landing of a group of blacks who had been emancipated on the Island of Guadeloupe. The citizens feared that the blacks were a threat to "the people of the southern States of the Union in particular...." See the *Annals of the Congress of the United States, 7th Congress, 2nd Session* (Washington: Gales and Seaton, 1851), 385-86.

11. *North Carolina Gazette*, May 5, 1775 and July 11, 1777.

12. *North Carolina Gazette*, July 18, 1777 and July 17, 1778.

13. *North Carolina Chronicle; or, Fayetteville Gazette*, May 10, 1790; *Minerva*, October 8, 1807.

14. See Littlefield, *Rice and Slaves*, 115-16 and his table on page 123 in which he quantified the number of African-born slaves with country marks, filed teeth, and brands. For examples of other African-born slaves who possessed the signature of their country on their face and body, see the *Raleigh Register*, February 10,1801 for the slave Prince who had scars upon his eye; *Hall's Wilmington Gazette*, June 8, 1797 for Sampson, a Guinea born fortune teller and conjurer who had a large scar on one side of his face that reached into his eye; *Washington Gazette and Weekly Advertiser*, July 24, 1807.

15. *State Gazette of North Carolina*, February 21, 1794; *Wilmington Gazette*, June 26, 1800.

16. *Wilmington Gazette*, June 26, 1800; *New Bern Herald*, May 13, 1809; October 15, 1811.

17. Gerald Mullin's study of Virginia slave runaways showed that of 1,280 slaves who fled between 1736 and 1801, 89 percent were males. Mullin, *Flight and Rebellion*, 40; Littlefield found that 82.4 percent of the runaways in South Carolina between 1732 and 1775 were males. Littlefield, *Rice and Slaves*, 144. For North Carolina, see Kay and Cary, "Slave Runaways in Colonial North Carolina," whose male-female flight percentages between 1748 and 1775 were 89 and 11 percent, respectively. See also Daniel Meaders, "South Carolina Fugitives as Viewed Through Local Newspapers With Emphasis on Runaway Notices 1732-1801," *Journal of Negro History* 60 (1975): 292. See also

Billy G. Smith and Richard Wojtowicz, *Blacks Who Stole Themselves: Advertisements for Runaways in the Pennsylvania Gazette, 1728-1790* (Philadelphia: University of Pennsylvania Press, 1989), 12-13; Betty Wood, *Slavery in Colonial Georgia, 1730-1775* (Athens: the University of Georgia, 1984), 172.

18. Slaveowners provided sufficient information for four children ten years of age who were taken along by their parents, enabling the writer to keep a computer record for each of them. They are, therefore, included in the 2,661 total. Computer records were not kept for the 110 children ten years of age (only one) and under because sufficient data were not given for them. This number added to the 2,661 is a total of 2,771 slave runaways.

19. Deborah G. White, "Ain't I a Woman? Female Slaves in the Antebellum South" (Ph.D. dissertation, University of Illinois at Chicago Circle, 1978), 88. Deborah White, "Female Slaves: Sex Roles and Status in the Antebellum Plantation South," *Journal of Family History* (Fall 1985): 251, see especially note 4.

20. A number of scholars have emphasized this point. See for example, Eugene Genovese, *Roll, Jordan, Roll: The World the Slaves Made* (New York: Pantheon Books, 1974), 649; Deborah White, *Ar'n't I a Woman? Female Slaves in the Plantation South* (New York: W.W. Norton and Company, 1985), 70-76; Kay and Cary, "Slave Runaways in Colonial North Carolina," 123; Windley, Profile of Runaway Slaves," 66; and Meaders, "South Carolina Fugitives," 292; Smith and Wojtowicz, *Blacks Who Stole Themselves*, 13-14.

21. *North Carolina Gazette; or Impartial Intelligencer and Weekly Advertiser*, October 26, 1793; *Raleigh Register*, May 19, 1820; *Wilmington Gazette*, January 23, 1801. For other examples in which female slaves fled with their child or children, see the notice in the *True Republican and Newbern Weekly Advertiser*, June 12, 1811 for Sophia who ran away from her New Bern owner April 25, 1811—carrying her two daughters, eight and five years old. Louisa absconded carrying her fifteen month old baby girl, *Carolina Federal Republican*, June 6, 1812. Arch'd McRae placed runaway notices in at least two newspapers for his slave Bess whom he purchased while she was in flight. Bess escaped with her three children sometime in 1827 or 1828. She was harbored and passed as free between the time she ran and

1835, the point at which McRae placed the notices in the newspapers for the apprehension of Bess and her three children. See the *People's Press*, March 18, 1835 and the *Carolina Observer*, July 21, 1835 for more information about Bess.

22. *North Carolina Gazette; or Impartial Intelligencer and Weekly Advertiser*, February 25, 1797; *The Star*, December 26, 1817, February 11, 1820. Also see the *Raleigh Register*, September 6, 1816 for Sarah, a female slave runaway who fled from her hirer, a Mr. Darby in Caswell County.

23. See Mullin, *Flight and Rebellion*, 103-04; Windley, "Profile of Runaway Slaves," 66.

24. Group flight is discussed in chapter 5.

25. Kay and Cary, "Slave Runaways in Colonial North Carolina," 13.

26. Census data on the slave population in North Carolina between 1820 and 1840 can be found in Department of State, *Census for 1820*; U.S. Census Office, *Aggregate Amount of each Description of Persons within the District of North Carolina Corrected at the Department of State*, 90-93; Department of State, *Compendium of the Enumeration of the Inhabitants and Statistics of the United States, From the Returns of the Sixth Census*, 40-42.

27. Windley, "Profile of Runaway Slaves," 79.

28. The Census data on the ages of slaves can be found in the volumes in note 26, same pages. My figures for the number of slaves in each of the age categories is an approximation since my age categories are different than those in the 1820 and 1840 censuses. However, they are similar. For example, the Census of 1820 breaks down slave ages "to 13" years of age, "14 to 25," "26 to 44," and "45 and older." In the 1840 Census, the age categories were "under 10," "10 to 23," "24 to 35," "36 to 54," "55 to 99," and "100 and upwards." Subtractions and additions were made from age category to category to get approximations. Kay and Cary, "Slave Runaways in Colonial North Carolina," 9, found that 62 percent of North Carolina's runaways between 1748 and 1775 were between 20 and 35 years of age. Also see Windley, "Profile of Runaway Slaves," who calculated that 72 percent of Virginia's and 64 percent of South Carolina's fugitives were between 20 and 39.5 years of age.

29. *State Gazette of North Carolina*, February 7, 1788; *State Gazette of North Carolina*, March 19, 1795; *True Republican and American Whig*, June 20, 1809; *North Carolina Gazette*, July 4, 1777; *Minerva*, February 8, 1808. For other examples of slave runaways in the 20 to 39 age category who had at least two owners, see *Minerva*, October 6, 1808, January 24, 1811, October 4, 1811, April 26, 1816 and October 26, 1816; *Hall's Wilmington Gazette*, April 6, 1797 and November 29, 1798; *Wilmington Gazette*, June 13, 1799, October 23, 1800 and October 15, 1801. For those slaves who had at least three owners, see the *Wilmington Gazette*, May 5, 1803, September 27, 1803, February 3, 1807, May 12, 1807; *American Recorder*, January 5, 1821, August 17, 1821; *Carolina Observer*, June 19, 1823, October 25, 1826. And for fugitives who had at least four owners, see the *Carolina Centinel*, March 17, 1821 for Dick who had lived in Bertie and Hertford counties before leaving his owner, William Griffin in March, 1818; *Western Carolinian*, July 16, 1822; *Carolina Observer*, February 27, 1817; *Charlotte Journal*, September 9, 1836 August 24, 1838, *Herald of the Times*, January 30, 1836; *Fayetteville Observer*, April 13, 1837, May 29, 1839; *Raleigh Register*, November 29, 1836; *North Carolina Standard*, April 7, 1836.

30. See Taylor, *Slaveholding in North Carolina*, 69-74 for the prices of slaves. Slaveowners preferred young slaves. Notices for the sale of slaves, for example, were primarily for young slaves. See *The American*, October 13, 1814 for the sale of "Eleven prime Negroes—consisting of men, women, boys and girls...." See the *Edenton Gazette*, May 8, 1827 in which J.S. Creecy offered for sale "Fifteen or twenty likely Negroes consisting of women and children, among whom are several boys." Also see the *New Bern Spectator*, June 18, 1831; *People's Press*, October 29, 1834. See also N.W. Alexander's notice in the *Miner's and Farmer's Journal*, November 16, 1833 for the sale of sixteen black slaves, "most of whom are young and likely." And the ad in the *Fayetteville Observer* quoted in Taylor, *Slaveholding in North Carolina*, 62, in which a subscriber wanted "to purchase 30 to 40 negroes of both sexes, not under ten nor over thirty years of age, for which the highest cash prices will be given." The average reward for slaves 50 years and older, for instance, was $16.30; the average reward for five of the six slaves 60 years of

age for whom the reward was given was $7.83. Rewards for fugitives are discussed in greater detail in chapter 5.

31. Kay and Cary, "Slave Runaways in Colonial North Carolina," 10, found that the average age of North Carolina runaways, 1748 to 1775 was 28 years; Windley, "Profile of Runaways," 83, estimated that the average age of all fugitives in Virginia and South Carolina was about 27 years; Smith and Wojtowicz, *Blacks Who Stole Themselves*, 13.

32. *North Carolina Gazette*, November 20, 1778; *State Gazette of North Carolina*, April 9, 1789; *Cape Fear Mercury*, August 7, 1775; *Wilmington Gazette*, October 15, 1801.

33. *Edenton Gazette*, November 12, 1821; *New Bern Spectator*, January 31, 1829, March 7, 1829, May 2, 1829, November 21, 1834; *Raleigh Register*, August 13, 1838. Also see the *Raleigh Register*, February 7, 1837; *Newbern Spectator*, February 4, 1835, November 25, 1836, and February 10, 1837 for Horace, depicted as "crow black"; *North Carolina Sentinel*, November 2, 1836; and the *Washington Whig*, February 12, 1839.

34. See Littlefield's comments about miscegenation in which he states that: "It is possible that some of those called "yellow" were also mulattoes, in which case the degree of race mixture was considerably larger." Littlefield, *Rice and Slaves*, 171.

35. Clark, *State Records*, XXIII, 65. The law was re-enacted in 1741, see same volume, 19.

36. Johnson, *Antebellum North Carolina*, 590-92. Also see Franklin, *The Free Negro in North Carolina*, 35-39. For a general discussion on miscegenation in the South, see Kenneth Stampp, *The Peculiar Institution: Slavery in the Ante-Bellum South* (New York: Alfred A. Knopf, 1956), 350-61. See also Genovese, *Roll, Jordan, Roll*, 413-431 and James H. Johnston, *Race Relations in Virginia and Miscegenation in the South, 1776-1860* (Amherst: University of Massachusetts Press, 1970); Winthrop D. Jordan, *White Over Black: American Attitudes Toward the Negro, 1550-1812* (Chapel Hill: The University of North Carolina Press, 1968), 136-50. One of the best studies on miscegenation in the South and the nation as a whole is Joel Williamson, *New People: Miscegenation and Mulattoes in the United States* (New York: The Free Press, 1980); John C. Mencke, *Mulattoes and Race Mixture: American Attitudes and Images, 1865-1918* (UMI Press, 1976); Leonard R. Lempel, "The Mulatto in United States Race

Relations: Changing Status and Attitudes, 1800-1940" (Ph.D. dissertation, Syracuse University, 1979).

37. John W. Blassingame, ed., *Slave Testimony: Two Centuries of Letters, Speeches, Interviews, and Autobiographies* (Baton Rouge: Louisiana State University Press, 1977), 128; Rawick, *The American Slave*, I, 341.

38. *North Carolina Journal*, July 3, 1797; *Free Press*, November 20, 1829 and June 15, 1832; *North Carolina Intelligencer and Fayetteville Advertiser*, June 17, 1808; *People's Press*, November 12, 1834.

39. *Carolina Centinel*, February 19,1820; *Western Carolinian*, April 8, 1823 and May 8, 1827; *Raleigh Register*, April 28, 1826. Also see the *Free Press*, February 18, 1825 for Harris's advertisement for Austin.

40. Similar findings were made in Virginia and in South Carolina. Of 667 runaways in Virginia for whom color was given, 420 (63 percent) were said to be mulattoes, yellow, and light. In South Carolina, 37 percent of the fugitives were described in this manner. See Windley, "Profile of Runaway Slaves," 87. In a very small sample of 62 runaways in New England, Lorenzo Green found that 11 of the fugitives were described as mulattoes. See Lorenzo Green, "The New England Negro As Seen In Advertisements for Runaway Slaves," *Journal of Negro History* XXIX (1944): 134.

41. See the *Raleigh Register*, April 27, 1809. Hunt's 1824 advertisements for Piety can be found in the *Raleigh Register*, August 20, 1824 and in the *Free Press*, August 27, 1824.

42. *Carolina Observer*, July 21, 1835. Bess was sold three times while she was in flight. McRae was the last purchaser of Bess and her children.

43. See the *State Gazette of North Carolina*, March 19,1795 for both George and Edwin. *Carolina Centinel*, October 6, 1821; *Carolina Observer*, February 25, 1830. For other examples of yellow-complexioned and mulatto slaves who were said to be passing as free—taking advantage of their color, see the: *North Carolina Gazette; or Impartial Intelligencer*, November 3, 1785, June 4, 1791; *Raleigh Register*, February 28, 1811, May 13, 1814, August 12, 1814, November 4, 1814, and May 23, 1826 for Peggy, a 16 year-old mulatto girl who would, no doubt pass as free and be in possession of a free pass. *The Carolina Federal*

Republican, August 23, 1817 for the mulatto slave Bill, an artful and ingenious fellow whom his owner believed had obtained an indenture or a free pass, so as to pass as free; *Carolina Observer*, March 1, 1826 and April 28, 1835; *Cape Fear Recorder*, May 9, 1818; *The Star*, August 15, 1817; *North Carolina Minerva*, March 23, 1799, August 27, 1799, May 28, 1804, the *People's Press*, November 12, 1834 for the mulatto slave, Jo, who was two-thirds white, "and when cleanly dressed, "might pass" for a white man."

44. Department of Commerce, *Negro Population, 1790-1815*, 207-208, 221. Also Williamson, *New People*, see especially his chapter entitled, "Genesis," in which he traces the growth of the mulatto population in the United States. Williamson contended that there were "two Souths" during slavery: the upper South, stretching from North Carolina to Pennsylvania, and the lower South, from South Carolina to the Gulf of Mexico. Because of the larger number of mulattoes in the upper South, Williamson referred to it as the "mulatto belt" and the lower South the "black belt," Williamson, *New People*, 25. For the total number of mulattoes in the United States, by region and by state, see *Negro Population, 1790-1915*, 221.

45. *Carolina Centinel*, July 25, 1818, November 7, 1818, and June 26, 1821; *Carolina Observer*, June 19, 1823; *Fayetteville Gazette*, October 12, 1789 and October 2, 1792; *North Carolina Journal*, February 18, 1836; *Newbern Spectator*, June 10, 1836, February 10, 1837, and October 31, 1840; *Tarboro Press*, August 25, 1838; *People's Press and Wilmington Advertiser*, August 9, 1839; *North Carolina Standard*, November 18, 1840

46. *Raleigh Register*, September 5, 1803, February 13, 1824. Joseph Hawkins advertisements for Harry can be found in *The Star*, April 25, 1823 and the *Raleigh Register*, July 13, 1824. Estimates by owners of their runaways' weight can be found in *The Star*, April 25, 1806; *Carolina Observer*, September 17, 1833; *Newbern Spectator*, March 17, 1837; *Western Carolinian*, February 13, 1836; *Fayetteville Observer*, April 17, 1839, November 18, 1840; *Carolina Patriot*, December 7, 1838.

47. *Western Carolinian*, August 1, 1820, July 24, 1821, December 4, 1827. Hundreds of examples can be found for descriptions of slaves who were said to be stout, fat, corpulent, chunky, slim, and slender. See the following runaway notices as

representatives of these descriptions: North Carolina Gazette; or Impartial Intelligencer, September 2, 1784, September 24, 1791, March 23, 1791, August 31, 1793, and March 29, 1794; *Wilmington Chronicle; and North Carolina Weekly Advertiser*, September 24, 1795; *Hall's Wilmington Gazette*, March 23, 1797, April 6, 1797, April 20, 1797, and March 8, 1798; *Wilmington Gazette*, June 13, 1799, June 26, 1800, and August 14, 1800; *Raleigh Register*, March 25, 1800, February 24, 1801, and January 12, 1802; *Minerva*, November 14, 1803 and December 15, 1808; *American Recorder*, March 15, 1816, November 19, 1819, and March 23, 1821; *North Carolina Journal*, October 26, 1826, August 29, 1827, and November 7, 1827; *Free Press*, September 26, 1828, January 30, 1829, and April 10, 1829; *Miner's and Farmer's Journal*, September 21, 1831, April 17, 1832, and April 19, 1834; *North Carolina Standard*, January 23, 1835, March 13, 1835, May 22, 1835, and September 17, 1835; *Charlotte Journal*, November 7, 1839; *Carolina Watchman*, December 10, 1836; *Fayetteville Observer*, June 10, 1840; *Raleigh Register*, February 7, 1837; *Newbern Spectator*, November 25, 1836; *Washington Whig*, February 12, 1839; *The Star and North Carolina Gazette*, July 25, 1838 for Hercules who was "stout" and said to be "made for strength."

48. *North Carolina Gazette; or Impartial Intelligencer*, April 8, 1797; *Raleigh Register*, April 18, 1803, October 1, 1804; *Hillsborough Recorder*, February 20, 1822. For other instances in which slaves were injured in some manner, see the following advertisements: *Raleigh Register*, April 23, 1805; *North Carolina Journal*, April 21, 1806, *The Star*, July 31, 1818; *Carolina Centinel*, October 30, 1821; *Western Carolinian*, October 5, 1824 and July 12, 1825; *New Bern Spectator*, March 13, 1830, December 14, 1830; *Hornet's Nest*, June 24, 1813; *Newbern Gazette*, March 9, 1804 for the slave Polladore who had a scar on his left hand and feet caused by an axe, and a lump on his right hand—which he received as a result of fighting; *Raleigh Register*, July 17, 1837, February 4, 1839; *Milton Spectator*, July 11, 1837; *The Star and North Carolina Gazette*, September 15, 1836, October 10, 1838.

49. *North Carolina Gazette; or Impartial Intelligencer*, April 30, 1796; *Carolina Centinel*, September 19, 1818; *Free Press*, July 12, 1831; *Charlotte Journal*, June 10, 1836. Jacob, a Craven

County slave had his right hand so badly burned that his fingers were drawn up, see the *Carolina Centinel*, May 29, 1824. Temp lost all of the toes on her feet from a burn when she was small, *The Star*, August 18, 1820. Toney's hand was burned as high as his wrist, *North Carolina Journal*, November 5, 1798; *Milton Gazette and Roanoke Advertiser*, September 11, 1830; *Fayetteville Observer*, November 13, 1839; *Greensborough Patriot*, June 8, 1836

50. See for instance, the *Wilmington Gazette*, March 25, 1806 for Jack who had a scar between his eyes, "occasioned by the kick of a horse." Isaac had a scar over his right eye as a result of a horse kick. See the *Raleigh Register*, February 9, 1809. Robin had scars across his fingers and hands from the cut of a cotton gin. See the *Western Carolinian*, May 7, 1822. For eye injuries and blindness, see the *Raleigh Register*, June 14, 1807 and October 11, 1816; *Elizabeth City Star*, October 7, 1826 for Croatan, whose eye was damaged and remained half shut; *The Star*, March 29,1822 and the *North Carolina Journal*, August 28, 1797; *Newbern Spectator*, May 16, 1840.

51. The advertisement for Carolina and Daniel can be found in *The Star*, July 10, 1825; *Carolina Centinel*, February 27, 1819; *Catawba Journal*, June 5, 1827. For the other two slaves who were advertised as being shot, see North Carolina *Gazette*; or *Impartial Intelligencer*, August 9, 1794 for the slave Bob who had been shot, cut, and wounded in the right foot. And the *Raleigh Register*, September 15, 1815 for Robin who was shot in 1812, but was able to flee to Petersburg, Virginia where he worked as a carpenter.

52. Owners did not specifically indicate that the runaways received the damage to their toes and feet while they were in flight, but other sources show that because of inadequate shoes and clothing, fugitive slaves sometimes suffered from exposure. See for example Rawick, *From Sunup to Sundown*, 73-74. The following are advertisements for slaves who had been frost-bitten at some point: *Fayetteville North Carolina Chronicle; or Fayetteville Gazette*, November 1, 1790; *North Carolina Journal* May 18, 1795 for Jim who lost several of his toes from being frost-bitten; Welcome was badly damaged by the frost, *Edenton Gazette*, April 6, 1819; and the *Cape Fear Recorder*, October 16,

1824 for Lucy who walked lame because she suffered from frost bites.

53. Windley, "Profile of Runaway Slaves," 96.

54. William Dosite Postell, *The Health of Slaves on Southern Plantations* (Gloucester, Massachusetts: Peter Smith, 1970), 159-163. See also Postell's discussion on slave injuries, 88-89.

55. *Hall's Wilmington Gazette*, April 20, 1797. See the *Edenton Gazette*, February 22, 1811 for L.O. Bryan's advertisement for Jerry; *The Star*, April 19, 1811. For other examples in which slaves were whipped, see *The Star*, December 24, 1813, October 27, 1815 for the slave Joe who had a scar on his right cheek caused by a flogging, May 10, 1816, August 9, 1816, October 11, 1816, July 4, 1823 for Ned who was given a whipping the day before he fled from his owner, Green Alford of Wake County, and December 17, 1824 for Edith, a female slave who had whip marks on her shoulders and arms, and who was said to have left with a free black man; *Edenton Gazette*, July 11, 1814; *North Carolina Journal*, September 28, 1795; *North Carolina Gazette; or Impartial Intelligencer*, September 24, 1791, January 7, 1797; *Raleigh Register*, February 4, 1805 for Cherry, who had a welt across her breast from a whipping and a scar on her leg caused by the bite of a dog, March 19, 1824, May 4, 1824, and December 9, 1825 for Isaac who was marked by the hickory.

56. Clark, *State Records*, XXIII, 202-203.

57. *Minerva*, March 21, 1803; *Raleigh Register*, March 3, 1808; *Carolina Federal Republican*, February 29, 1812; *State Gazette of North Carolina*, December 9, 1789. See the following notices for slaves who had cropped ears: *Raleigh Register*, August 18, 1801, February 23, 1802, July 22, 1805, April 22, 1814, April 28, 1815, and October 11, 1816.

58. See Daniel Mannix and Malcolm Cowley, *Black Cargoes: A History of the Atlantic Slave Trade* (New York: Penguin Books, 1976), 47; Littlefield, *Rice and Slaves*, 123; Windley, "Profile of Runaway Slaves," 91.

59. *North Carolina Gazette; or Impartial Intelligencer*, February 25, 1797, July 4, 1795; *The Star*, September, 22, 1820. *North Carolina Standard*, July 18, 1838

60. *State Gazette of North Carolina*, July 4, 1795; *Raleigh Register*, January 9, 1818; *New Bern Spectator*, November 21,

1834. Descriptions of slaves who were branded by their present owner (the subscriber), or by a previous owner can be found in the fugitive notices that follow: *True Republican and Newbern Weekly Advertiser*, July 16, 1810; *State Gazette of North Carolina*, February 21, 1794; *Raleigh Register*, November 19, 1804, July 21, 1826 for the slaves Ben and Mike; *The Star*, September 30, 1814; *Edenton Gazette*, February 26, 1806 for Jacob who was branded with the letters J.S., the initials of his owner James Sutton, October 19, 1810, February 1, 1811, and June 5, 1820 for the fugitive George, a house servant who was burned with the letter R. George made several attempts to flee to Philadelphia, declaring that he would be free; it was for that reason that his owner Peter Evans branded an "R" on each cheek.

61. Hatch listed his address as Jones and Craven Counties from the 1790s through the 1820s. The Hatch's owned substantial land and large numbers of slaves in Jones County.

62. McLean, "A Yankee Tutor," 64.

63. *Carolina Centinel*, June 13, 1818, July 11, 1818. See the following runaway notices for slaves who were branded by Hatch: *Hall's Wilmington Gazette*, August 30, 1798; the *Carolina Federal Republican*, April 3, 1813 and August 6, 1814. Edmund Hatch and Hatch, Junior and a number of relatives advertised for several dozen slaves from the 1790s to the late 1820s. Their advertisements can be found in several Wilmington and Craven County newspapers, including the *Encyclopedia Instructor*, *True Republican and Newbern Weekly Advertiser*, *Newbern Herald*, *North Carolina Gazette; or Impartial Intelligencer*, and others.

64. *The Star*, July 11, 1823; *Raleigh Register*, January 25, 1822, April 27, 1809 for the first advertisement for Piety, and August 20, 1824 for Hunt's second notice describing Piety and her second flight from bondage. See the *Carolina Observer*, July 21, 1835 for Bess. Examples of reported bad teeth can be found in the following runaway notices: *State Gazette of North Carolina*, February 7, 1788 for the female slave Clary; *North Carolina Chronicle; or Fayetteville Gazette*, September 13, 1790; *State Gazette of North Carolina*, January 28, 1791; *North Carolina Intelligencer and Fayetteville Advertiser*, April 16, 1806, March 22, 1811; *The American*, October, 13, 1814; *Raleigh Register*,

July 27, 1821; *Carolina Federal Republican*, September 24, 1814, and February 22, 1817.

65. *Milton Spectator*, November 7, 1832; *People's Press*, November 12, 1834.

66. For a variety of these descriptions, see the *Edenton Intelligencer*, June 4, 1788; *Newbern Gazette*, November 24, 1798; *Encyclopedia Instructor*, May 21, 1800; *American Recorder*, January 19, 1816, February 27, 1824; *Carolina Federal Republican*, July 23, 1814, September 24, 1814, July 15, 1815; *Raleigh Register*, September 8, 1815, May 3, 1816, May 16, 1821; *New Bern Spectator*, May 2, 1829, October 24, 1829, December 18, 1830, May 25, 1832; *North Carolina Journal*, November 7, 1827, October 7, 1835; *People's Press*, August 21, 1833, February 19, 1834.

67. See Postell, *The Health of Slaves*, 88.

68. See Johnson, *Antebellum North Carolina*, 527-529 on the health of slaves in North Carolina, and on general health problems and diseases, 722-743. See also Postell, *Health of Slaves*, 74-88. For an excellent discussion on diseases and maladies suffered by slaves, see Todd L. Savitt, *Medicine and Slavery: The Diseases and Health Care of Blacks in Antebellum Virginia* (Urbana: University of Illinois Press, 1978). Although Savitt's book focuses on Virginia slaves, many of the diseases discussed were obviously present in North Carolina among black slaves and whites alike.

69. John Pettigrew to Charles Pettigrew, May 27, 1797 in Sarah McCulloh, ed., *The Pettigrew Papers* (Raleigh: State Department of Archives and History, 1971,), I, 210-211, 430-432. For other maladies, see the same volume, pages 240-241, 292, 355, and 405-406. Tom, described as a fiddler by Trotter in his correspondence to Ebenezer Pettigrew was no doubt, the same slave who fled from Trotter on at least three occasions between 1815 and 1824. See the *American Recorder*, May 15, 1815, May 23, 1821, and March 18, 1824.

70. Joel N. Shurkin, *The Invisible Fire: The Story of Mankind's Triumph over the Ancient Scourge of Smallpox* (New York: G.P. Putnam's Sons, 1979), 26. See also Donald Hopkins, *Princess and Peasants: Smallpox in History* (Chicago: The University of Chicago Press, 1983), see especially his chapter on the impact of smallpox in the United States, 234-281.

71. *True Republican and Newbern Weekly Advertiser*, August 7, 1811. The notice for Argyll, and Brunetta's second flight from slavery can be found in the *Wilmington Gazette*, January 8, 1805. Her escape in 1800 is in the same paper, October 23, 1800.

72. Notices for slaves with smallpox, or for those who had been afflicted with the disease can be found in newspapers across the state from the 1790s through the 1830s. See for example the *North Carolina Gazette*, May 8, 1778; *State Gazette of North Carolina*, July 2, 1789, August 27, 1790; *North Carolina Chronicle; or Fayetteville Gazette*, November 1, 1790, November 15, 1790; *Hall's Wilmington Gazette*, August 24, 1797; *North Carolina Journal*, June 4, 1798; *Wilmington Gazette*, June 10, 1806; *Raleigh Register*, February 9, 1809, March 22, 1810; *Edenton Gazette*, November 20, 1820; *Carolina Centinel*, June 3, 1820 and February 7, 1824. *North Carolina Standard*, May 16, 1838.

73. *Carolina Observer*, February 10, 1825. See also Johnson's discussion on North Carolina's reluctance to accept the smallpox variolation, Johnson, *Antebellum North Carolina*, 734-737. In reference to the inoculation, see Charles Pettigrew to Ebenezer Pettigrew, June 30, 1802 in Lemmon, ed., *The Pettigrew Papers*, 288-289.

74. Savitt, *Medicine and Slavery*, 219.

75. *Fayetteville Observer*, October 30, 1792. Stampp, *The Peculiar Institution*, 306. For maladies, including colds, warts, cancer, and others, see the following runaway notices; *Carolina Federal Republican*, August 20, 1814 for the slave Daniel who had an ulcer on his head; *Halifax Minerva*, July 23, 1829 for Arthur who was said to have a cancer on the bottom of his foot; *Western Carolinian*, July 12, 1825; *The Star*, April 18, 1817; *Raleigh Register*, August 16, 1836; *North Carolina Standard*, November 18, 1840.

76. *Raleigh Register*, May 24, 1816, March 19, 1824. See also the *North Carolina Journal*, November 3, 1806 for the slave Abraham who was subject to rheumatic pains. The notices for Isham and Kit are in *The Star*, May 25, 1820 and *North Carolina Journal*, November 7, 1827, respectively.

77. *Cape Fear Recorder*, August 2, 1823. Some of the same descriptions were found by Postell in his survey of plantations

and medical records, Postell, *Health of Slaves*, 160-163; Savitt, *Medicine and Slavery*, 49-80.

78. On the relationship between nutritional deficiencies and disease, see Savitt, *Medicine and Slavery, 86-98*; Leslie H. Owens, *This Species of Property: Slave Life and Culture in the Old South* (New York: Oxford University Press, 1976), 50-69; Kenneth F. Kiple and Virginia H. King, *Another Dimension of the Black Diaspora: Diet, Disease, and Racism* (Cambridge: Cambridge University Press, 1981), 117-133.

79. See the *Wilmington Gazette*, August 23, 1808 for Hannah; *Edenton Gazette*, September 17, 1821; *People's Press and Wilmington Advertiser*, June 30, 1837.

80. *Edenton Gazette*, July 20, 1819.

81. The advertisement for Jin can be found in *The Star*, November 12, 1819. Notices for the slave women who were destined for other states are in the *Hillsborough Recorder*, March 29, 1820; *Western Carolinian*, February 12, 1828; and *Halifax Minerva*, August 27, 1829.

82. The runaway notices for these expectant mothers who fled with their husbands can be found in the *North Carolina Gazette; or Impartial Intelligencer*, July 29, 1784; *North Carolina Minerva*, November 4, 1797; *The Star*, February 5, 1819; *Raleigh Register*, July 20, 1824 and September 10, 1838; *North Carolina Standard*, September 17, 1835. The advertisement for the African born slaves is in the *Raleigh Register*, November 24, 1806.

83. See Johnson, *Antebellum North Carolina*, 523-524; Taylor, *Slaveholding in North Carolina*, 91-92; Genovese, *Roll, Jordan, Roll*, 550-552; Stampp, *The Peculiar Institution*, 289-292; Postel, *The Health of Slaves*, 38-43.

84. For recent discussions on slave clothing and descriptions in advertisements for runaway slaves, see Randall M. Miller and John David Smith, *Dictionary of Afro-American Slavery*. (Westport, Connecticut: Greenwood Press, 1989), 117-21; Patricia Campbell Warner and Debra Parker in Barbara M. Starke and others, *African American Dress and Adornment* (Dubuque, Iowa: Kendall/Hunt Publishing Company, 1990), 82-91. See in particular pp. 85-90 where the authors discuss types of cloth used in slave clothing, fabrication, and other sources of clothing for slaves. See also Gloria M. Williams and Carol Centrallo in the

same source, 51-65. An excellent source is Jonathan Prude, "To Look Upon the 'Lower Sort': Runaway Ads and the Appearance of Unfree Laborers in America, 1750-1800," *Journal of American History* (July 1991): 125-59.

85. On the purchase of slave clothing and garments made by the slave mistress and the slave seamstresses, see the sources in the preceding note. See also Thomas Trotter to Ebenezer Pettigrew, October, 28, 1810 in Lemmon, ed., *The Pettigrew Papers*, 432 in which Trotter wrote that Mrs. Trotter was "obliged...to see about Negro clothing."

86. *North Carolina Gazette*, February 20, 1775; *State Gazette of North Carolina*, March 25, 1791; *The Star*, September 11, 1812.

87. Below are examples of descriptions of clothing worn by fugitive slaves between 1775 and 1840. The effort is to show the variety of garments and the dress of slaves across the state. See the *North Carolina Gazette*, March 24,1775, July 4, 1777, August 1, 1777; *State Gazette of North Carolina*, April 9, 1789, July 9, 1790; *Newbern Gazette*, November 24, 1798; *North Carolina Journal*, March 4, 1799; *Raleigh Register*, June 3, 1800, May 4, 1802, July 11,1803, August 22, 1803; *Wilmington Gazette*, September 25, 1804, December 4, 1804; *Minerva*, May 19, 1806, February 25, 1808, October 6, 1808, January 17, 1812, March 29, 1812; *American Recorder*, March 23, 1821; *Carolina Centinel*, December 4, 1824, April 8, 1826, July 8, 1826; *Greensboro Patriot*, December 27, 1826, March 24, 1830; *North Carolina Spectator and Western Advertiser*, June 18, 1830, December 10, 1831; *Oxford Examiner*, October 4, 1832; *Western Carolinian*, March 29, 1834, December 6, 1834, August 22, 1835; *Newbern Spectator*, March 10, 1837; *The Star and North Carolina Gazette*, May 29, 1839; *Western Carolinian*, February 13, 1836; *North Carolina Standard*, July 28, 1836.

88. See for example, the *Minerva*, June 5, 1812 for James H. Keys's elaborate description of his mulatto slave Jacob. Keys maintained that: "To describe him by his dress would be impossible, as he carried off several articles of clothing of different colours." See also the *American Recorder*, November 19,1819.

89. *Raleigh Register*, July 13, 1824.

90. *Free Press*, August 1, 1818; the notice for Alford is in the *Newbern Spectator*, November 24, 1837. For other examples of fugitives who took their clothing, see as representatives, the *Raleigh Register*, January 19, 1816, March 9, 1821 for the slave John, who left Governor John Branch's plantation in Wake County on February 25, 1821, carrying clothes tied up in a red handkerchief, and April 27, 1821 for Welcome and his daughter Betsy, who both took a fine supply of clothing, including some made of silk; *Carolina Observer*, March 4, 1819; *New Bern Spectator*, August 7, 1830, November 8, 1833; April 27, 1838 *Charlotte Journal*, February 17, 1840, March 5, 1840; *Raleigh Register*, January 29, 1838; *Fayetteville Observer*, October 18, 1837; *Hillsborough Recorder*, July 25, 1839, September 5, 1839; *Greensborough Patriot*, June 8, 1836; *Tarboro Press*, August 8, 1840; *Western Carolinian*, February 13, 1836.

CHAPTER FOUR

Slave Personalities

There are dozens of theories of personality. Psychologists, such as, Sigmund Freud, Alfred Adler, Carl Jung, Harry Stack Sullivan, Gordon Allport, and others have all made significant contributions to our understanding of what constitutes personality. In 1937, Gordon Allport categorized fifty definitions of personality into six broad areas. The definitions ranged from overt behavior and appearance of the individual, to Freud's belief that the unconscious mind and childhood experiences largely determined the behavior and actions of individuals. Between these two definitions of personality lie the belief that motives, feelings, thoughts, and emotions made individuals unique human beings. And finally, some psychologists state simply that personality is the aggregate of a person's "inherited and mental qualities."[1] In sum then, personality can be looked at as the mental, physical, emotional, and spiritual attributes that make human beings who they are.

Whatever present day definitions are used to describe what personality is, slaveowners who advertised for their runaway slaves in the late eighteenth- and early nineteenth- centuries, described what must be considered, important aspects of their slaves' personalities. Owners provided descriptions of their fugitives' countenance, or facial expressions; a number of slaveowners also noted their runaways' deportment, or the kind of conduct and behavior they exhibited. Masters also described their slaves' ability to communicate orally, including, their proficiency in English, speech impediments, and whether or not they spoke other languages. These portrayals were less concrete than the physical delineations discussed earlier. They were not constant and obviously changed according to the situation in which slaves found themselves. But these were basic personality traits that owners believed would prevail under most circumstances.

In a description of countenance, slaveowners were concerned with providing clues as to how slaves would present themselves when approached by whites. Hundreds of subscribers noted that their slaves possessed "a good countenance," "a pleasing or pleasant look," "a grum sullen countenance," and other features.[2] Durant Hatch's description is indicative of the facial expressions that some slaves wore. He wrote that his sixteen-year-old fugitive Mary, "generally wears a pleasing countenance, and is very likely." Alexander Peden of Wilmington, likewise, wrote that his runaway, Sarah, was lively in her conversation, "and frequently accompanied with a smile." The slave Jack and an unnamed slave fled from their Currituck County owners on June 18, 1791. The July 18, 1791 advertisement in the *State Gazette of North Carolina* (Edenton) described Jack as having a "boyish and down look," while the other slave was portrayed as possessing "a very smiling countenance, and when he laughs shows his upper gums...." Some slaves exhibited "mild countenances," while others looked "humble," and generally displayed pleasant, non-threatening dispositions.[3]

Many runaways could be identified by their "grum," "sullen," and "sulky" temperaments. These were slaves who were somewhat withdrawn; no doubt, they were dispirited, angry, and their melancholy appearance was used by their owners to describe them. Dick, for example, a slave who escaped from Henry C. Hatch's plantation in Jones County had a "sulky countenance." Dick had good reason to be angry, dispirited, and even a bit rebellious because he was separated from his family. Dick's father lived on a farm near Kinston, and his wife and mother resided in two different areas of Newbern. Hatch believed that the man would probably lurk about the areas in which his family lived. William B. Shepherd, who lived four miles below Elizabeth City in Pasquotank County, noted that his fugitive, Jerry, who left him on September 29, 1807, "when spoken to has a very grum look." Pompey's "sullen countenance" may have been due to his being purchased from his Suffolk, Virginia owner by William Anderson of Caswell County, North Carolina. Anderson, Pompey's new owner wrote that the runaway would, no doubt, find his way back to Suffolk.[4]

While some slaves presented themselves with a congenial demeanor, and others in a withdrawn fashion, there was another group of runaways who made no attempt to hide their feelings. They were bold, confident, and proud-looking. Some were even described by their owners as having a "nasty," "surly," and arrogant disposition. The slave Bill was such a person. He left his owner Nehemiah Hearn of Montgomery County on the night of November 28, 1825. Hearn's advertisement—which appeared in the *Western Carolinian* (Salisbury) nearly two months later—was explicit about the runaway's disposition. Hearn described Bill as having "a brazen saucy countenance; when spoken to, [he] speaks in a very impolite, abrupt manner..." Bill also chewed tobacco, and found the means to secure several articles of clothing, including, four suits, two hats, two pairs of shoes, and two coats, one of which was "of the very best quality, lined with new red flannel." The yellow-complexioned slave also took forty to fifty dollars with him. Hearn believed that Bill had obtained a free pass, and would go to Carroll County, Tennessee where he would pass as a free man.[5]

The facial expressions that slaves wore did not always reflect their true personalities. A smiling, pleasing, down cast, and pleasant countenance, in many instances, was the mask that slaves wore. After all, eluding captivity was their paramount concern. And many individuals played the role that their status as slaves called for—that of an unassuming, meek, and submissive character. Other slaves, without doubt, did internalize the roles ascribed to them, and played them well. On the other hand, the "bold and forward countenance" displayed by the slave John, and the "bad disposition" exhibited by Sam, did not occur as frequently.[6] Perhaps slaves were aware that it was "suicidal" to present a brazen, "ugly" portrait of themselves.

Men were more likely to show a "sullen," "sulky," "bad" countenance. The appearances that runaway slaves presented did not necessarily mirror their conduct or actions either. Those fugitives who looked as if they were meek and humble, for example, also committed felonies and were often deceptive and manipulative in their actions. Bold, surly looking runaways, on the other hand, were sometimes submissive in their relationships with whites.

Slaveowners also provided information about their slaves' ability to speak the English language. This was especially true in the case of foreign-born slaves. Several African-born fugitives had not been acculturated to the extent that they had learned any English. This was usually due to their length of time in America. For instance, the five African-born slaves—Kauchee, Boohum, Ji, Sambo Pool, and Peg Manny—who escaped from Edward Batchelor and Company in Newbern in February 1775 were "incapable of uttering a word of English..." He also believed that the fugitives had been enticed "away by some infamously principled Person, of a fairer Complexion, but darker Disposition than theirs." In November 1806, William Baxter's runaway notice for "Four African Negro Slaves" appeared in the *Raleigh Register*. Only one of the slaves who escaped from Baxter near Rutherfordton, North Carolina on September 23, 1806, could speak any English. Baxter believed that the two men and two women would soon be jailed in North or South Carolina.[7]

Most African-born runaways, however, did exhibit some knowledge of the English language. And slaveowners were careful to point out their slaves' degree of proficiency in English. Such phrases as, "he speaks broken English," or "he speaks bad English," were often used to describe both African-born and creole slaves' use of English. Thus, the thirty year-old slave, Dublin, who had filed teeth was a "New Negro," who spoke broken English..." Dick, a slave who belonged to Everitt House of Dobbs County, and who had a number of physical markings, including missing toes, a large scar on his right knee, and country marks over his face and body, spoke "very much broken..." According to Bajieu Laporte, Suck, an African-born runaway, looked and talked like a newly imported slave. The slaves Toby, Sampson, Joe, Bill, Anthony, and Austin all were reported to have spoken "broken English."[8] A number of other African-born fugitives could speak English, but their owners maintained that they spoke the language poorly. Ben, described by his owner as being between 30 and 40 years of age, and marked on each arm with the signature of his country, spoke "bad English..." Jinkin Avirett, noted also, that his Guinea-born slave, Sampson, who was a "fortune teller and conjurer," spoke "bad English."[9]

While a few African-born slaves lacked the ability to speak the tongue of their masters, and others could barely speak the language, a number of them spoke English rather proficiently. If the African-born slave did not have filed teeth, or if he had not been scarified, his speech pattern and facility with English were the most significant elements in identifying him. Slaves who spoke English fluently, and spoke their native tongue as well could have easily beguiled unsuspecting whites. This was especially true if owners described their slaves as African-born without mentioning their facility in English.

Typically, slaves who spoke proficiently were depicted in the following manner. Although Surry, a thirty year-old slave, who once belonged to Governor William Tryon was a "new Negro," he spoke "pretty good English." Lang, an African-born runaway, spoke "very good English." And because he was brought to America at a very young age, the African-born slave, George, had very little memory of his native tongue, and no doubt, spoke English well.[10] Owners sometimes indicated that their slaves spoke English well, but they failed to provide any information about their place of origin. Considering the dates of the advertisements, it is likely that those slaves were also foreign-born.[11]

Slaveowners also described the ability of West Indian-born slaves to speak English. In addition, masters pointed out their slaves' familiarity with other languages. Slaves were imported to the United States from non-English speaking, as well as, English speaking nations and owners were concerned with providing readers with as much information as possible about their fugitives' knowledge of different languages. F. Briols of Chowan County, for instance, wrote that his runaway slave was a "French Negro Man" who spoke "tolerable good English." Oliver Smith's slaves, Anthony and John, spoke "broken English" and French. Smith believed that the two fugitives, who escaped from him in Pitt County in April, 1796, had intentions of boarding a vessel to return to the West Indies. The runaways—But Easter Gardner, Grudge, Prince, Joe, and Isham—spoke French and English "tolerably well."[12]

In their descriptions of creole slaves, owners seemed to have focused less on how well their fugitives spoke English, and more on the manner, disposition, tone, and craftiness of their speech.[13] It was in these descriptions that slaveowners attempted to alert white citizens about the way in which their fugitives would respond verbally when addressed by them. These accounts shed light on the slaves' personality and their view of the dominant white class. The notices are also a testimony to the diversity of slave discourse, their world views, and their ideas about themselves as individuals. Slaveowners used numerous phrases to describe the style and linguistic peculiarities that their slaves used to express themselves.

Slaves expressed themselves verbally very much in the manner they presented themselves in their countenance. Some slaves were described as being soft-spoken, timid, polite, and slow-spoken in their conversation. Toney, a slave who lived in Beaufort County, had a sly look and spoke very politely. Alexander Johnson's slave, Joe, spoke low and humble. John Watson indicated that his slave, Peter, who fled from Wadesboro, North Carolina in July 1828, was "rather slow spoken." Sandy and Anthony, two slaves who escaped from their owner, Samuel Potter of Wilmington in July 1834, "spoke slowly." Potter maintained that Sandy was able to speak plainly because he spoke slowly.[14]

Hundreds of slaveowners noted that their runaways spoke "quickly" and "abruptly." The most common phrase used by masters was that their slaves "talked fast." In addition, a number of masters pointed out that their fugitives spoke with confidence, with assurance, and with boldness. Other runaways were portrayed as individuals who spoke freely, while many were loquacious. Some runaways were reported to have been intelligent in their oral communications. This was often reported when owners believed their fugitives would use their ability to speak plainly and effectively to deceive whites and to elude captivity. The picture painted by slaveowners is at variance with the "Sambo" image of slaves that has survived over the years. In most cases when owners described their slaves' speech characteristics, they portrayed men and women who were anything but "Sambos."

The thirty-five year old slave Rachel, for example, walked "very pert," and answered quickly when she was addressed. Henry Swink, who lived near Salisbury, wrote that his "rather chunky built" twenty-six year old slave, Easter, was "bold in her looks" and spoke fast. Although Easter was pregnant, she fled alone during the winter of 1828, taking with her, a considerable amount of clothes. Swink believed that Easter had obtained a free pass, and would travel to Tennessee, or go to Granville County where she "came from." Jack, a Sampson County slave also had a bold look, and was quick spoken. Joseph B. Skinner of Edenton described his forty year old fugitive, Andrew, as having a sharp visage, a retreating forehead, a rather surly countenance, and a man who answered "short and quick." Andrew fled because his wife—who belonged to a man near Edenton—was about to be sent to Philadelphia or to New York. Skinner surmised that his runaway was going to one or both of those Northern cities to see his wife. And finally, S.M. Stewart of Chapel Hill, placed an advertisement in the *Hillsborough Recorder* for James, a slave who was a servant at The University of North Carolina for four years before he fled on November 20, 1829. According to Stewart, the fugitive was a man who spoke quickly "and with ease, and is in the habit of shaking his head while in conversation." Stewart added that James was probably well-dressed, and had also taken considerable clothing with him. He believed that the runaway would either attempt to reach a free state via Norfolk or Richmond, Virginia, or would associate himself with the Colonization Society.[15]

Many slaves had a lot to say. They were talkative; and often, as owners pointed out, slaves who were loquacious could talk themselves out of being captured. And owners warned whites that their slaves would attempt to do such. Many fugitives were reported to have the capacity to tell plausible stories.[16] And because of their artful, cunning ability—they, no doubt, eluded captivity for long periods of time.

In a lengthy advertisement for his absconded slave Anthony, Ebenezer Burnap of Onslow County, wrote that the fugitive was "very active and ingenious...[and] quite talkative." Not only was Anthony well-dressed, but he also "stole some good clothes" from his owner. Burnap warned that Anthony "is a cunning, artful fellow...and has no doubt obtained forged free papers and will probably attempt to go to some of the northern states." In route to the North, Anthony could have used his "competent knowledge" of the blacksmith trade to aid him in his quest for freedom. Alice Heron wrote in 1809 that her slave, Lucy, was "remarkable for her loquacity." Concerning his runaway slave, Essex, John Drew of Edenton noted that the forty-five year old slave was, "palavering in his discourse, a great villian, for which he has been lately branded..." Primus, a yellow-complexioned slave, scarred on one of his temples, spoke plain English and was very talkative. His owner, Susanna Bordeaux maintained that Primus would pass as a free man and hire himself out to one John Campbell in Fayetteville.[17] According to many subscribers, talkative, chattering slaves were common—and this was instrumental in their ability to deceive and to further advance their chances of securing freedom.[18]

The runaway advertisements clearly indicate the variety of ways in which slaves responded to whites verbally. And although slaves were expected to play the submissive, subservient role, many did not. A number of slaveowners were quick to reveal that some fugitives spoke in a defiant, "repugnant" manner. Consider for example, the fugitive Adam, a slave who fled from Osborn Hunter in Johnston County. According to Hunter, Adam was a man who answered "uncommonly bold" when spoken to. Believing that the runaway would lurk about Raleigh or Sampson County, Hunter offered "a generous Reward to any Person who will secure him with Irons in any Jail convenient to where he may be taken..." William C. Nelson of Craven County in advertising for his runaway Marcus, who had been hired out to Roger Jones, wrote that the forty year-old slave spoke boldly. Other slaves responded arrogantly to whites. Although the slave Nero had an impediment in his speech, he was nevertheless, "insolent in his address."[19]

Other slaves could be identified by their remarkably confident, assured, open, bold, and free speech. Despite the fact that Virgin had a "downish" look when he was spoken to by whites, his response to their questions was full of confidence. Granderson, a carpenter who belonged to John D. Hawkins of Franklin County was "blunt spoken" and also spoke with assurance. D.W. Davis's slave, Emanuel, spoke quickly, and with great confidence. Mary Moor of New Hanover County, noted that Sarah—who fled from her on August 12, 1804, and who was going to Fayetteville—was "very free spoken."[20]

Slaves possessed a wide range of unique speech patterns, and slaveowners were not hesitant in describing their diversity. Coupled with their portraits of slave discourse, owners revealed much more about slaves and who they were. For instance, the fugitive Simbo, was an Onslow County Methodist preacher who spoke very distinctly. Nathaniel Hunt of Franklin County noted that his runaway Henry, "talks short and appears dissident when spoken to." A number of owners emphasized the intelligence level of their slaves, which was usually an indication of their belief that the slave would pass as free, leave the state, or deceive would-be captors. Frank, for example, had a pleasing countenance, and spoke plainly and intelligently.[21]

Some slaves had "rough," "coarse" voices, while some owners noted that their slaves possessed "weak," "effiminate," "soft" voices. The Oxford, Granville County slave, Oliver, was described in such a manner. Thomas B. Littlejohn, in a rather detailed advertisement, wrote that his slave, who had been employed as a waiter in Oxford, "is very polite and courteous in his address, has rather a soft, effiminate voice, and has a short quick step when he walks." Littlejohn requested that two other newspapers, the *Carolina Federal Republican* and the *Charleston Courier*, also insert the advertisement. Littlejohn believed that Oliver, who left by horseback, was bound for Newbern or some other seaport.[22]

Some owners indicated that their runaways were "smooth spoken," or "sensible" when speaking. Moses, reportedly was "smooth spoken, and humble to white people." Caroline, a fifteen year-old female slave who fled from her owner, Joseph F. Anthony in June 1835, spoke "very sensibly." And because of her sensible speech Rachel was able to lurk about the suburbs of Newbern for at least six months without being captured, as Anthony's notice for her absence did not appear until December 25, 1835. In an elaborate description of his slave Ben, Alexander Sorsby of Nash County, specified that his slave spoke "broad and quick, and endeavors to speak proper language." Ben was also described as a very intelligent man who had escaped before, and was familiar with several other states, "seaport towns, and other noted places."[23]

An examination of the newspaper advertisements for slave runaways, shows that some slaves suffered from speech disorders. Slaveowners revealed that a number of fugitives had lisps—a speech defect characterized by improper pronunciation of certain sibilants, while other runaways stuttered or stammered.[24] Some owners were not as precise in denoting their runaways' specific speech defect, and simply resorted to noting that they possessed a "speech impediment." It is likely that these individuals stuttered too, as owners sometimes used the term "stuttering" and the phrase "he has a speech impediment" in the same notice. The etiology of speech disorders among slaves has been debated for a number of years—with the subject of stuttering and stammering receiving most of the attention.

In his study on runaway slaves in eighteenth-century Virginia, Gerald Mullin theorized that a relationship existed between slave occupation and stuttering. He found that waitingmen and sailors were "heavily represented among stutterers," and it was their "mobility and frequency of contact with whites" that caused them to stutter. Mullin posited that the environment in which these slaves found themselves was "highly stressful." Other slave occupations, such as, carpentry, blacksmith, and shoemaking were not represented among the stutterers that Mullin found in the runaway notices, leading him to speculate that these craftsmen did not stutter because they "characteristically worked by themselves, at their own pace, and with a minimum of direct and persistent supervision."[25] Mullin, then, attributed slave stuttering to the psychological stress that resulted from contact between waitingmen, sailors, and whites.

John Blassingame maintained that there were many causes of stuttering among slaves. He contended that: "Much of the hesitation, stuttering, or rapidity in speech may have resulted from their slave's unfamiliarity with European languages, missing teeth, and other physical infirmities. The peculiarities may have had no relation to any extreme anxiety about white people." Other scholars have also attempted to construct a physiological framework for understanding slave stuttering. In their study on runaways in colonial North Carolina, Kay and Cary wrote that speech impediments possibly "stemmed from physiological reasons." Latham Windley believed that psychological stress was related to stuttering because slaves lived "under the condition of permanent slavery." He averred, however, that the psychological stress that slaves experienced, and their occupations did not satisfactorily explain why slaves stuttered. Windley, for instance, found that of 94 runaways who stuttered in Virginia and South Carolina, 22 (23.4 percent) were skilled. Obviously, the question is, how do you explain the disorder in the 76.6 percent of stutterers who were unskilled?[26]

Between 1775 and 1840, slaveowners in North Carolina advertised for at least 120 fugitives who stuttered or stammered, had a speech impediment, or a lisp. Based on the notices, 88, or 73.3 percent of all speech disorders were classified as stuttering or stammering. Twenty-three (19.2 percent) had a "speech impediment," while 9 (7.5 percent) slaves reportedly had a lisp. Nearly five percent of the 2,661 runaways had a speech disorder. Only 4, or 3.3 percent of the slaves with speech disorders were female (see table 8). This disparity confirms twentieth century scholarship on stuttering. It is a disorder that is characteristically male, in which four out of five people who stutter are boys and men.[27]

Of the 120 fugitives who had a speech disorder, only 26, or about 22 percent were advertised as having a skill. Eleven of these twenty-six fugitives worked as carpenters, or as shoemakers. Twelve of the runaways were employed in at least eleven different occupations, ranging from waiting to blacksmith, tannery, ditching, saw-milling, carriage driving and hostling, coopering, cobbling, and house service, while three of the men were boatmen (see table 9). One of these men stuttered only when he was frightened or alarmed; one of the boatmen had a "slight" speech impediment; and the third man stuttered, but no explanation was given for the disorder. Three other boatmen who fled from their owners had no speech disorders whatsoever.[28] The notion that waiters and sailors stuttered because of their contact with white authority is not supported by these findings. It appears then that there was no correlation between specific occupations and stuttering. All slaves, whether they were skilled or unskilled, had contact with whites in North Carolina. Absentee ownership did not exist in the slave South. Most farms and plantations were relatively small, containing less than twenty slaves, which meant that white slaveowners and their children were in constant contact with their slaves.

Table 8

Slaves with Speech Disorders in Skilled Occupations

Number of Stutterers		Total	Percent	Number of Skilled Slaves
Male	Female			
86	2	88	73.3	21
Speech Impediments				
22	1	23	19.2	4
Lisp				
8	1	9	7.5	1
		120	100.0	26

Source: North Carolina Extant Newspapers, 1775-1840

Slaveowners offered a number of explanations as to what caused their slaves to stutter. It appears that one group of slaves were "true stutterers"—that is, they probably began stuttering as children, as most stutterers do. It was a disorder that continued through adulthood, and, in no way related to their fear of whites.[29] A number of owners noted without further explanation

Table 9

Occupations of Skilled Runaways with Speech Disorders

Occupation	Number	Percentage
Blacksmith	2	7.7
Boatmen	3	11.5
Carpenter	5	19.2
Cobbler, cooper, carpenter	1	3.9
Cooper	2	7.7
Cooper, shoemaker	2	7.7
Ditcher, sawyer	1	3.8
Hostler, carriage driver	1	3.9
House servant	1	3.9
Shoemaker	6	23.0
Tanner	1	3.8
Waitingmen	1	3.9
Total	26	100.0

Source: North Carolina Extant Newspapers, 1775-1840

that their slaves stuttered. William Davis of New Hanover County, for instance, wrote that the slave Bob, a carpenter, stuttered so badly that he could hardly be understood. Emery, a slave who belonged to James Williams of Duplin County stammered "very much in his speech." The fugitive Sam, who had attempted to run to Norfolk, Virginia on a previous occasion, stuttered in his speech. According to their owners, Ranson, Lucy, David, Toney, and Charles all stuttered for no apparent reason.[30]

Many owners were more certain about when their slaves would stutter, or why they would display a speech impediment. Some slaves, out of sheer fear of being caught, "stumbled" in their speech. Consider for example, George Klutts's fugitive John. According to Klutts, John—whom he feared would alter his and his owner's name—stammered when he was angry or afraid. In reference to his runaway Harry, Charlton Leary wrote that, "when scared [he is] apt to stutter. Andrew Murdock, who lived near Hillsborough, reported that his twenty year-old fugitive Stephen, had "a stoppage in his speech, and when either scared or surprised [stuttered] a good deal." Other slaves stuttered when they were in a hurry, or spoke fast. Bill, a New Hanover County slave, who to the dismay of his owner, endeavored to board a vessel and leave North Carolina with bedding blankets, stammered "in his speech when the least hurried." Muse's speech impediment was due to his rapid speech. W.B. Grist of Beaufort County, likewise described his runaway Jesse, as a man who "stuttered when talking fast." And the country-born fugitive Minor, stammered a little in his speech when he talked fast.[31]

Some slaveowners were aware that their slaves stuttered when they were questioned by a white person. Fear of the whip, and of white authority, without doubt, placed many slaves under stress; and although they were bold enough to run away, the interrogation by whites caused nervous conditions, of which stuttering was a symptom. Peter Maxwell wrote in 1797 that his slave had absconded with another slave named Parker. Although Parker was a man who appeared bold, and "had gained notions of being free," his running mate stammered "when spoken to by a white person." D.W. Davis of Franklin County indicated in his runaway notice for Simon, that he was "inclined to stutter, particularly when closely interrogated." The fugitive Frank possessed a pleasing countenance, and spoke plainly and intelligently, but stammered in his speech when interrogated. Shadrack Stallings of Duplin County pointed out in his notice for his Wake County born, artful slave, Aston, that he stuttered "sharply when spoken to." Peter, a Chatham County slave who belonged to John Headen, had "an impediment in his speech, and when closely examined or agitated, stutters."[32]

Some slaves exhibited disfluencies when confused, embarrassed, or implicated in a "wrongdoing." Gloster, for example, stuttered "particularly when confused." Will, a slave who lived on James S. Battle's Coal Spring plantation near Tarboro, stuttered "in his conversation and considerably when confused." James G. Cuthbert's eighteen year-old slave possessed a pleasant countenance, and stammered whenever he was "accused of anything improper..." The slaves' oral hygiene also played a role in the cause of their speech disorders. As discussed earlier, a number of slaveowners specified the poor condition of their fugitives' teeth. Simon's speech impediment, for instance, had nothing at all to do with psychological stress and fear of whites. His owner, David D. Frater of Craven County, attributed his condition to "the loss of some of his front teeth." The absence of some of Dinah's incisors interfered with her speech.[33]

The affliction of stuttering for many slaves was, no doubt, neurophysiologically-based. This is a theory which holds that motor muscle behavior of human beings is controlled by the neocerebellum. The cerebral cortex carries messages to the cerebellum, in which specific behaviors are programmed. In turn, the message is transmitted to the cerebral motor strip, "which then initiates the muscle behaviors necessary to carry out the program"—in this case—speech. Children, two to four years of age experience normal cerebellar function, yet they stutter. It is at this age, according to Charles Overstake, that "the onset of stuttering is a normal developmental phenomenon," that "is remediated as the nervous system grows, matures, and becomes increasingly myelinated." Stuttering continues when there is a "neurophysiological aberration," or an alteration in thought-to-speech behavior. In other words, a small percentage of children, for some unknown reason, continue to stutter because they change their "thought-to-speech behavior so that they do not think or speak as a fluent speaker."[34]

Although hundreds of books and articles have been written on stuttering, researchers maintain that the etiology of the affliction remains an enigma. Dozens of theories exist on its cause, as well as the treatment of the disorder. If clinicians are perplexed when they observe stutterers in their offices, and are unsure about the cause of their patients' speech impediment, then it is dangerous for twentieth-century scholars to attempt to apply definitive causes to slave stuttering in the eighteenth- and nineteenth-centuries. Eugene Genovese, for example, warned in regard to stuttering that: "Recent psychological researches cannot be projected back in an attempt to construct a depth psychology of strangers long since dead."[35] Several different causes can be advanced for slave stuttering and other speech disorders. And though some slaveowners did seek to explain why their slaves had a speech impediment, most simply mentioned the condition, and sought not to note its cause.

The wide array of speech characteristics that slaves exhibited reflected the diversity of slave personality types.[36] There has been considerable debate over the years concerning slave personality. Scholars, seemingly, have been in search of the "typical" slave. Did slaves internalize their prescribed roles? Was American slavery "closed" to the extent that it produced a "Sambo" personality type? Did North American slaves rebel against slavery on the order that West Indian slaves did? For Stanley Elkins, the answer to the first two questions is yes, and to the last, it is no. Elkins maintained that the unique feature of slavery in the United States was that it was "closed." The "closed" system of slavery, according to Elkins, was based on the totality of the slaves' powerlessness, and their complete dependence on their owners. The slaves' very existence was tied—in every way—to their masters. And it obviously follows that slaves engaged in little if any protest against the system of slavery. Elkins concluded that the system produced "Sambos"—slaves who were docile, irresponsible, loyal, lazy, "humble but chronically given to lying and stealing; his behavior was full of infantile silliness and his talk inflated with childish exaggeration. His relationship with his master was one of utter dependence and childlike attachment: it was indeed this childlike quality that was the very key to his being."[37] Elkins viewed this personality type as typical among American black slaves.

Scholars have responded to Elkins since 1959, and as a result, there has been a profusion of books and articles on slave personality. An analysis of data that, theretofore, had not been carefully examined, showed indeed, that Elkins's views were parochial, and to some extent, unfounded.[38] The use of slave narratives by scholars, for example, shed some light on slave personalities. Elkins did not analyze the narratives, nor did he examine fugitive slave advertisements. The runaway notices provide a vivid portrait of the diversity of slave personality types, and in no way, do they present a picture of slaves who completely internalized roles, and who lived totally within the realm of their owners' wishes. Slaveowners who advertised for runaway slaves were candid in their notices because they wanted to secure their slaves—property in which they had invested significant amounts of money. They had no reason to be dishonest in describing their slaves. If slaves were docile, impudent, intelligent, loquacious, stubborn, artful, defiant, keen, or shrewd—owners were likely to report that fact. Why, for example, would they describe a bold, artful, defiant slave as someone who was meek, humble, and passive? Candor served their interests. Although Southern lore and literature portrayed slaves as being "Sambos," newspaper advertisements, on the other hand, revealed that slaves were complex; they possessed personalities that were ambivalent and inscrutable.[39]

Slaveowners used a number of terms to describe their slaves' personalities—that is, their unique behavioral and emotional characteristics. Hundreds of fugitives were portrayed as being artful; others were reported to be "keen," "shrewd," "intelligent," "defiant," "sensible," "cunning," "humble," and "ingenious." The significance of noting these qualities, obviously, was tied to the owners' belief that runaways would exhibit these characteristics most of the time, thus aiding citizens in their identification.

In this regard, the term "artful," by far, was most commonly used by slaveowners to describe their absconded slaves. To portray a slave as artful meant that he was "outside" the alleged "closed" system of slavery. His ingenuity allowed him a degree of psychological and physical freedom that surely was not characteristic of an individual who labored under a "closed" system of enslavement. Consider in this case, the fugitive Ceasar, a slave who belonged to Nancy Simmons of Windsor, Bertie County. The twenty-three year-old, black complexioned slave left Simmons on December 26, 1818. In a lengthy advertisement for Ceasar, Simmons portrayed him as "very artful and always dressed well and frequently wears a watch..." Simmons's fear was that Ceasar would endeavor to reach a free state, "under an idea of there having his freedom, or will ship on board of the first vessel whose Captain can be deceived, or is villian enough to secret him away, as he crossed the ferry from Salmon Creek to Edenton, and has not been heard of since." Because Simmons believed that Ceasar was heading North, she had the advertisement published in two other newspapers, the *Baltimore Telegraph* and the *Norfolk Beacon*.[40]

The duality in a slave's personality can be seen in Joseph H. Bryan's portrait of his mulatto slave Stephen. Although Stephen had a "down look" when he was spoken to and also stammered a little when he spoke, he nevertheless, was well known in many parts of Bertie County...as "an artful cunning man, 'a Jack at all trades,' he can cobble, cooper, do rough carpenter's work, & make almost every thing that can be useful on a plantation." Bryan informed readers that Stephen would lurk about Robert Peterson's plantation in Bertie County, where his wife lived. Artful, cunning slaves often took money and other goods from their owners to aid them on their journey. There are dozens of examples where these slaves—both male and female—broke open their owners' trunk and took valuable goods, sometimes thousands of dollars in value. The fugitive, Sam, who left his Onslow County owner John Fullwood, was a plain speaking, "very artful fellow". Fullwood noted that the fugitive broke into his trunk and took eighty dollars. That money was probably used by Sam to aid him in his quest to leave Washington, North Carolina by ship, no doubt, headed for a free state.[41]

A number of owners warned citizens that their slaves were so artful that they would tell plausible stories to elude captivity or to secure their release. Elijah Ratcliff's slave, Peter, was "quite artful in telling tales" to maintain his freedom. Carolina, a well made, dark-complexioned man also was said to be artful and plausible in his tales. John Fleming, his Bladen County owner, believed that he would be harbored by the blacks in Wilmington. The New Hanover County slave Bob, knew how to beguile whites to get what he wanted. Bob, an African-born slave, was well known in Wilmington as a ship carpenter. He had been hired out to a Captain Thomas Hunter in Wilmington for six years prior to his flight from bondage on Tuesday, June 23, 1807. Henry Urquhart, the slave's owner, wrote in the *Wilmington Gazette* that Bob was "very tricky, and very plausible and coxing when he has any favor to ask, and is apparently pleased and in good humor til he obtains his end ..." Bob also persuaded another slave to give him three dollars in order to purchase fowls for the man. Urquhart believed that Bob took the money, absconded, and purchased himself new clothes. The slave was in flight for at least a month before the advertisement appeared for him on July 28, 1807. Urquhart suspected that Bob intended to make his escape via an outbound vessel, and so warned that "from the date hereof all masters of vessels are cautioned, against carrying him to sea, and all others black or white harboring him."[42]

Some slaveowners were quick to point out that their runaways were "artful," "sensible," or "intelligent" to the extent that they had acquired the ability to read and write. All of the slaveholding states enacted legislation which banned the teaching of reading and writing to slaves. Stiff penalties were meted out to citizens who broke the law. Some slaves learned to read and write despite the laws. Between 1775 and 1840, North Carolina slaveowners advertised for at least 99 slaves who could read and write. This number represented 3.7 percent of the 2,661 slaves for whom advertisements exist. Male slaves were more likely to learn how to read and write, as 96 (97) percent of those who could read and write were men, while only 3 (3 percent) were women.

Owners' fears were that these slaves would forge "tickets" or free passes. Of the slaves who could read and write, 39, or nearly 40 percent reportedly wrote passes for themselves and other fugitives who accompanied them. William Kirkland of Hillsborough, for instance, described his female slave Jenny as "a very artful, cunning woman, and as she can write a little, it is probable she may have wrote a pass for herself and daughters." Jenny fled with her two daughters, Docia and Elsa, aged fifteen and twelve, respectively, on July 2, 1804. Kirkland warned citizens that Jenny, aged thirty-five, and her daughters would probably try to get back to Fayetteville, where they were purchased by a former University of North Carolina professor a few years prior to their escape in 1804. The slave Jim was depicted by his owner as "an artful fellow [who could] write a tolerable hand, and [would] no doubt forge passes for himself or attempt to pass for a freeman." Although the African-born slave Tom spoke English badly, he was described by J. Martin as an artful man who would "procure or forge a pass as he can write a little..." Benjamin Boykin of Halifax County illustrated his slave's ability when he wrote that: "Steward is quite a genteel and intelligent negro, can read and write, and has a very pleasing address when spoken to; it is supposed that he will forge free papers and attempt to pass as a free negro." John's ingenuity and his literacy aided him in his quest to be free. The twenty-two year-old six foot tall Montgomery County slave left his owner, David Bruton, during the early part of March 1828. Taking with him a bundle of clothes, "a Testament, a Spelling Book, Scott's Lessons, Watts' Hymn Book, and a printed notebook, with inkstand and black paper"—John, according to Burton's other slaves—left with the intention to "take shipping for a free state." Bruton was convinced that his slave would write a pass for himself.[43]

Many slaves used their shrewd, keen, artful, and cunning abilities to deceive whites and to advance their objectives. Whether it was to visit relatives, to be reunited with family members, or to find freedom in or out of North Carolina, their ingenuity was instrumental in helping them to attain their goals. The descriptive phrases used by owners to identify features of their fugitives' personalities, revealed a lot about the slaves' complexity and the difficulty in attempting to put them in distinct categories.[44]

Many of the "artful, cunning" runaways to whom owners referred, were skilled artisans. In addition to their agricultural duties (if they had any), a number of slaves brought skills from Africa, the West Indies, or learned them in the United States that were useful on and off the plantation. The acquisition of a skill hastened their acculturation because it placed them into direct contact with whites, primarily, in the towns of North Carolina.

Skilled artisans used their training in towns, on neighboring plantations, in industry, and aboard ships. This access to the mainstream of North Carolina life, widened these slaves' horizons and introduced them to a degree of freedom not enjoyed by their brethren back on the farms and plantations.[45]

Skilled slaves also produced income for their owners by being hired out. And it was while they were under hire that many of these slaves absconded. The value to their owners was evident in the size of the rewards offered for them.[46] Of the 2,661 slaves who fled between 1775 and 1840, 339 or about 13 percent reportedly had at least one skill. An additional twenty-five fugitives were house servants. These findings are within a range that existed for slave artisans in South Carolina. Latham Windley found that 14 percent of the runaways in South Carolina between 1730 and 1787 had acquired skills that took them beyond the farms and plantations. In the case of Virginia, however, Windley and Gerald Mullin found that 30 to 31 percent of Virginia's fugitives were skilled artisans and domestics. [47]

A majority—250, or 74 percent of the skilled fugitives in North Carolina had one skill; 68 (20 percent) had two skills; 20 (6 percent) were knowledgeable in at least three different trades, while 1 fugitive was proficient in four job areas—that of blacksmith, cooper, shoemaking, and carpentry. Seven of the skilled slaves were females, working as seamstresses, weavers, knitters, and cooks. On the other hand 16, or 64 percent of the 25 house servants were females. When owners did not specify their slaves' occupation, it is assumed that the fugitives were field hands. If indeed an owner's slave had a skill, it is likely that he would acknowledge that fact in the runaway notice. This information was a valuable item on the menu of descriptions given to ensure the slave's capture.[48]

Slaves in North Carolina were engaged in dozens of skilled jobs. Nearly one-third were blacksmiths and carpenters, followed by shoemakers and coopers. Table 10 shows the wide range of occupations in which fugitive slaves were employed. Owners not only indicated the trade or occupation in which their fugitives were engaged, but they also provided significant information about that skill and its relationship to the slaves' personality, character, abilities, plans and destination.

Table 10

Occupational Breakdown of Slave Runaways in
North Carolina, 1775 to 1840

Occupations	Number
Baker	1
Barbers	4
Barber, shoe cleaner	1
Basketmaker	1
Blacksmiths	52
Blacksmith, carpenter	1
Blacksmith, sawyer	2
Blacksmith, shoemaker	2
Blacksmith, cooper	1
Blacksmith, cooper, shoemaker, carpenter	1
Blacksmith, rockblaster	1
Boatmen	6
Boot and shoemaker	2
Boot, shoe, and harness maker	1
Brick and stonemason	1
Bricklayer, plasterer	2
Brickmasons	5
Brickmason, plasterer	1
Brickmaker	1
Brickyard worker	1
Butcher	1
Cabinet and chair maker	1
Carpenter, painter, joiner	1
Carpenter, shoemaker, painter	1
Carpenter, joiner	2

Table 10 (cont'd)

Occupations	Number
Carpenter, millwright business	3
Carpenter	55
Carpenter, shoemaker	7
Carpenter, painter, barber	1
Carriage driver	3
Carriage driver, hostler	1
Caulker	2
Caulker, ship carpenter	1
Chairmaker	1
Chairmaker, carpenter, cabinetmaker	1
Cobbler, cooper, carpenter	1
Cook	2
Cook, sailor	1
Coopers	24
Cooper, sawyer	2
Cooper, carpenter	2
Cooper, pressman	1
Cooper, shoemaker	9
Cooper, corker	1
Cooper, sawyer, shoemaker	1
Ditcher	4
Ditcher, sawyer	1
Fisherman	2
Gardner, hostler, waggoner	1
Gold miners	2
Hatter	3
Hewer, sawyer	1

Table 10 (cont'd)

Occupations	Number
Hewer, timberman, shipyard worker	1
Hostler, barber, millwright business	1
Hostlers	4
House and cabinet workman	1
Miller	1
Miners	2
Nail cutter	1
Nail cutter, blacksmith	1
Overseer	1
Painter	1
Plasterer	1
Rope-walker, rigging	1
Sailors	3
Sawyers	8
Sawyer, basketmaker	1
Sawyer, carpenter	1
Sawyer, shoemaker	1
Sawyer, shoemaker, waggoner	1
Seamen	6
Seamstresses	4
Seamstress, knitter	1
Seamstress, weaver	1
Shingle weaver	1
Ship carpenters	3
Ship worker	1
Shoemakers	30
Shoemaker, basketmaker	1

Table 10 (cont'd)

Occupations	Number
Shoemaker, tanner	1
Stonemason	1
Tailors	3
Tailor, barber, horseman	1
Tanner	1
Tanners, curriers	2
Tanner, currier, shoemaker	1
Waggoners	7
Wagon and stagemaker	1
Waiters	8
Waiter in a tavern	1
Waiter, hostler	1
Waiting man, waggoner	1
Weavers	3
Weaver, spinner	1
Whip-saw, plantation business	1
Total	339

Source: North Carolina extant Newspapers, 1775-1840

A number of skilled fugitives carried the tools of their trade with them when they absconded. Their intention, according to their owners, was to practice their trade wherever they went. Isaac Hilliard of Halifax County, wrote in 1816 that his twenty-two year-old carpenter Joe, who served his apprenticeship under John R. Cary of Raleigh, absconded around April 25, 1816, taking with him clothes, boots, and carpenter's tools. Joe was well known in Raleigh because he also had worked there for a while. Hilliard, however, believed that his slave would go to Petersburg, Virginia. Petersburg was a likely place for skilled slaves in 1815 and 1816 because much of the town was destroyed by fire. Samuel Thorn, also of Halifax County felt that his fugitive Robin, would carry his carpentry skills to Petersburg, primarily, because of the high wages paid to restore the town. John Burgwin promised to prosecute anyone who hired his runaway carpenter, Abram, who had been employed without his consent. Burgwin pointed out that he had suffered a loss as a result of Abram hiring his own time. The slave fled in November 1801, taking his clothes and "sundry tools."[49]

Because of their special situation in slave society, skilled and domestic slaves were more likely able to read and write. A disproportionate number of skilled and domestic slaves acquired these abilities. Of the 99 slaves, for example, who could read and write, 21 (21.2 percent) were artisans and domestics.[50] These fugitives also were more apt to have a "ticket" or free papers and to pass as free. Nearly 6 percent of all slaves (157), reportedly were in possession of a pass of some sort. Of this number, 49, or 31.2 percent were craftsmen and house servants.[51] A similar proportion also existed for slaves whom owners believed would pass as free. Some 434 runaways passed as free. Of those, 98 had a trade or were employed as domestics. So, though skilled slaves and domestics made up 16 percent of the runaway population, they composed 23 percent of the fugitive population that passed as free.

The color of fugitives had little to do with their access to particular skills. In this regard, owners seemingly were not selective in who would be allowed to rise through the ranks to practice a skill. Aptitude for the skill, no doubt, weighed heavier than any other factors. Skin color was provided for 242 of the 339 craftsmen. Sixty skilled artisans were described as "mulatto." Of the 242, 110 (45.4 percent) were "black," "dark," and "brown." The remaining 72 skilled slaves were described as "yellow," "light," and "bright." Overall, 14.8 percent of all light-complexioned fugitives and 11.1 percent of all "distinguishably Negro" runaways were proficient in some craft.

This, however, was not the case for house servants. Skin color was provided for eleven of the fugitive house servants. Additionally, six domestics were reportedly mulatto. Of these 17 runaways, 14 (82.3 percent) were "fair," "light," "yellow," and "mulatto," whereas only 3 (17.7 percent) were black and dark.

Boatmen, who usually traversed the rivers, sounds, and inlets in North Carolina, and seamen who were employed in out-going vessels, obtained a degree of latitude that was not enjoyed by land-based skilled slaves. They were in constant contact with passengers and Northerners.[52] Jack, for example, was hired out by his owner, James Simms, as a boatman in the Contentna Creek and Neuse River, between Stantonsburg and Newbern. He was known as Captain Jack, and according to his owner, the fugitive had "obtained free papers from some malicious person, and will probably pass as a free man." A. Backhouse offered a reward of $150.00 for Sam, a carpenter and seaman. The "remarkably black," twenty-eight year old man "procured a Seaman's Protection and obtained forged Free Papers." Backhouse believed that his slave had "already gone or will attempt to go to some of the Northern sea-ports." Boatmen and mariners, as well as ship carpenters—having access to the waterways and vessels leaving North Carolina—were all in better positions to abscond, putting slavery behind them.[53]

There is little doubt that house servants, most of whom were women, enjoyed privileges, and received a degree of freedom that field hands did not.[54] Edah, for instance, who lived in Hertford, Perquimans County was treated very kindly according to her owner James Wood. He was therefore at a loss to explain why she absconded, "having always been used more like a free person than a slave." Wood further described his twenty-two year old mulatto slave as having a "very light complexion, modest pretty countenance, red cheeks, and a remarkable handsome figure." Domestic slaves were less likely to have the scars, bruises, and other occupational afflictions that were common among slaves who worked outside. Nearly one-third of the house servants passed as free. George, "an intelligent, well made, genteel-looking" house slave made several attempts to escape to Philadelphia, "where he says he will be free." George's owner, Peter Evans branded an "R" on each of his cheeks to identify the fugitive as a persistent runaway.[55]

Not only did "shrewd," "artful," "keen," and cunning fugitives pose a problem for their owners, but defiant, arrogant, and obstinate slaves did so as well. Passivity, humility, and docility did not characterize these slaves. Slaveowners reported that a number of their slaves—males in particular—defied white authority. Defiant slaves killed, robbed, and committed other felonies against slaves and whites, showing little regard for the law, or for their "place" in Southern society.[56] Such was the case of the slave Brister, who escaped from his Wake County owner Christopher Robertson on August 10, 1811. According to Robertson, Brister killed one of Robertson's sons with a hoe. Giving his notice the title, "STOP THE VILLIAN!!!, Robertson maintained that: "For the apprehension of such an offense it would almost seem unnecessary to offer a reward—Justice and the good of society require his apprehension and punishment." Robertson, nevertheless, offered a "liberal reward" for the slave, dead or alive. Elizabeth Cromwell revealed the implacable nature of her slave Tom in a notice published in the *Tarboro Press*, October 22, 1836. Tom, who was fifty-six years, fled on Tuesday night, September 6, 1836. He had been in flight more than a month when Cromwell's advertisement appeared for him. Tom lurked in the community during that time killing and injuring his owner's cattle, hogs, sheep, and other animals. Cromwell wrote that Tom was a "malicious negro and will certainly resist an attempt to take him...."[57]

George McKenzie of Chowan County met with stiff opposition from his runaway slave Dick Pepper, who was a caulker by trade. Pepper escaped from McKenzie in 1793, and five years later on April 7, 1798, by chance, McKenzie encountered his slave in Chowan County. McKenzie wrote that Pepper "knocked down my servant and endeavored to get me down..." Pepper had been working at his trade for five years eluding captivity in Chowan and the neighboring counties. The fugitive had a number of passes in his possession—"granted to him by people of property." He was able to escape from his owner again, and McKenzie vowed to prosecute those who had aided the runaway, averring that "as it is a most villainous practice to harbour any persons property, and deprive the master of his slave's labor, and of which the owner and family might stand in need of." Cordal Hunter's fugitive Peter, who had whip marks on his back and breast, stabbed a man who attempted to apprehend him. Hunter warned that: "It would do well for people to be on the guard"...and "no advantage of the law will be taken by me of any person, who may kill the said negro in taking or confining him."[58]

Other notices were placed in the state's newspapers for a number of slaves who either committed felonies, or challenged their owners' authority. John Burgwin's slave Frank, who had been recently whipped for a felonious act, escaped with an iron on one of his legs. Burgwin believed that another one of his slaves, Ned, was persuaded by Frank to elope with him to file off his iron clogg. The fugitive Trim, escaped from his owner, Margaret M'Klan, but returned a few nights later and robbed her house. Elizabeth P. Dickinson described her fugitive, Frank Mutton, as "a very desperate blood-thirsty fellow," who lurked about Edenton, "braving the power of white men to take him." In an extremely lengthy advertisement for his slave Jacob, James H. Keys of Warren County noted the daring, bold personality, and strength that we are to believe were uncharacteristic of black American slaves. Describing a man who surely was not representative of the "Sambo" personality type, Keys wrote that Jacob "had been heard by the overseer to throw out some hints that all should be free, and that he saw no reason why the sweat of his brow should be expended in supporting the extravagance and idleness of any man...This principle, I am informed, he wished to impress upon the minds of my other negroes: and I doubt not will attempt to do the same wherever he goes. It therefore becomes not only the duty, but the interest of every person possessed of such property, to apprehend such a fellow, and thereby arrest the progress of such dangerous principles."[59]

A number of owners revealed the intractable nature of their slaves by noting that many of them had fled on previous occasions. These were slaves who exhibited a very strong determination to rid themselves of slavery permanently. At least 6 percent of all runaways had escaped before. They were either apprehended by citizens and returned to their owners, captured by law enforcement authorities and jailed, or they returned of their own free will. Once slaves were in captivity, slaveowners no doubt, forced them to reveal where they had been, why they fled, and with whom they had any contact. This information was important because owners used it to plot their slaves' possible destination if they ran away again.

The Chatham County owner William Brantly, for example, surmised that since his fugitive Davy had escaped to Ohio before, there was no doubt that he would again attempt to make it to that free state. Kate, a slave who also lived in Chatham County had made a previous attempt to get back to Norfolk, Virginia where she was raised. The fugitive's owner believed that she would again chart a course for Norfolk.[60] Some slaves fled from each master to whom they were sold, and from one master several times. Tom Whitfield, a Craven County slave, left Rachel M'Cabe in November 1821. After her death, Whitfield was sold to R.J. Powell of Smithfield, Johnston County, from whom he escaped in the summer of 1823. Whitfield was apprehended and later sold to Warry Kilpatrick, but was again sold. His new owner, Henry B. Mitchell of Craven County advertised in 1829 that Whitfield ran away from him in January 1829. Whitfield, a house painter, was evidently so rebellious that Mitchell wrote concerning his apprehension: "if in the act of taking him he should resist and be killed, I will not hold the person so killing, responsible for his value." S. Cochran's slave, Sam, a hatter by trade, fled in September 1821, in December 1821, and again on April 18, 1825.[61]

A number of fugitives were able to secure their freedom again after they had been taken out of jails by owners or overseers and were returning home. Dempsey, Brutus, Simon, Ralph, Bill, and Minor were in the custody of their owners on their way home when they fled again.[62] The taste of freedom for many slaves prompted their quest for more and more liberties, and contributed to their absconding several times. Johnston, for example, was a "noted runaway, this being the third time that he has attempted to make his escape." Benjamin Rogers of Wake County noted that Lewis, who was "active in almost any farming business," escaped in 1819 and passed as free in the towns of Milton and Oxford. Calling himself Lewis Petteford, the fugitive glimpsed freedom for a while, but was apprehended. However, he escaped again in 1823. There is little doubt that the fifty-three old runaway Abram grew accustomed to the freedom he experienced while passing as free, using the name Reuben

Wiggins in Washington County. Reuben was captured, or returned on his own, but escaped again on December 1, 1824.[63]

Owners' frustrations with recalcitrant runaways was evident in their granting permission to would be apprehenders to kill their slaves if they rebelled when attempting to capture them. The North Carolina General Assembly enacted legislation in 1791 that theoretically protected the slaves from "willful and malicious killing." Offenders were "adjudged guilty of murder" under the new law, whereas before, they may have been given a prison sentence and required to pay the owner the slave's value. The law, however, did not apply "to any person killing a slave outlawed by virtue of any act of Assembly of this state, or to any slave in the act of resistance to his lawful owner or master, or to any slave dying under moderate correction."[64] In effect, the law did little or nothing to prosecute those who killed slaves because the burden of proof was always on the dead slave. Owners and their witnesses could argue that the slave was killed because he resisted. Fugitives as well as slaves on the farms and plantations were shot and beaten to death without the fear of judicial reproach.[65]

Slaveowners, therefore, were in "good legal standing" when they advertised that there would be no attempt to prosecute those who terminated their fugitives' lives.[66] Farmers and planters had yet another weapon in their arsenal to deal with their impudent fugitives—that of outlawing them, offering a reward for their head, dead or alive. Over the sixty-five year period 1775-1840, owners had at least 70, or 2.6 percent of all fugitives outlawed. Of these runaways, 65 (92.9 percent) were male and 5 (7.1 percent) were female.

As discussed earlier, some owners offered a greater reward for killing their fugitive than for capturing the slave alive. Typical was the Craven County slave mistress Rebekah Delastatius who offered four dollars for the return of her slave Nan, and ten dollars if she were killed. Joseph Mares—also of Craven County—was willing to pay twenty-five dollars for killing his runaway Joe; he, however, offered only five dollars for the return of the slave. The slave Sampson—who was branded on the left cheek with the letter "T"—was legally outlawed. His owner, Robert Franklin offered five dollars for the return of the slave, but fifty dollars for his head. Harod Pitman of Edgecombe

County offered ten dollars in reward money for Peyton's return, and twenty-five dollars if he were "killed or seriously wounded." Described as an "impudent rascal," Peyton was only seventeen years old.[67] The fact that the state compensated owners for the death of their slaves, no doubt, was an incentive to outlaw runaways. Most owners, however, resolved to use less stringent means to secure their fugitives.

Beyond identifying their slaves' speech patterns and behavior, disfluencies, deportment, and other aspects of their personality, slaveowners also provided readers with other unique features of their fugitives. Hilliard Fort described Issac as an "expert in wrestling, jumping, and running."[68] A number of slaves played the fiddle, and a few took their instruments with them when they fled. The mulatto fugitive Ben, played "the fiddle very well and formerly played for a black dancing master...."[69] Slaves' ability to sing and to dance also were alluded to by owners. Slave vices were revealed as well by owners. Peter for instance, a Warren County fugitive, was a "gambler at heart." Several subscribers noted that their slaves were alcoholics or that they were fond of "intoxicating drinks.".[70]

Special reference was made to ministers and other slaves who were deeply religious. Owners were quick to report that slaves often used religion to beguile whites and to attain their objectives. March was such a man. A.F. MacNeill of New Hanover County, the slave's owner, contended that March was a "smooth spoken," artful man who used "religion to cloak his designs." Slave ministers could be identified by their irrepressible urge to preach to whomever they came in contact. Willis, for example, a shoemaker and preacher, always carried a Bible and "attempted to preach or exhort among" the slaves. Other slaves were said to have been proficient in the scriptures, professed Methodism, or were devout Baptists.[71]

The runaway advertisements are a testimony to the differences in slave personality. They refute the notion that slaves were monolithic in their responses to whites, and that slavery was an all-consuming system that allowed no degree of physical and psychological freedom. Slaves varied in their looks; many presented themselves in a pleasing, non-threatening manner, while others looked despondent and withdrawn. On the other hand some looked bold, assertive, and impudent.

They, by no means, spoke alike. Slaves were identified as "slow," "fast," "abrupt," and "insolent" speakers. Their countenance, deportment, and discourse reflected the wide range of personalities; and although "Sambo" was present among them—the evidence that he dominated is extremely weak. A few insolent slaves were outlawed, or owners gave permission to citizens to kill their fugitives if they resisted. Despite their reasons for running and the risks that flight entailed, all runaways were in search of what they regarded as sacred. Flight, indeed, was a testimony to the intrepid nature of hundreds of slaves.

Notes

1. Gordon W. Allport, *Personality: A Psychological Interpretation* (New York: Henry Holt and Company, 1937), 24-54. Jess Feist, *Theories of Personality* (New York: Holt, Rinehart, and Winston, 1985; Dominick A. Barbara, *Your Speech Reveals Your Personality* (Springfield, Illinois: Charles C. Thomas, Publisher, 1958); Norman N. Markel, ed., *Psycholinguistics: An Introduction to the Study of Speech and Personality* (Homewood, Illinois: The Dorsey Press, 1969), 197-219; William B. Arndt, Jr., *Theories of Personality* (New York: Macmillan Publishing Company, Incorporated, 1974), 7-8.

2. The following are common descriptions used by slaveowners to describe their slaves' countenance: "Pert countenance," "frowning countenance," "pleasant countenance," "a down look," "smiling countenance," "a mild look and genteel appearance," "downcast countenance," "good countenance," "a sour look," "a mild inoffensive countenance," "grim countenance," "a grinning countenance," "a bashful countenance," "an abject countenance," "a pert lively countenance," "a sneaking look," "sly appearance," "bold and forward countenance," "an open, agreeable countenance," "a sullen, down, and guilty look," "a suspicious countenance," and "a forbidding countenance."

3. See the *Carolina Federal Republican*, February 14, 1818 for Mary; *Cape Fear Recorder*, July 31, 1819; *State Gazette of North Carolina*, July 8, 1791. *North Carolina Journal*, May 19, 1836; *Washington Whig*, March 5, 1839; *The Star and North Carolina Gazette*, January 31, 1838. Examples of runaways who had these favorable appearances can be found in notices in the following newspapers: *Wilmington Gazette*, October 31, 1799; *Raleigh Register*, October 1, 1807 for the slave Kingson who had a "smiling countenance," March 20, 1812, August 12, 1814, and March 8, 1822 for Phagon of Warren County who had "a downcast look"; *Carolina Federal Republican*, April 16, 1810 for Mesback Always's who was described as "very humble," and October 16, 1816; *The Star*, April 8, 1814, July 1, 1814, September 30, 1814, and October 30, 1814 for the Oxford, Granville County slave Oliver, who was described by Thomas B. Littlejohn as having a "pleasing, smiling countenance, is very

polite and courteous," a rather "soft, effiminate voice, and has a short quick step when he walks." *North Carolina Journal*, May 6, 1805; *American Recorder*, February 22, 1822; *Carolina Observer*, January 5, 1826, October 25, 1826; *Western Carolinian*, April 19, 1825 and June 6, 1826; *Newbern Herald*, May 13, 1809; *North Carolina Journal*, October 9, 1833 for Alexander Johnson's notice for his runaway, Joe, who spoke "low and humble" when spoken to, and who also had a pleasing countenance, and July 30, 1834.

4. *True Republican and Newbern Weekly Advertiser*, August 7, 1811. The notice for Jerry is in the *Elizabeth City Gazette*, December 31, 1807; the advertisement for Pompey can be found in the *Raleigh Register*, August 26, 1814. For other examples of slaves who possessed "grum looks" and "sulky appearances," see the *Raleigh Register*, April 14,1806; *Carolina Observer*, February 27, 1823; *Western Carolinian*, November 2, 1830, January 20, 1834 for Willis Scott's slave Jerry, who had a "grum sulky look"; *Free Press*, January 20, 1824 for the slave Shadrack; *Carolina Federal Republican*, August 17, 1816.

5. *Western Carolinian*, January 24, 1826.

6. See the *Wilmington Gazette*, September 24, 1801 for John, and the *Western Carolinian*, June 24, 1823 for Sam, and February 12, 1828. See also the *Edenton Gazette*, March 2, 1810; *The Star*, November 15, 1816 for the slave, Jerry, who possessed an "impudent look," November 6, 1818; *Miner's and Farmer's Journal*, September 21, 1831 for Jacob who was said to have "an impudent and ill look; *American Recorder*, July 10, 1818 for the Beaufort County slave, Harry; *The American*, October 13, 1814 for Jim who had a pert appearance; *Hillsborough Recorder*, May 17, 1820; *North Carolina Gazette, or Impartial Intelligencer*, September 24, 1791; *North Carolina Journal*, November 7, 1792; *Milton Gazette and Roanoke Advertiser*, July 31, 1830 for Thomas Jefferson Faddis's mulatto slave who had a "rather impertinent look"; *North Carolina Standard*, June 9, 1836; *Charlotte Journal*, June 10, 1836; *Newbern Spectator*, December 8, 1837; *Raleigh Register*, February 18, 1839.

7. See the *North Carolina Gazette*, February 24, 1775 for Batchelor's runaways and the *Raleigh Register*, November 24, 1806 for Baxter's four fugitives. See also the *North Carolina Gazette*, May 1, 1778 for Peter, a "new Negro" who could not or

would not speak English. J. Lanier's African born slaves—Jack, Aka, Sam, and Botswain—spoke no English at all. *North Carolina Minerva*, October 8, 1807.

8. *North Carolina Gazette*, July 11, 1777, July 18, 1777, January 16, 1778, and July 31, 1778; the notice for Toby is in the *North Carolina Chronicle; or Fayetteville Gazette*, May 10, 1790; see the *Carolina Federal Republican*, August 23, 1817 for Easler Killpatrick's description of his fugitives, Sampson, Joe, and Bill; the advertisement for Anthony is in the *North Carolina Gazette, or Impartial Intelligencer*, May 14, 1796; and John B. Smith's notice for Austin, a Guinea-born slave can be found in the *New Bern Spectator*, March 13, 1830. See also the *Catawba Journal*, December 4, 1827 for the slave Charles; *North Carolina Gazette*, June 27, 1777; *North Carolina Journal*, January 5, 1795, June 5, 1805; *Hall's Wilmington Gazette*, August 30, 1798; *Raleigh Register*, November 24, 1806 for the slave, Jack; *North Carolina Gazette or Impartial Intelligencer*, July 4, 1795 for Prince, an African-born slave who spoke "the English tongue, so that he may be hardly understood"; and the *Carolina Centinel*, March 27, 1819 for the fugitive Ephraim, described by his owner as "a native of Guinea, speaks very broken...[and] a very ignorant fellow, but a good hand at work."

9. *North Carolina Gazette*, July 17, 1778; Avirett's notice for Sampson is in *Hall's Wilmington Gazette*, June 9, 1797; see also the *North Carolina Journal*, April 21, 1800 for the Mecklenburg County slave, Jack, who did not speak very good English; *State Gazette of North Carolina*, October 4, 1787; *Fayetteville Gazette*, October 12, 1789 for the African-born fugitive, London, who spoke "bad English."

10. See for instance, *North Carolina Gazette*, July 25, 1777; *North Carolina Gazette, or Impartial Intelligencer*, April 12, 1794; *North Carolina Journal*, November 10, 1800; *North Carolina Minerva*, June 16, 1796; *State Gazette of North Carolina*, December 22, 1796, August 29, 1798.

11. See Frances Batchelor's runaway notice for the slave Salem, who fled from Newbern in 1775. Batchelor noted that the fugitive spoke "good English," *North Carolina Gazette*, April 3, 1778; *North Carolina Chronicle; or, Fayetteville Gazette*, November 22, 1790.

12. *Herald of Freedom*, March 27, 1799; *North Carolina Gazette, or Impartial Intelligencer*, May 14, 1796; the notice for But Easter is in the *State Gazette of North Carolina*, October 28, 1795; J. Bruin's advertised for Gardner can be found in the *North Carolina Journal*, September 24, 1798; and the ads for Grudge and Prince appeared in *Hall's Wilmington Gazette*, August 30, 1798, and for Joe, June 26, 1800; see the *North Carolina Journal*, June 5, 1805 for Isham, purchased in Norfolk, Virginia in 1793 by William Williams and who spoke "broken English," but spoke "French very well." See also the *Wilmington Chronicle and North Carolina Weekly Advertiser*, September 24, 1795; the *New Bern Herald*, May 13, 1809; *North Carolina Minerva*, December 2, 1814 for the female slave Ruth, who spoke Dutch; and the *Fayetteville Gazette*, May 21, 1793 for Jame, a twenty-one year old slave who spoke "the Dutch and English languages plainly."

13. Several owners, however, did report their creole slaves' proficiency in English. See representative examples of country-born slaves who spoke English "plainly," or "good," in the following newspaper notices: *North Carolina Gazette, or Impartial Intelligencer*, September 24, 1791 for James, a twenty-one year old Jones County man who spoke "good English." See also Simon Foscue's runaway notice for Joe, who spoke good English. See the same newspaper, August 9, 1796; *Wilmington Chronicle; and the North-Carolina Weekly Advertiser*, February 4, 1796 for the fugitive Allick; the *Fayetteville Gazette*, October 2, 1792 for a male and a female slave, who fled together from Gray's Creek, twelve miles below Fayetteville, August 1792. According to their owner James Jackson, the two fugitives, aged about forty, spoke "good English," *North Carolina Chronicle, or Fayetteville Gazette*, February 21, 1791.

14. See the *North Carolina Gazette, or Impartial Intelligencer*, March 25, 1797 for Toney; *North Carolina Journal*, October 9, 1833, June 10, 1829; *People's Press*, July 23, 1834. For other examples of fugitives who were described in these ways, see the *Milton Spectator*, November 7, 1832; *North Carolina Minerva*, July 11, 1803; *Raleigh Register*, April 22, 1814; *Miner's and Farmer's Journal*, September 6, 1834; *Free Press*, July 21, 1827 and January 30, 1829.

15. *North Carolina Journal*, November 16, 1801; *Western Carolinian*, February 12, 1828 for Easter; *Wilmington Gazette*, September 5, 1799; *Edenton Gazette*, March 2, 1810; *Hillsborough Recorder*, November 25, 1829 for James, the University of North Carolina servant. The "Colonizing Society" to which Steward referred was probably the American Colonization Society. Scores of other slaves were described as speaking quickly. See the advertisements in the following newspapers as examples: *Carolina Centinel*, February 12, 1820; *New Bern Spectator*, June 19, 1823 for the slave Caesar, who spoke and moved quickly; *The American*, July 23, 1818 for Luke, a fast talker; *Western Carolinian*, May 14, 1822 for the runaway Peyton, who spoke quickly and "rather abruptly"; *Raleigh Register*, November 1, 1810; *Edenton Gazette*, August 21, 1820 for James Coffield's notice describing his slave Joe as speaking quickly, and who was "very knowing and artful"; *Hillsborough Recorder*, October 22, 1828; *Roanoke Advocate*, May 17, 1832; and the *Warrenton Reporter*, July 8, 1825 for Silla, described as having a "honey-yellow complexion," and "quick spoken"; *People's Press*, March 25, 1836; *Hillsborough Recorder*, March 23, 1838; *Raleigh Register*, November 5, 1838.

16. See for example, *Hall's Wilmington Gazette*, February 9, 1797; *Wilmington Gazette*, March 8, 1798, May 13, 1802, September 27, 1803 for Quash who could tell a plausible story, December 15, 1807, March 14, 1809, April 24, 1804, June 19, 1810, and June 26, 1810 for Harry who was "plausible in his conversation, April 27, 1815; *The Star*, June 29, 1809, July 27, 1821; *Western Carolinian*, October 14, 1823, June 6, 1826, October 2, 1828 for Solomon, described as "intelligent and plausible"; *Wilmington Chronicle*, February 4, 1796. *People's Press*, November 13, 1835.

17. *Carolina Centinel*, February 3, 1821; *Wilmington Gazette*, March 14, 1809; *Edenton Gazette*, April 20, 1810, February 4, 1802.

18. Other examples of slaves who were said to have talked excessively can be found in dozens of newspaper advertisements. See for example, Edward Witty's notice in the *North Carolina Gazette, or Impartial Intelligencer*, March 23, 1793 for Ned, a country-born slave described as being "very talkative"; *North Carolina Journal*, February 29, 1796 for the slave Seneca,

December 12, 1796 in which Samuel Johnston wrote that his slave Manuel, was "a pert, chattering, remarkably active fellow," and by trade, a tailor, barber, and "excellent horseman"; *Encyclopedia Instructor*, May 21, 1800. Durant Hatch described his slave Isaac, as being remarkably "talkative"; *Hall's Wilmington Gazette*, October 11, 1798 for Cato, portrayed as "very talkative and deceitful"; *Carolina Federal Republican*, February 15, 1812, August 16, 1817 for the fugitive Charles, described as "talkative," and also did "some tricks by the slight of hand"; *Edenton Gazette*, October 16, 1820; *Carolina Centinel*, April 15, 1820; *American Recorder*, May 5, 1815, in which Thomas Trotter specified that his slave Tom, was "very black, very talkative, and impudent..."; *The Star*, December 26, 1817.

19. See the *Raleigh Register*, August 5, 1805 for Hunter's notice. The advertisement for Marcus is in the *Carolina Federal Republican*, May 30, 1815; *Carolina Centinel*, April 17, 1819. Other examples of slaves who spooke in a bold fashion can be found in several newspapers. See, for example, *The Star*, August 20, 1813 in which Cyrus Whitaker described his runaway Dick as a "pert spoken" man, August 18, 1820, May 10, 1827, July 5, 1827, May 20, 1830 for Abby who absconded with her two male children, and was described as being "a bold spoken woman," January 4, 1833, December 6, 1833; *Western Carolinian*, June 24, 1823, February 27, 1827 for Abram, who was "rather bold spoken"; *Carolina Federal Republican*, May 30, 1815; *North Carolina Standard*, December 31, 1835.

20. *North Carolina Journal*, May 6, 1805; *Raleigh Register*, June 24, 1825, November 10, 1810; *Wilmington Gazette*, September 4, 1804. See also the *North Carolina Minerva*, January 19, 1809.

21. The advertisement for Simbo is in the *Newbern Gazette*, August 15, 1800; *The Star*, January 14, 1814, September 30, 1814. For other examples, see the *Carolina Federal Republican*, January 4, 1812; *Milton Gazette and Roanoke Advertiser*, February 26, 1824.

22. The notice for Oliver is in the *North Carolina Minerva*, October 7, 1814; *State Gazette of North Carolina*, May 9, 1794; *New Bern Spectator*, December 25, 1835; See also *The Star*, January 13, 1826.

23. *State Gazette of North Carolina*, May 9, 1794; *New Bern Spectator*, December 25, 1835; *The Star*, April 10, 1818. For the wide variety of speech peculiarities among slaves, see the following: *The Star*, February 24, 1815, October 23, 1818; *Raleigh Register*, December 5, 1803, March 22, 1816, September 13, 1816, October 22, 1807, October 27, 1808, November 19, 1804; *Halifax Minerva*, August 27, 1829; *People's Press*, November 12, 1834; *North Carolina Intelligencer and Fayetteville Advertiser*, March 22, 1811 for Tom, a Methodist preacher, who "spoke in a low tone of voice," and Jacob, who could be identified by his "deliberate and hesitating discourse"; *Elizabeth City Star and North Carolina Eastern Intelligencer*, October 21, 1829 for Jack, having "rather a whinning voice when earnestly engaged in conversation"; *Carolina Observer*, August 14, 1823, October 23, 1828 for the slave Sandy, who articulated badly, July 29, 1830, June 11, 1833, March 24, 1835, in which the fugitive Jim was "slow spoken, and in answering utters a kind of laugh," July 7, 1835; *Cape Fear Recorder*, July 31, 1819 for Alexander Peden's female slave, Sarah, who "in her conversation" was "lively and frequently accompanied with a smile"; *The Star*, July 8, 1814, for Jim, who was "fluent in discourse with a quick and wrapped utterance, particularly when a little intoxicated...."

24. It is likely that slaveowners used the terms "stutter" and "stammer" interchangeably. Twentieth century scholars, however, note a difference between the two.

25. Mullin, *Flight and Rebellion*, 101; see also 80-81, 185n and 186n for examples of stutterers and theories on etiology of the affliction. See also Stampp, *The Peculiar Institution*, 381-82.

26. Blassingame, *Slave Community*, 203; see also 204-205; Kay and Cary, "Slave Runaways in Colonial North Carolina," 32; Windley, "Profile of Runaway Slaves," 159. There were forty-seven stutterers in Virginia's runaway population between 1736 and 1787, of whom twelve were skilled. In South Carolina, Windley found that ten fugitives had one or more skills, 158-60.

27. Jock A. Carlisle, *Tangled Tongue: Living With a Stutterer* (Toronto: University of Toronto Press, 1985), xiii. See also Charles Van Riper, *The Nature of Stuttering* (Englewood, New Jersey: Prentice-Hall, Incorporated, 1971), 45-48 for his theories on why males were more likely to stutter.

28. For the boatmen who stuttered, see *Wilmington Gazette*, October 15, 1801; *North Carolina Centinel*, June 22, 1836; and the *Newbern Spectator*, July 25, 1840. Boatmen who had no speech disorders can be found in the *Carolina Federal Republican*, April 30, 1824; *Newbern Spectator*, December 18, 1830; and *Raleigh Register*, December 22, 1835.

29. Stuttering is a speech disorder that has its onset in children between two and four years of age. See, for example, Charles P. Overstake, *Stuttering: A New Look at an Old Problem Based on Neurophysiological Aspects* (Springfield, Illinois: Charles C.Thomas, Publisher, 1979), 10; Edward G. Conture, *Stuttering* (Englewood, New Jersey: Prentice-Hall, Incorporated, 1982), 11-14.

30. *Wilmington Gazette*, September 16, 1806, February 3, 1807; *Raleigh Register*, October 29, 1804, November 29, 1825; *State Gazette of North Carolina*, August 17, 1793; *Carolina Federal Republican*, February 6, 1813, April 3, 1813; *Wilmington Gazette*, October 15, 1801, March 18, 1802. For other examples of slaves who stuttered, see the *Carolina Centinel*, May 30, 1818, April 12, 1823; *Western Carolinian*, October 30, 1821 for the slaves Paris and Charles; *New Bern Spectator*, January 30, 1830, March 13, 1830; *Free Press*, March 28, 1828; *Edenton Gazette*, May 8, 1827; *True Republican and Weekly Advertiser*, October 24, 1810; *North Carolina Minerva*, June 3, 1797, October 29, 1804, July 28, 1808.

31. See the *Western Carolinian*, July 3, 1827 for Klutts's notice for John; *The Star*, June 21, 1827; see the *Raleigh Register*, November 9, 1809 for Stepheny; *Wilmington Gazette*, April 6, 1816; *State Gazette of North Carolina*, February 20, 1799; *North Carolina Journal*, September 25, 1797; *New Bern Spectator*, March 7, 1829, May 2, 1829; *Carolina Federal Republican*, February 6, 1813 for the runaway, David, a carpenter, who stammered a little when speaking fast.

32. *Hall's Wilmington Gazette*, April 20, 1797; *The Star*, November 15, 1811, September 30, 1814; *Wilmington Gazette*, April 19, 1799. *Western Carolinian*, October 14, 1823 for Neptune; *Raleigh Register*, June 7, 1825, June 28, 1825, October 21, 1834 for Peter; *Edenton Gazette*, November 2, 1810, September 17, 1811, in which the fugitive Glasgow was described as a man who "when suddenly accosted, stutters a

little..." See the *North Carolina Journal*, April 21, 1806 for the slave Monmouth who had a speech impediment and was unable to look at a white person in the face. His owner William Pugh also pointed out that the fugitive could not give a "ready answer"; *Carolina Centinel*, August 9, 1828; *North Carolina Centinel*, June 22, 1836; *Raleigh Register*, November 29, 1836; *Fayetteville Observer*, May 2, 1838; *Newbern Spectator*, August 17, 1838; *Tarboro Press*, September 14, 1839.

33. See the *Raleigh Register*, June 24, 1825 for Gloster; *Free Press*, August 26, 1831; *Carolina Centinel*, December 4, 1824 and November 4, 1835 for Simon; the notice for Dinah is in the *Wilmington Gazette*, February 7, 1804.

34. Overstake, *Stuttering: A New Look at an Old Problem*, 11-12.

35. Genovese, *Roll, Jordan, Roll*, 646-47. In addition to the sources previously cited on stuttering, a number of other works proved indispensable to my understanding of the speech disorder. One common thread in all the sources on stuttering that I examined is that the authors admit from the outset that stuttering is a complex subject and nobody really knows why about one percent of the world's population stutters. See Dominick Barbara, *A Practical Self-Help Guide for Stutterers* (Springfield: Charles C. Thomas, Publisher, 1983), 3, 35; Gerald Jonas, *Stuttering: The Disorder of Many Theories* (New York: Farrar, Strauss and Gioux, 1977); Ann Irwin, *Successful Treatment of Stuttering* (New York: Walker and Company, 1980), 3-31. There are as many definitions of stuttering as there are theories on its cause, but I found Charles Overstake's definition particularly interesting. According to Overstake, "Stuttering is a speech disorder characterized by disruptive tonic and clonic muscle behavior and comprised of a complex of neurophysiological symptoms, which alter the normal rhythmic flow of speech to the extent that it interferes with communication and attracts attention to itself." Overstake, *Stuttering: A New Look at an Old Problem*, 9.

36. The following are common phrases used by slaveowners to describe their slaves' speech: "Apt to swear in conversation," "intelligent in conversation," "quick spoken," "well spoken," "speaks low when spoken to," "stutters when spoken to," "speaks

quick and abruptly," "speaks in a very impolite, abrupt manner," "speaks broken English," "speaks slow when spoken to," "a very coarse voice," "very talkative," "talks loud," "speaks with a droaning voice," speaks plain and slow," "clear spoken fellow," "speaks slow and drawls out his words," "speaks good English," "speaks very distinct," "stutters very badly," "has an impediment in his speech," "stammers in his speech," "speaks bad English," "speaks tolerably well," "speaks plain English," "has a stoppage in his speech," "speaks French," "smooth spoken," "speaks short," "speaks lively," "glib spoken," and "affable speech."

37. Stanley Elkins, Slavery: *A Problem in American Institutional and Intellectual Life* (Chicago: The University of Chicago Press. 2nd edition, 1968), 82 for the quote, and all of chapter three.

38. See, for instance, Paul D. Escott, *Slavery Remembered: A Record of Twentieth-Century Slave Narratives* (Chapel Hill: The University of North Carolina Press, 1979), 18 especially, and chapter one, entitled, "Two Peoples and Two Worlds," 18-35; Blassingame, *Slave Community*, 202, chapters 6 and 8; Ann J. Lane's edited volume, *The Debate Over Slavery: Stanley Elkins and His Critics* (Urbana: University of Illinois Press, 1971); Rawick, *From Sundown to Sunup*, 95-96; Julia Floyd Smith, *Slavery and Rice Culture in Low Country Georgia, 1750-1860* (Knoxville: The University of Tennessee Press, 1985), 186.

39. Elkins, *Slavery*, 82; Rawick, *From Sundown to Sunup*, 95; Blassingame, *Slave Community*, 228-30.

40. *Edenton Gazette*, January 12, 1819.

41. *Edenton Gazette*, July 27, 1819; *Wilmington Gazette*, July 23, 1805 for Sam.

42. *Carolina Observer*, September 17, 1833; *Wilmington Gazette*, April 24, 1804, July 28, 1807 for Bob; see the same newspaper March 14, 1809 for the runaway Jacob, who was "plausible in conversation and very artful," June 19, 1810, June 26, 1810; *North Carolina Minerva*, January 24, 1811 for the fugitive Hector, who possessed "art sufficient to invent the most plausible tales to prevent his being arrested."

43. *North Carolina Minerva*, July 9, 1804 for Jenny and her daughters, November 4, 1803 for Jim, December 27, 1816; *Free Press*, August 15, 1828; *Carolina Observer*, March 20, 1828 for John. For other examples of slaves who wrote their own pass,

see: the *Edenton Gazette*, September 29, 1808, January 14, 1812 for Nathaniel C. Bissell's runaway Jack, who forged himself a free pass; *North Carolina Minerva*, November 14, 1803, July 28, 1808; *Raleigh Register*, April 27, 1821 for Isaac Wright's rather lengthy notice for Welcome and his daughter Betsey, who fled from Bladen County on April 10, 1821. According to Wright, Welcome was a man of fine understanding, who could read and write, and also had some knowledge of figures. Wright also believed that his slave had taken books, pen and ink, papers, and money with him; *New Bern Spectator*, November 28, 1829; *The Star*, April 8, 1814; *Carolina Centinel*, March 17, 1821 for Hammond, who could read and write, generally carried a book with him and would, no doubt, "write himself a pass." An excellent source on slave literacy is Janet Duitsman Cornelius, *"When I Can Read My Title Clear": Literacy, Slavery, and Religion in the Antebellum South* (Columbia: University of South Carolina Press, 1991).

44. Slaveowners described scores of fugitives in this manner. Typical are the notices for Dublin, printed in the *North Carolina Gazette*, February 7, 1788 for Duplin and Clary; *State Gazette of North Carolina*, December 4, 1788, June 25, 1789; *North Carolina Gazette, or Impartial Intelligencer*, March 23, 1793, August 31, 1793, August 9, 1794; *North Carolina Journal*, November 9, 1795, July 4, 1796, July 10, 1797 in which Robert Freeman wrote that his fugitive, Jubloe, was noted for his art and cunning abilities; *Raleigh Register*, October 22, 1807 for Joe, a basketmaker, April 17, 1812, May 10, 1816 for two Surry County slaves, Tom and Ben, both of whom were blacksmiths, December 26, 1817, February 13, 1824; *Elizabeth City Star and North Carolina Eastern Intelligencer*, October 21, 1829 for Jonathan H. Jacocks who described his slave Jack, as a "shrewd, ingenious, and artful" man; *The Star*, February 18, 1814, April 8, 1814, December 5, 1815 for Zaccheus, "an ingenious, sensible fellow, July 19, 1816 for the fugitive Jo, who was a "cunning" man who would "induce people to let him go," March 10,1826; *Edenton Gazette*, November 14, 1814, August 21, 1820; *North Carolina Journal*, July 10, 1797; *Wilmington Gazette*, June 3, 1802, April 28, 1803, April 24, 1804, October 14, 1804, July 23, 1805; *Carolina Observer*, July 14, 1825 for the "intelligent and artful" violin player, Manual, June 7, 1826, June 28, 1826,

February 10, 1831, September 17, 1833 for the Anson County, runaway, Peter, who was "quite artful in telling tales"; *Herald of the Times*, April 30, 1836; *Newbern Spectator*, February 10, 1837; *Raleigh Register*, September 14,1839.

45. See Catherine W. Bishir, "Black Builders in Antebellum North Carolina," *North Carolina Historical Review*, LXI (October 1984): 423-61; Peter H. Wood, "Whetting, Setting, and Laying Timbers: Black Builders in the Early South," *Southern Exposure* VIII (Spring 1980): 3-8; Leon Stavisky, "The Origins of Negro Craftmanship in Colonial America," *Journal of Negro History*, XXXII (July 1947): 417-29; James E. Newton and ronald L. Lewis, *The Other Slaves: Mechanics, Artisans and Craftsmen* (Boston: G.K. Hall & Co., 1978); Judith W. Chase, "American Heritage from Ante-bellum Black Craftsmen," *Southern Folklore Quarterly* 42 (1978): 135-58; Phil Peek, "Afro-American Culture and the Afro-American Craftsman," *Southern Folklore Quarterly* 42 (1978): 109-34; Robert W. Fogel and Stanley L. Engerman, *Time on the Cross: The Economics of American Negro Slavery* (Boston: Little, Brown and Co., 1974), 38-43.

46. Rewards for fugitives are discussed in detail in chapter 5. Owners sometimes offered up to $150.00 for skilled slaves. See *People's Press*, August 21, 1833 for the twenty year old slave, Bill; *Wilmington Gazette*, May 13, 1802 for the New Hanover County cabinet and chairmaker, John, April 28, 1803; *Carolina Centinel*, February 3, 1821, June 3, 1820, and July 11, 1818.

47. Windley, "Profile of Runaway Slaves," 137; Mullin, *Flight and Rebellion*, 94-96; Johnson, "Runaway Slaves and the Slave Communities in South Carolina"; Littlefield, *Rice and Slaves*, 136 (Table 8); Philip Morgan, "Colonial South Carolina Runaways," 64 (Table 4). Morgan found that of 5,599 runaways between 1732 and 1782, 13.8 percent were skilled. For colonial North Carolina, see Kay and Cary, "Slave Runaways in Colonial North Carolina," 14 (Table 3). They found that 12.7 percent of the fugitives in their sample of 134 were skilled workers. For other British colonies, see Gad Heuman, "Runaway Slaves in Nineteenth-Century Barbados," *Slavery and Abolition* (December 1985): 99.

48. See Johnson, *Antebellum North Carolina*, 476-77. In a section entitled, "Slave Labor," Johnson discusses labor division on typical North Carolina plantations. Her list included house

servants, mechanics, cooks, maids, butlers, coachmen, gardeners, blacksmith, carpenters, and field hands.

49. The notice for Joe is in the *Raleigh Register*, May 31, 1816; see the same newspaper, September 15, 1815 for Robin; *Wilmington Gazette*, December 10, 1801. For others, see the *State Gazette of North Carolina*, March 3, 1796 for Perquimans County slave Peter, who took with him "sundry shoemaking tools; *True Republican and New Bern Weekly Advertiser*, August 8, 1810; *Catawba Journal*, November 28, 1826; *Charlotte Journal*, September 28, 1838. The General Assembly enacted legislation as early as 1794 which disallowed slaves to hire their own time. Owners found guilty of violating this law had to pay a penalty of forty dollars. Additionally, if found guilty, the sheriff was to hire out the slave for one year. Proceeds from the hire were to go into the state's treasury, to be used for the poor in the County in which the offense occurred. See Iredell and Battle, *Revised Statutes*, 579-80.

50. Slaves who were literate and who were skilled can be found in the following: *Carolina Centinel*, April 15, 1820, November 4, 1826 for the fugitive Isaac who also had "knowledge of figures," had carpentry skills, and had an "itching" for a free state; *North Carolina Minerva*, March 23, 1821; *Hall's Wilmington Gazette*, October 26, 1797; *New Bern Spectator*, February 17, 1832; *State Gazette of North Carolina*, October 28, 1795; *Raleigh Register*, April 13, 1807, September 6, 1816, October 1, 1824 for Sam, who fled from his owner before, and was apprehended in Virginia; he was a carpenter, painter, and barber, April 28, 1826, November 14, 1826; *North Carolina Journal*, August 21, 1797, November 6, 1797; *The Star*, April 12, 1811, November 15, 1816, April 18, 1817; *Free Press*, August 15, 1828; *Edenton Gazette*, January 14, 1812.

51. For examples, see *State Gazette of North Carolina*, January 18, 1798, July 4, 1798; *Herald of Freedom*, March 27, 1799; *Carolina Federal Republican*, August 23, 1817; *Raleigh Register*, June 3, 1800, April 13, 1807, March 29, 1816, January 17, 1817, January 9, 1818, April 25, 1826; January 19, 1836; *The Star*, January 22, 1819, May 20, 1830, October 21, 1830; *Hillsborough Recorder*, November 27, 1822; *Edenton Gazette*, June 16, 1808, November 14, 1814; *North Carolina Minerva*, December 27, 1816, March 23, 1821; *Carolina Centinel*, February 3, 1821; *New*

Bern Spectator, December 18, 1830, December 30, 1836; *Western Carolinian*, November 16, 1824; *Wilmington Gazette*, September 16, 1806, September 13, 1838; *Wilmington Advertiser*, January 12, 1838.

52. Kay and Cary, "Slave Runaways in North Carolina," 19-20; Windley, "Profile of Runaway Slaves," 132.

53. For James Simms's slave, see the *New Bern Spectator*, December 18, 1830; *Carolina Centinel*, June 3, 1820. For other examples, see the *State Gazette of North Carolina*, March 19, 1795; *Wilmington Gazette*, April 19, 1799; *American Recorder*, May 14, 1819; *Carolina Federal Republican*, August 23, 1817.

54. Such an impression is obtained from interviews with ex-slaves. See for example, the interview of the Orange County former slave, Sarah Debro in Norman R. Yetman, *Voices From Slavery* (New York: Holt, Rinehart and Winston, 1970), 98-101; see also Blassingame, *Slave Testimony*, 83 for the Newbern house servant, James Wrial, and 131 for the narrative of the Person County slave, James Curry. See also C.W. Harper, "House Servants and Field Hands: Fragmentation in the Antebellum Slave Community," *North Carolina Historical Review* LV (Winter 1978): 42-59.

55. The notice for Edah is in the *North Carolina Minerva*, September 9, 1814; *Edenton Gazette*, June 5, 1820. Advertisements for house servants can be found in the following newspapers: *State Gazette of North Carolina*, February 7, 1788; *North Carolina Gazette, or Impartial Intelligencer*, April 29, 1784, June 4, 1791; *North Carolina Journal*, May 15, 1797, April 4, 1800, February 2, 1807, October 16, 1809; *Hall's Wilmington Gazette*, February 8, 1798, June 7, 1808; *Raleigh Register*, August 5, 1814, June 29, 1817, April 27, 1821; *The Star*, April 25, 1823, March 4, 1829; *Edenton Gazette*, November 24, 1809, June 5, 1820; *Free Press*, August 1, 1828; *Carolina Centinel*, January 24, 1829; *New Bern Spectator*, December 25, 1834.

56. See Catterall, *Judicial Cases Concerning the Negro*, II, 12-13 for the case, *Connor v Gwin*, and 15, *State v Sue*.

57. The notice for Brister is in *The Star*, October 4, 1811; *Tarboro Press*, October 22, 1836 for Tom. See also *Western Carolinian*, September 18, 1827.

58. See the *State Gazette of North Carolina*, July 4, 1798 for Dick Pepper; *Free Press*, July 21, 1827 for Peter.

59. *Hall's Wilmington Gazette*, April 20, 1797, October 5, 1797; *Edenton Gazette*, October 13, 1809; *Raleigh Register*, June 5, 1812. For other instances of defiance, the commission of crimes by fugitives, bad, and rebellious attitudes, see *North Carolina Gazette*, January 13, 1775, March 24, 1775; *Wilmington Gazette*, October 31, 1799 for Elijah, who committed a capital offense; *North Carolina Journal*, June 4, 1810; *The Star*, November 14, 1817, June 20, 1823; *Raleigh Register*, March 16, 1822; *Edenton Gazette*, March 8, 1827 for the Chowan County slave Flora, who was described as a "raw bone ugly Negro" and was as bad as she was ugly. *American Recorder*, June 27, 1823 for the fugitive Abram, described as a resolute and determined villian, who would not be taken easily; *Carolina Observer*, July 28, 1825 for Lawrence who allegedly broke into a store in Richmond County.

60. See *The Star*, July 20, 1809 for Davy; September 14, 1809 for Kate. For other examples, see *Edenton Gazette*, June 5, 1820; Carolina Centinel, September 2, 1826; *North Carolina Journal*, June 11, 1798; *Raleigh Register*, July 9, 1813 for Watt who made two previous attempts to reach Tennessee, October 1, 1824; *The Star*, January 13, 1815; *North Carolina Journal*, November 7, 1827.

61. See the *Carolina Centinel*, December 8, 1821, December 3, 1825, and October 10, 1829 for Whitfield; the notices for Sam are in the *Raleigh Register*, October 12, 1821, January 11, 1822, and the *Hillsborough Recorder*, April 27, 1825.

62. See the *Raleigh Register*, October 29, 1833; *Carolina Federal Republican*, September 17, 1817; *The Star*, May 31, 1811; *Catawba Journal*, April 22, 1833; *Western Carolinian*, August 19, 1823; *North Carolina Journal*, September 25, 1797. See also October 1, 1804; *Western Carolinian*, November 16, 1824.

63. *Raleigh Register*, January 9, 1818; *Hillsborough Recorder*, March 5, 1823; *Free Press*, December 3, 1824. Below are just a few examples of fugitives who fled more that once: *Western Carolinian*, June 13, 1826 for Joe and his wife Anniky, both of whom escaped at least two times, May 17, 1827; *Wilmington Gazette*, April 9, 1801, in which A.B. Toomer reported that his slave Sparrow fled in 1801 and in 1802, carrying with him two pistols and a sword; *The Star*, April 4, 1823; *Raleigh Register*,

December 19, 1803, October 4, 1816, September 29, 1820, April 28, 1816; *Carolina Federal Republican*, December 14, 1816; *State Gazette of North Carolina*, March 12, 1795; *North Carolina Minerva*, August 27, 1799; *Catawba Journal*, June 5, 1827; *Carolina Observer*, January 12, 1826; *Carolina Centinel*, July 11, 1818.

64. Potter and others, *Laws of the State of North Carolina*, I, 659. See also Don Higginbotham and William S. Price, Jr., "Was It Murder for a White Man to Kill a Slave? Chief Justice Martin Howard Condemns the Peculiar Institution in North Carolina," *William and Mary Quarterly* (Fall 1980): 593-601.

65. Catterall, *Judicial Cases Concerning the Negro*, II, 14 for *State v Weaver*, and 15, *State v Primer*.

66. See the *Carolina Centinel*, July 28, 1821 for John Franklin's notice; he gave permission to kill his slave Sam Maddon if violence occurred in attempting to apprehend him, December 1, 1821 for two fugitives.

67. *New Bern Gazette*, March 16, 1799; *Carolina Federal Republican*, April 4, 1812; *True Republican & Newbern Weekly Advertiser*, July 16, 1810; *Roanoke Advocate*, August 18, 1831. See as other examples, *Carolina Federal Republican*, August 23, 1817 for Enoch Foy's fugitive Bill, who was outlawed and for whom $100.00 was offered for his return, and $110.00 for his head; *Free Press*, July 30, 1824 for George, who "was known as a rascal all over." Hilliard Fort offered twenty dollars in reward money for the fugitive's return, and forty dollars for his death; *The Statesman and Third Congressional District*, February 7, 1835. Joseph R. Hanrahan offered $100.00 "for the delivery" of Syphax's head. See also the *Carolina Centinel*, March 18, 1820 for the female runaway, Silvey of Craven County, for whom Eden T. Jones offered fifty dollars for her head, September 6, 1823 for Jerry; his owner was willing to give $200.00 for his head, or $100.00 for his return; *Wilmington Gazette*, April 19, 1799. For outlawed slaves in general, see *North Carolina Gazette*, January 13, 1775, March 24, 1775, May 5, 1775, October 6, 1775, May 1, 1778; *True Republican & Newbern Weekly Advertiser*, July 16, 1810; *Carolina Federal Republican*, July 6, 1816; *The Carolinian*, August 8, 1812; *Raleigh Register*, September 5, 1803; *The Star*, July 31, 1818, March 29, 1822; *North Carolina Journal*, June 23, 1806; *Hillsborough Recorder*,

March 5, 1828; *Edenton Gazette*, October 1, 1807, July 16, 1811, November 19, 1811; *American Recorder*, July 10, 1818, June 27, 1823 for Abram, described as a "resolute and determined villian; *Cape Fear Recorder*, April 5, 1817, April 14, 1821; *Carolina Centinel*, June 2, 1821; *New Bern Spectator*, July 10, 1830.

68. *Free Press*, July 30, 1824.

69. *North Carolina Journal*, February 11, 1805. For other fiddle and violin players, see the *North Carolina Journal*, February 8, 1796; *North Carolina Gazette, or Impartial Intelligencer*, March 25, 1797; *Wilmington Gazette*, June 26, 1800, December 10, 1801; *Edenton Gazette*, February 10, 1808, February 1, 1811, October 8, 1811; *The Star*, August 2, 1810; *American Recorder*, May 5, 1815; *Carolina Observer*, July 14, 1825; *Western Carolinian*, August 8, 1835.

70. The notice for Peter is in *The Star*, March 17, 1810. For slaves who were described as alcoholics, or who were fond of liquor, see the *North Carolina Gazette, or Impartial Intelligencer*, October 31, 1795; *Carolina Observer*, December 24, 1828.

71. See the *Wilmington Gazette*, March 12, 1812 for March; the notice for Willis appears in *The Star*, April 12, 1811. For examples of descriptions of slave religiosity, see the *Wilmington Gazette*, March 24, 1807; *Edenton Gazette*, July 16, 1811; *The Star*, January 13, 1815, October 14, 1830; *Raleigh Register*, January 20, 1831.

CHAPTER FIVE

Flight, Destination, and Rewards

In a discussion of slave flight, one of the most obvious questions is, why did slaves runaway? Where were they going, and how could they expect to remain free in a nation where their color was the badge of servitude? Slave runaway notices tell us a lot about what motivated slaves to run away. Many advertisements also reveal where owners believed their slaves were headed. Herein is a discussion of those factors which prompted slave flight, their possible destinations, and the rewards that slaveowners offered to citizens who captured their fugitives.

The internal slave trade existed in North Carolina down to 1865. Owners sometimes sold their slaves when they experienced financial hardships. At other times, estates were divided, and slave families were split as a result. On other occasions, slaveowners sold obstinate, "troublemaking" slaves. Whatever their reasons for selling their property, the slaves who were sold, and the family members who were left behind, were the ones most affected by the sale.[1]

It is no surprise then that many slaves ran away to be reunited with their family members. In many instances, slaveowners provided information about their slave's quest to return to their wives, husbands, children, and other relatives. According to slaveowners, 282 (11 percent) of the fugitives ran away to restore the familial bonds that had been severed by a sale. Male slaves were more likely to be sold in North Carolina. Their value was usually greater, and the tasks that they could

173

perform on the farms and plantations made them prime candidates for the slave markets. Of the 282 slaves who sought family members, 149 (53 percent) were men in search of their wives, children, and parents. At least 15 female slaves were in search of their husbands; and the other 118 slaves—mostly males—reportedly lurked about the plantations and farms on which their relatives lived.[2]

In most cases, fugitives did not have to go far to be reunited with their loved-ones. Slaves were often sold to slaveowners in the county in which they lived, or to farmers and planters in adjoining counties. The fugitive Jack was typical. He fled from his Chowan County owner, John M. Bond, on October 1, 1820. Bond's notice for Jack appeared in the *Edenton Gazette* on October 16, 1820. According to the advertisement, the slave lurked near a Chowan County plantation where his wife lived. Ricks Fort, a Halifax County slaveowner disclosed that he purchased the runaway slave, Peter, in Scotland Neck, Halifax County in August 1827. Peter absconded from Fort on March 24, 1828, just seven months after he was purchased. Fort believed that Peter had returned to Scotland Neck, and that the slave would conceal himself and visit his wife whenever he could. Thomas H. Hill of Jones County had no doubts that his runaway, Jerry, would make an attempt to visit his wife and mother in neighboring Craven County before going to Wilmington to board a vessel to leave the state.[3]

Some slaves traveled great distances to return to farms and plantations from which they had been sold, and to areas where they believed their spouses, children, and other relatives had been taken. There were a number of cases in which slaves, both male and female, escaped to follow their spouse to another state. As discussed in Chapter 1, many slaveowners moved to the deep South during the 1820s and the 1830s to more fertile soils to grow their crops. A number of them carried their slaves with them, creating a problem for slaves who had husbands, wives, and children belonging to those masters. The Duplin County slave Joe, faced such a dilemma in 1828. Joe's wife belonged to John Rhode, also of Duplin County. She was taken "South" by Rhode and his family in 1828. Joe's guardian, Charles Hines, concluded that his fugitive was following his wife. A year later, William B. Collins's slave Sam, escaped to find his wife who was taken to Alabama by the Hatton family. In 1830, William Boylan, a notable Wake County planter, who owned 39 slaves and nearly 5,000 acres of land, advertised for his slave David who was in pursuit of his wife whose owner had taken her to Alabama. Finally, the female slave Winny escaped from her Robeson County master John M'Phail in March 1800. Winny took additional clothing, and M'Phail concluded that it was "probable that she may have made toward Turtle River in Georgia, as her husband has been taken there."[4]

The 282 fugitives who endeavored to be reunited with family members is undoubtedly a conservative figure. Slaveowners did not always specify that slaves ran away to rejoin relatives. They, however, disclosed other information which suggested that runaways fled to be with family members. Hundreds of slaveowners stated that their runaways would probably visit former farms and plantations on which they had once lived. There is little doubt that these fugitives returned simply to visit their former masters. It is likely that they too were visiting relatives and possibly enticing them to run as well. Runaways such as Mingo, Peter, and Tim who reportedly lurked near the plantations of their former owners, no doubt, attempted to resume their family ties.[5]

Slaveowners revealed that at least 517 runaways would lurk about their former owners' plantations in and outside of North Carolina. These slaves, added to those whom owners specifically indicated would visit relatives, amounts to 784 slaves. Masters provided destinations for 1,380 fugitives, or nearly 52 percent of the 2,661 slaves who absconded. Based then on the owners' report, about 57 percent of the fugitives for whom destinations were given, made an attempt to be reunited with family members.

Many slaves, for instance, who attempted to return to Virginia, Maryland, other slave states, and even places outside of the United States were, no doubt, in search of loved ones. The slaves, Ben and Alice fled from their Caswell County owner Elish Brown on June 23, 1814. Both fugitives were purchased from two different slaveowners in Southampton County, Virginia. Brown noted in his advertisement that they "are supposed to be gone towards their former home." William Anderson, also of Caswell County, bought two slaves from owners in Virginia. The two slaves, Charles and Pompey ran away from Anderson on August 15, 1814. Charles was purchased at the Isle of Wight County court house, while Pompey was bought in Suffolk, Virginia. Anderson was convinced that the men would return to the places where they were purchased. The twenty-year-old fugitive slave Paris, was brought from Maryland Eastern Shore, and his owner John Martin assumed that Maryland was his destination. The slave Adam ran away on November 24, 1816 shortly after he was purchased by Joshua Gay in Frederick County, Maryland. Gay surmised that his fugitive would try to reach his former home.[6] Most slaves who were headed for other slaveholding states were en route to neighboring Virginia—North Carolina's major supplier of slaves.

Slaveowners also provided some insight into why slaves ran, and their possible destinations when they made references to the number of former owners their slaves had. At least 876 (33 percent) of the fugitives had previous owners. Most runaways, 745, had at least one other owner prior to the master who advertised for their recovery; 116 fugitives had a total of three owners; 12 had four owners, including the subscriber; 2 runaways had five owners, and 1 slave had a total of six different owners (see figure 6). This slave, who was named Isaac, had been the property of four different men in Gates, Northampton, and Bertie Counties in North Carolina, and Suffolk, Virginia. His last owner, Josiah Collins advertised for the forty-four year-old man in September 1807. Collins wrote that the fugitive was "well known at all those places." Slaveowners obviously faced more difficulty in attempting to pinpoint where their slaves were when they had been owned by several people. In some cases, these slaves had family and had made acquaintances with people everywhere they had once lived. James Engram of Lenoir County revealed this problem when he advertised for his slave March, who had been owned by four previous slaveholders. Engram concluded that he was not sure where March would go because he had "great acquaintance[s]" on all four plantations where he had been a slave.[7]

Many slaves who ran away to their former owner's plantation, or to find family members, were assured of being harbored by their relatives. This action by relatives infuriated slaveowners because it increased their fugitives' chances of

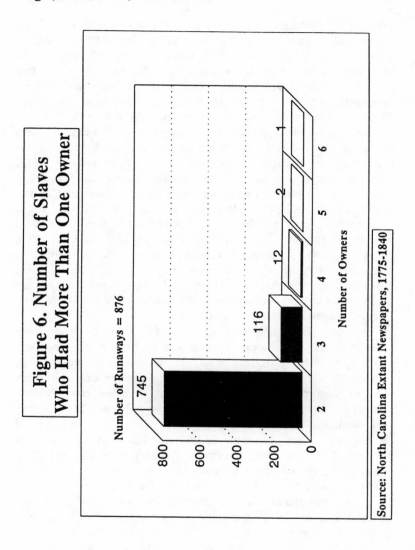

Figure 6. Number of Slaves
Who Had More Than One Owner

Number of Runaways = 876

Source: North Carolina Extant Newspapers, 1775-1840

permanent freedom. Some slaves were concealed until they could find passage to the North or elsewhere. William Nash of Caswell County believed that his runaway, a blacksmith, would be harbored by the fugitive's brothers in Newbern "until he can get off." Other slaves found solace and aid from their wives, husbands, and parents. Abigail, for instance, escaped on March 25, 1801 with her infant and young son John. Her owner William Green of New Hanover County contended that she and her children would be harbored by her husband, Jim, a slave belonging to William Campbell in the same county. John Burgwin revealed a similar story in advertising for Manuel, a slave whom he hired from David Jones of New Hanover County. According to Burgwin, Manuel was concealed "by a Negro Woman belonging to Mrs. Heron, who he has for a wife, and was there last Sunday night." The twenty-five year-old slave Harry, ran away from his Pasquotank owner, Samuel Nixon in February 1825. It was not until May 27, 1826 that Nixon advertised for his fugitive. Harry had been concealed by his mother and father in neighboring Perquimans County during the fifteen months he was in flight.[8]

Fugitive slaves who were concealed by relatives, sometimes enticed them to run away. Typical was Nicholson Washington's slave, Jack, who harbored his fugitive wife for about three months. Washington assumed that Jack was then enticed by his wife to also run away. The two fled together from Wayne County on October 27, 1818. Washington believed that the man and woman would hide-out near Newbern, or conceal themselves on the plantation of William Gaston where Jack was purchased. Moses, Clara, Denny, and Nancy were all enticed by runaway family members to leave their owners.[9]

. The desire by slaves to sustain familial bonds tells us a lot about the importance of the slave family. Although the family suffered as a result of separation of its members, and from the castigation of authority figures, it was an institution that slaves highly valued. The fact that so many runaways attempted to keep it to together, testifies to the potential and real strength of the black slave family unit. The fugitive slave notices give support to recent scholarship which stresses the positive role that the slave family played in the lives of its members.[10]

Not only did slaves respond to the need to maintain intact family structures, but they also escaped from their owners for fear of being sold. It is likely that thousands of slaves made the best out of their bondage. Some, no doubt, reasoned that life on their present farm or plantation was not the best, but it was better than life on other farms and plantations, and was preferred over the unknown. Toney, a Craven County slave, who belonged to Elijah Clark believed that being sold was the fate that awaited him. He "was sent to Mr. Gildersleeve's with a note, on business, and it is understood that he took up the idea that he was going to be sold or sent away, which was not so." Being illiterate, the slave apparently assumed that the note which he carried contained information about him. Described by Clark as a first rate hewer, timber-getter, and shipyard worker, Toney fled from his owner on October 19, 1833. The fact that he carried additional clothing meant that his plans were not to return soon. The female slave, Rose, confronted the some problem in 1835. According to her owner, Jere Nichols, Rose "took a fright from a false report of her being or about to be sold to the speculators, by M.L. Rivera, from whom I hired her." Nichols believed that Rose would return "after word had been given out that there was no intention of any thing of the kind; and if she will now return without further trouble, she will not be disturbed." Rose was in flight at least one month before Nichols's advertisement for her escape appeared in the *People's Press and Wilmington Advertiser*.[11]

The fear of being flogged, or an actual whipping provoked some slaves to run away. It is difficult to determine if these slaves returned to their owners shortly after they fled, or if indeed they sought permanent freedom. There is insufficient evidence to sustain the notion that they fled and returned when they had gotten over the pain, the humiliation, an the anger felt for their owners. A case in point was the slave Esther. Her decision to run away with the slave Jubloe, was probably made easier because she carried "the marks of a whipping she received the day before her departure." Robert Freeman, owner of the two slaves, made no indication whatsoever about the slaves' possible destination. Ned, a man who belonged to Green Alford of Wake County, ran away in May, 1823 because of a beating he received the day before he absconded. Unlike the fugitive Esther, however, Ned reportedly would secure a free pass, and pass as free," as he is connected with free negroes." According to William Cain, Senior of Hillsborough, Jim "had no cause for going off except for striking his overseer for which he expected correction."[12]

The number of slaves who fled to avoid a whipping or because they were flogged, appears to be relatively small. However, there was another group of slaves who fled for no other reason than to claim their freedom. These were men and women who desired to escape the complete ravages of their enslavement. Slaves who passed as free, and especially those whom owners believed would leave North Carolina and go to a free state, clearly illustrate this point. At least 181 (7 percent) of the bondsmen and bondswomen were headed for a free state. Slaves were destined for such places as Indiana, Illinois, New York, Pennsylvania (Philadelphia most often), and Ohio. In most cases, slaveowners simply indicated that their slaves were going "North," "Northward," or to a "free state."

Owners believed that a number of these fugitives would attempt to secure their freedom by boarding vessels leaving the state. It was for this reason that hundreds of them warned shipowners and "masters of vessels" not to harbor, or carry their slaves out of the state. Consider, for example, Nathan B. Whitfield's notice for his four slaves, Isaac, Scipio, Jerry, and Kasey, all of whom fled together in September, 1826. Whitfield noted that the runaways were "endeavoring to go northwardly to some non-slaveholding State, as Isaac for some time has a disposition that way, and no doubt has enticed the rest away with him." Whitfield warned "Masters of Vessels and others... against harboring or carrying off said fellows." Reuben Dennis's slaves, Cuff, David, and Moses were in a perfect place in the state to leave by water. Located in Beaufort, Carteret County, on the southeastern coast of North Carolina, the slaves were believed to have joined a group of other runaway slaves from their community who endeavored "to escape into some of the Northern States." Dennis likewise, warned seamen not to conceal or transport his fugitives out of the state. Slaves who fled North, obviously stood a better chance of securing their freedom than those who remained in their communities. Their northern flight, however did not quell the efforts of some owners to attempt to retrieve them. Whitmill Hill of Bertie County who advertised for his slave Yarmouth for instance, declared that the fugitive was worth the price of four slaves, and that he would pursue him throughout the North, where he believed the slave had fled.[13]

A number of other slaves fled to northern states via land routes. At least two slaves attempted to run to Indiana. Ephraim, a Wayne County slave who altered his name to John Artis, and who was in possession of a free pass, reportedly joined a group of blacks from Guilford County who were en route to Indiana. Ephraim left his owner, Peter L. Peacock on January 8, 1827, but the notice for him did not appear in the newspaper until August 16, 1827. Chances are the slave had already reached his destination when the advertisement appeared for him in *The Star*, a Raleigh newspaper. Seven years later, the Chatham County slave, Peter obtained free papers, and joined a group of "emigrants" who were bound for Indiana. Ten slaves, according to their owners, were headed for Ohio. Davy, a slave who procured a free pass and could also write, was believed to have run away to Ohio, where he had once run before. Several other slaves also had been to free states before, but for some reason returned of their own free will, or were captured. Seven fugitives also were headed for Pennsylvania; nine runaways made their destination New York, while three other slaves were en route to New England. The other slaves who were going "North," or to a "free state" were probably bound for these same areas (see table 11).[14]

Many slaveowners were at a loss to explain why their slaves fled. They had no idea where they were going and what prompted them to runaway. A number of subscribers simply stated that their slaves ran "without provocation." When owners indicated that their slaves ran away without "cause or provocation," they undoubtedly meant that they had been "spared the rod." John W. Charles of Wake County, for instance, did not understand why his thirty-five year-old slave, Robbin left him in April 1821. Charles maintained that although Robbin's back was "cut by former owners," he had never beaten the slave. John Curtis, also of Wake County, failed to understand that the desire for freedom alone, provoked Sam to leave his plantation in 1816. Curtis wrote that Sam was headed to Pennsylvania.[15] Owners who had no knowledge of why their slaves fled is an

Table 11

Destinations of Runaway Slaves
Leaving North Carolina

Destination	Number of Runaways
Alabama	5
Georgia	13
Illinois	1
Indiana	4
Louisiana	1
Maryland	17
Massachusetts	1
Mississippi	1
New England	1
New York	9
Ohio	10
Pennsylvania	7
South Carolina	18
Tennessee	6
Virginia	147
West Indies	6
North or to a free state	148
Total	395

Source: North Carolina Extant Newspapers, 1775-1840

indication that perhaps they did not know their slaves as well as they thought. Masters were sometimes misled by their slaves' congenial, mild-mannered, pleasing personalities, and were naive enough to believe that their slaves were content in bondage. As a result, they found it difficult to explain why their slaves escaped.

Whether flight was planned well in advance, or if it were spontaneous, slaves had to consider a number of important variables. For example, the mode of escape, or the means that runaways used to leave their owners was surely a factor that received considerable attention by slaves. However long they pondered their method of leaving their owners, overwhelmingly, the decision was to leave by foot. This form of departure was safest. Fugitives were better able to elude captivity, as they could hide in the woods and the swamps. They were in a better position than those slaves who took horses, or carriages when they ran away. The freedom that "foot flight" afforded fugitives was responsible for the small number of slaves who escaped by horseback. Only 42 slaves fled by horseback. It appears that the decision to use horses to flee was based on the slave's desire to quickly put distance between himself and his owner. A few of these runaways, for example, eventually abandoned their horses and resorted to travel by foot. Horses drew attention to slaves, and also required feeding and rest—all of which were impediments to the fugitive's objectives. Owners sometimes offered rewards for both the fugitives and the horses.[16] An even smaller number of slaves fled by boat. Only three runaways used a sail boat, or canoe to escape. This number does not include the dozens of runaways whom owners believed escaped initially by foot and then left on an outgoing vessel leaving North Carolina.[17]

The decision by slaves to run was not closely tied to climatic conditions in North Carolina. It seems that slaves would have selected the warmest months to run. This, however, was not the case. And it was probably due to the nature of flight, that is, the decision to run away was usually a spontaneous one, in which little calculated planning took place. This is not to say that some slaves did not entertain the idea of running weeks and months in advance of their departure, but there is little evidence in the runaway notices that slaves mapped out strategies that would ultimately lead them to their goals. If flight were planned in advance, it appears that slaves would have been more selective in the time of year they absconded.[18]

Slaveowners provided information on dates of departure for 2,262 fugitives, including 75 of the 110 children who were taken along by their parents. Figure 7 shows the frequency distribution of flight by months. It can readily be seen that nearly as many slaves escaped in January (202), one of the coldest months, as in June (208), July (203), and August (214), the three hottest months of the year. Twenty percent of the fugitives fled in March (237) and April (221). The pattern of monthly flight was consistent for male and female slaves, with similar percentages for both groups. It has been suggested by some scholars that many slaves escaped to simply avoid work. They have pointed to large numbers of slave escapes in the spring and early fall months as evidence—pointing out that heaviest farm labor began in the spring and ended with the harvesting of many crops in late summer and early fall. If slaves fled simply to avoid work, owners seemingly, would have indicated this important variable in their notices. No Subscriber, however, listed work avoidance as a motivation for flight. Slaves ran to fulfill more specific objectives—that of visiting relatives, escaping the wrath of cruel owners, or to find freedom from slavery.[19]

Seasonally, there was not a significant difference in the prevalence of slave flight. Fifty-five percent of the fugitives fled between March and August, while 45 percent ran off during cool and cold months, September through February. Slightly more fugitives escaped during the winter than the fall months. Seasonally, the percentages for male and female flight were 23 versus 24 percent during the winter months; 28 and 25 percent in the spring; 27 percent for men and 28 percent for women during the summer; and 22 percent versus 22 percent, in the fall of the year (see figure 8).[20] Women, like men were not highly selective in the months that they chose to abscond. Their immediate situation, and their goals dictated flight more than anything else. The almost equal distribution of male and female flight by month can also be attributed to the fact that 46 percent of all females ran away in groups, usually consisting of men.

When slaves ran away, they usually "stole themselves" individually—that is, they fled alone.[21] However, there were cases in which two or more slaves ran away together. In his study on group flight in South Carolina between 1799 and 1830, Michael

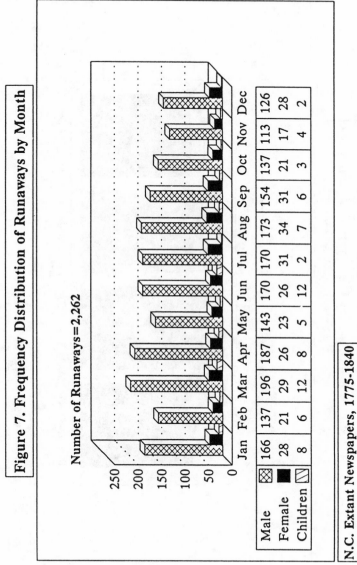

Figure 7. Frequency Distribution of Runaways by Month

Number of Runaways=2,262

	Jan	Feb	Mar	Apr	May	Jun	Jul	Aug	Sep	Oct	Nov	Dec
Male	166	137	196	187	143	170	170	173	154	137	113	126
Female	28	21	29	26	23	26	31	34	31	21	17	28
Children	8	6	12	8	5	12	2	7	6	3	4	2

N.C. Extant Newspapers, 1775-1840

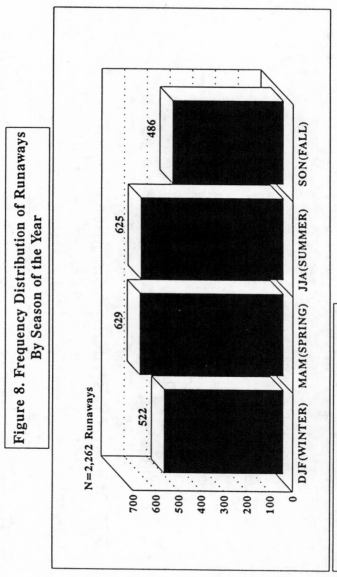

Figure 8. Frequency Distribution of Runaways By Season of the Year

N=2,262 Runaways

522 629 625 486

DJF(WINTER) MAM(SPRING) JJA(SUMMER) SON(FALL)

700
600
500
400
300
200
100
0

Source: N.C. Extant Newspapers, 1775-1840

P. Johnson concluded that..."the same community ties that had to be severed to run away alone could and did strengthen slaves of both sexes and a wide range of ages to run away together, in groups. These groups exemplified the bonds of affection, loyalty, and trust that knit the larger slave community and gave collective expression to the spirit of resistance."[22] There is no doubt that companionship eased a number of burdens that flight entailed. However, group flight increased the risks of betrayal, discovery, and apprehension.

Nevertheless, slaveowners indicated that 870, or 31.4 percent of the 2,771 slaves who fled between 1775 and 1840, ran away in groups. Some 212 women, or 44 percent of all females, and the 110 infants and children ran away in groups, while 548 (25.1 percent) of the male runaways ran off in groups. Numerically then, 270 female and 1,631 male slaves absconded alone. Discretion dictated small group sizes; and it was probably for that reason that 498, 57.3 percent of the fugitives ran away in groups that contained only two slaves. Fourteen slaves ran away in groups that consisted of free blacks and whites; there were 51 groups that contained three slaves; 24 groups were composed of four fugitives; 6 groups contained six slaves; 7 groups had five runaways; and 3 groups contained seven, eleven, and fourteen slaves each (see table 12).

It is interesting to look at the composition of these groups of runaways. Table 13 shows that about 40 percent (345) of the runaways were men who fled together. In most cases, they were field hands. Only 16 women ran away together; 176 slaves ran away in mixed groups, consisting of men and women; 218 family members, including parents and children, brothers and sisters, infants and other relatives fled; 28 family members and friends absconded in groups; and 35 married couples left their owners. Slaves who fled in groups ran for the same reasons as those who ran off alone. Slaves who were purchased at the same time from their owners often fled together. Jim and Solomon, for example, were purchased in Maryland just about six few weeks before they ran away together in 1833. Their owner, Armstid Branch of Mecklenburg County, stated that the two slaves would attempt to get back to Maryland. Male and female slaves who ran away together often were attempting to get back to areas where they were reared. Married couples fled

Table 12

Frequency Distribution of Slaves
Who Ran Away in Groups

Number of Slaves in Group	Number of Groups	Total Number of Slaves in Groups	Percentage
1	14	14	1.6
2	249	498	57.3
3	51	153	17.6
4	24	102	11.7
5	7	35	4.0
6	6	36	4.1
7	1	7	0.8
11	1	11	1.3
14	1	14	1.6
Total	354	870	100

Source: North Carolina Extant Newspapers, 1775-1840

for the same reason. A few men and women kidnappd their wives and husbands, or enticed them to run after returning to the farm or plantation, or finding them after they had been sold. Family flight often involved females running away with their children. At least 56 of the children (more than half) were taken

Table 13

Composition of Groups of Runaways

Composition	Number of Slaves	Percentage
All Men	345	39.6
All Women	16	1.9
Mixed Group (Males & Females)	176	20.2
Husbands and Wives	70 (35 couples)	8.0
Family Flight	218	25.1
Family Flight & Others	45	5.2
Total	870	100

Source: North Carolina Extant Newspapers, 1775-1840

by female slaves who were unaccompanied by adult male or other female slaves. The remainder of the children were taken along by their mothers, fathers, and other slaves. Jack and his wife Tamer, for instance, absconded from their Craven County owner, Wilson Blount on February 24, 1798, taking their four children. In a remarkable departure from slavery in 1837, the female slave Nancy escaped with her ten children and three other slaves. The subscriber even referred to the children by name. These fourteen slaves fled from the heirs of Elkanah Ailen of New Hanover County and passed as free in several neighboring counties in eastern North Carolina.[23]

Owners were obviously angered by the loss of several slaves at one time. Taking into consideration that slaveholding in North Carolina was relatively small, many slaveowners were at a sizeable disadvantage when groups of runaways robbed them of their labor. William Dew, for instance, advertised for four slaves—two men and two women—who left his plantation in Edgecombe County in August 1798. Dew, who owned 11 slaves, sent his notice for the four slaves to the editor of the *Newbern Gazette* just days after the four ran away.[24] Zenas Alexander of Mecklenburg County had seven of his slaves to leave him in 1816. Tom, one of those who fled, took his three children, a shotgun and two pistols. Alexander was also confronted with the dilemma again in 1822. Four of his slaves, all men, absconded together, taking with them a rifle, a shotgun, and a screwdriver. The slaves' escape, no doubt, placed a strain on Alexander, as he only owned fifteen slaves in 1820, one-half of whom were children under fourteen years of age.[25] Edmund Hatch of Jones County suffered the loss of slaves who ran off in groups on at least seven different occasions.[26] Finally, George Clitherall of New Hanover County advertised for a group of eleven slaves, including two children, who left him on January 10, 1803. The slaves had been recently purchased from John Burgwin, also of New Hanover County. Clitherall described the fugitives as being "young and likely, and all speak very plain English, and are extremely plausible in deception." Five of the fugitives were family members, and half of the other six slaves, according to Clitherall, were going to various plantations to be with their wives.[27]

Slaveowners provided information about the origins of flight, or the counties from which slaves fled, for 2,733, or 98.6 percent of the runaways, including the infants and children. Although slaves ran away from their owners in every county in North Carolina, the eastern section of the state was most plagued with the problem of slave flight. As we have seen, the slave population was heaviest in the eastern counties of the state. Halifax, Edenton, Newbern, and the Wilmington districts, for example, contained almost 64 percent of the state's slave population in 1800; and in 1840, the same areas held nearly 53 percent of the slaves in North Carolina. Tobacco, cotton, and naval stores production in the southeastern section of the state were main staples. In addition to these staples, slaveholders used slave labor to grow and harvest Indian corn, wheat, and rice.[28]

Table 14 lists the number of slaves who fled in each North Carolina county between 1775 and 1840. Craven and New Hanover Counties were hardest hit by slave flight. Ten years before the American Revolution began, New Hanover County had 1,476 black and 529 white taxables. By 1786, the town of Wilmington, the County seat of New Hanover, and one of the major shipping cities in North Carolina for decades, contained four times as many blacks as whites. In 1800, 57.5 percent of the inhabitants of New Hanover County were black. Although their proportion of the population was smaller in 1840 (47.8 percent), numerically, blacks in New Hanover County increased from 4,058 to 6,376 between 1800 and 1840. In 1800, blacks—slave and free—made up almost 44 percent of the population in Craven County; and in 1840, blacks constituted 50.7 percent of the population.[29]

Twenty-two percent of all slaves for whom advertisements exist, ran away from owners in Craven and New Hanover Counties. Craven County owners lost 302, while New Hanover County owners reportedly lost 314 slaves. A number of possible explanations can be advanced to explain flight in these two counties. First, the sizeable black populations in both counties, including the cities of Newbern and Wilmington, were known for harboring slaves. Slaves and free blacks, for example, constituted 67.7 percent of the population in Wilmington in 1800, and 58.4 percent of the population in Newbern at the same time. In 1840, 59.3 percent of Wilmington's population was black, while 54.2 percent of the people in Newbern were black.[30] Slaves who fled to these towns had willing protectors. Slaves in Craven and New Hanover Counties lived in two of the leading commercial centers in the South. There was always a steady stream of ships importing and exporting goods into and out of those cities. Slaves seized the opportunity to board vessels to leave the state. It was not uncommon for ship captains and theirs crews to conceal, employ, and even carry

Table 14

Frequency Distribution of Runaways by County,
Sex, and Children Taken

County	Male	Female	Child	Total
Anson	31	8	—	39
Beaufort	52	8	2	62
Bertie	37	9	—	46
Bladen	23	4	—	27
Brunswick	13	2	—	15
Buncombe	6	—	—	6
Burke	7	—	—	7
Cabarrus	17	1	—	18
Camden	1	—	—	1
Carteret	18	4	—	22
Caswell	34	2	—	36
Chatham	49	9	—	58
Chowan	99	26	—	125
Columbus	1	1	—	2
Craven	206	73	23	302
Cumberland	112	25	7	144
Currituck	9	—	—	9
Davidson	5	1	—	6
Dobbs	4	—	—	4
Duplin	20	4	1	25
Edgecombe	70	14	6	90
Franklin	42	3	6	45
Gates	3	2	—	5
Granville	34	6	—	40

Table 14 (cont'd)

County	Male	Female	Child	Total
Greene	9	—	—	9
Guilford	21	5	—	26
Halifax	96	18	5	119
Hertford	7	2	—	9
Hyde	7	—	—	7
Iredell	16	2	—	18
Johnston	36	5	5	46
Jones	60	15	2	77
Lenoir	34	6	—	40
Lincoln	13	3	—	16
Martin	11	2	—	13
Mecklenburg	83	14	1	98
Montgomery	10	4	—	14
Moore	10	4	—	14
Nash	14	2	2	18
New Hanover	225	62	27	314
Northampton	12	1	—	13
Onslow	30	8	1	39
Orange	76	17	1	94
Pasquotank	11	4	—	15
Perquimans	8	5	—	13
Person	24	2	—	26
Pitt	26	6	5	37
Randolph	20	—	—	20
Richmond	21	8	1	30

Table 14 (cont'd)

County	Male	Female	Child	Total
Robeson	30	3	—	33
Rockingham	12	1	—	13
Rowan	50	10	1	61
Rutherford	9	4	—	13
Sampson	14	—	—	14
Stokes	6	—	—	6
Surry	10	—	—	10
Tyrrell	6	—	—	6
Vance	2	2	—	4
Wake	161	45	6	212
Warren	39	8	—	47
Washington	12	3	—	15
Wayne	22	6	2	30
Wilkes	5	1	—	6
Yancey	3	—	—	3
Total	2,153	479	99	2,733

Source: North Carolina Extant Newspapers, 1775-1840

fugitive slaves out of the state. And it was for that reason that runaways from remote places in North Carolina fled to Newbern and Wilmington looking for passage out of the state. And finally, the relatively large number of slaves who reportedly ran away in these counties may be explained by slaveowners having access to newspapers to advertise for their fugitives. No fewer than a dozen newspapers were published in both Newbern and Wilmington between 1775 and 1840.

The fact that several newspapers were published in Raleigh partially explains the number of slaves who reportedly fled from their owners in Wake County. Slaveowners turned to the *Raleigh Register*, *The Star*, the *North Carolina Minerva*, and the *North Carolina Standard* to advertise for their absconded property. Owners across the state also used these newspapers. As a matter of fact, notices for 30 percent of all slaves were published in newspapers in Raleigh, the state's capital.

It is not as easy to explain the low incidence of slave flight in counties where the black population was greater than the white. For example, both Northampton and Warren, two major tobacco-producing counties, had large black populations, but a small number of reported runaways. In 1800, slaves and free blacks made up almost 55 percent of the populations in both counties. In 1840, slaves alone constituted 50.5 percent of the population in Northampton County, and 63.4 percent of the population in Warren County. Only 13 slaves reportedly ran away in Northampton County, while 47 left their owners in Warren County. One possible explanation for the proportionately small number of reported runaways in these two counties is that few, if any newspapers were published in these counties. In this study, for example, not a single Northampton County paper was located; only one Warren County newspaper, the *Warrenton Reporter*, has survived the time period under consideration here. This, however, does not mean that slaves did not run away in these counties. Slaveowners simply did not have the advantage afforded owners who resided near towns with newspapers.

The low level of slave flight in western North Carolina, to a great extent, reflected the small number of slaves in that section of the state. The slave population, like the white population grew slowly in the Salisbury and Morgan districts, containing such counties as Rowan, Guilford, Stokes, Surry, Iredell, Wilkes, and Mecklenburg. In 1800, for instance, no counties in these areas contained more than a 20 percent black slave population, while on the other hand, 27 of the 45 counties in the central and eastern sections of North Carolina were comprised of at least 30 percent black populations. Only Mecklenburg and Rowan Counties, both located in the Salisbury district, had any measure of slaves to have reportedly run away. Blacks made up 19.1 percent of the population in Mecklenburg County in 1800, and in Rowan County, they were 14.2 percent of the overall population. The proportion of slaves grew to 34.2 percent in Mecklenburg County, and to 27.7 percent in Rowan County by 1840. Slaveowners advertised for 98 fugitives in Mecklenburg County, and for 61 runaways in Rowan County. At least seven newspapers were published in Charlotte and Salisbury, the respective county seats.

It is difficult to determine the number of slaves who were apprehended by slave catchers, citizens, and slaveowners themselves. It is likely that some slaves who fled were killed, used by whites in and out of the state of North Carolina, and hundreds, no doubt, found a measure of freedom. Slaveowners provided an incentive to whites to apprehend and return their fugitives to them, or to carry them to jail, by offering monetary rewards. Rewards were offered for 2,294, or 86.2 percent of the fugitives. In terms of gender, slaveowners offered rewards for 1,888 (87 percent) of the male slaves, and for 406, or 84.2 percent of all female runaways.

Many owners did not specify the amount of money they were willing to pay apprehenders. They simply stated that captors would be generously rewarded, or paid for their troubles. Sarah Gee's notice for her slave Jenny was typical. Gee wrote that: "A generous reward will be given for taking up said runaway and delivering to me.[31] Slaveowners sometimes offered two different rewards. The lower amount was to be paid if the slaves were apprehended in the county in which they ran, and the higher reward would be given if the fugitives were caught outside the county or the state.[32]

Rewards for runaways ranged from 25 cents to 500 dollars. The reward amount offered most often was ten dollars. This amount was offered for slightly more than 29 percent of the runaways. This amount was consistent for both male and female runaways. Table 15 shows the frequency distribution of rewards for the 2,294 fugitives between 1775 and 1840. Proportionately, higher rewards were offered for skilled artisans. Skilled slaves comprised 13 percent of the runaway population, but 20 percent of rewards of fifty dollars and above were offered for them. Specifically, 20 percent of the rewards for fifty dollars were promised for skilled slaves; 30 percent of the rewards for 100 dollars were promised for artisans; two of the six rewards for 150 dollars were for them; and one of the two rewards of 200 dollars was promised for John Buck, a blacksmith, "possessing more intelligence than usual."[33]

On the average, slaveowners were willing to pay less for the return of their female slaves. This was probably due to owners' perceptions that female slaves were less valuable than male slaves. For example, subscribers offered less than ten dollars for 91 females, or 22.4 percent of women for whom rewards were listed. On the other hand, masters promised less than ten dollars for 163 male runaways, or 9.4 percent of all males for whom rewards were offered (see figure 9). Subscribers offered two dollars to twenty-five dollars for 87.6 percent of the female slaves, while twenty-five cents to twenty-five dollars was consented to for 78.2 percent of male fugitives. Rewards of thirty dollars and above were promised for 12.3 percent of female runaways, and 21.7 percent of the men. The average reward for male runaways was $24.19, and for female slaves, it was $17.88. The overall average reward for runaways was $23.07. Slaveowners offered even less for older slaves. For example, they promised an average of about $16.30 for slaves fifty years to fifty-nine years of age. The average reward for five of the six slaves 60 years of age was $7.83. Older slaves were of less value to owners. Only two owners offered more than twenty-five dollars for runaways fifty and older.

During the years 1775 to 1799, notices appeared for an average of seventeen fugitives per year in North Carolina. Due to the American Revolution and the fact that only a few newspapers were published in colonial North Carolina at that time, partially explains why there were fewer reportings of runaway slaves. No advertisements were found during the years 1779 to 1786 in the two newspapers that were published in the colony at that time. However, thousands of slaves escaped from

Table 15

Frequency Distribution of Rewards
Offered for Runaways by Sex

Reward in $	Male	Female	Total
.25	1	—	1
1.00	1	—	1
2.00	3	1	4
2.50	1	—	1
3.00	1	2	3
4.00	3	3	6
5.00	128	74	202
6.00	7	2	9
6.66	3	—	3
7.00	2	2	4
7.50	1	1	2
8.00	10	4	14
8.50	2	2	4
10.00	534	135	669
12.00	7	—	7
12.50	18	8	26
13.00	7	—	7
15.00	77	18	95
16.00	6	—	6
16.50	4	2	6
20.00	364	54	418
25.00	297	48	345
30.00	69	7	76

Table 15——(cont'd)

Reward in $	Male	Female	Total
32.50	2	—	2
33.00	8	1	9
33.33	1	—	1
35.00	1	1	2
40.00	31	6	37
50.00	228	26	254
60.00	2	—	2
75.00	3	1	4
80.00	1	1	2
100.00	54	6	60
110.00	1	—	1
150.00	6	—	6
180.00	—	1	1
200.00	3	—	3
500.00	1	—	1
Total	1,888	406	2,294

Source: North Carolina Extant Newspapers, 1775-1840

their owners in North Carolina, Virginia, South Carolina, and other southern colonies during the Revolution. Many fled to aid the British against the colonists during the early stages of the

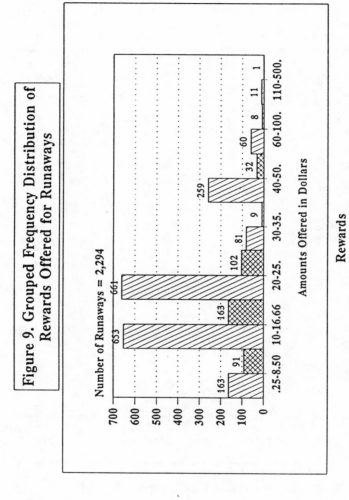

Figure 9. Grouped Frequency Distribution of Rewards Offered for Runaways

Source: N.C. Extant Newspapers, 1775-1840

war. And hundreds of slaves followed the British General, Charles Cornwallis, on his trek through Virginia and the Carolinas during the latter stages of the conflict between the English and the American colonists. So, slaves were fleeing but their flight to what they hoped would lead to freedom was not recorded.³⁴

Between 1800 and 1840, notices were found for an average of fifty-four runaways per year. It is difficult to associate the prevalence of slave flight with particular events in North Carolina. It seems, for example, that there would have been more reportings of slave flight during the 1830s. These years witnessed the surge in abolitionist activity, the era of the publication of David Walker's *Appeal*, and of Nat Turner's revolt in Southampton County, Virginia. But these events also ushered in tighter control of slaves throughout the South. As pointed out in Chapter 2, North Carolina enacted a series of laws in the 1830s to better manage both the slave and free black populations. If slave flight were impacted by these events, the advertisements do not yield any such evidence. Slave flight after 1800 was consistent annually, as there was nearly an equal distribution of runaways each year from 1800 to 1840. The increase in the reporting of slave runaways after 1800 was probably due to the increase in the number of published newspapers. There were nearly four times as many newspapers published between 1800 and 1840 as before.

Many slaveowners advertised for their fugitives as a last resort. Owners sometimes waited weeks, months, and occasionally, one to two years before advertising for their slaves. Others, no doubt, concluded that it was useless to place a notice for their runaways in distant newspapers because they believed their runaways were simply "lurking" in the county in which they lived. And it must be noted again that all slaveowners did not use the press to advertise for their fugitives. Some refused to pay the advertisement costs that ranged from fifty cents to one dollar for three insertions. Many slaveowners relied on citizens in their communities, and on their and the slaves of other masters to provide information about where their slaves were. Others simply waited patiently, hoping that their slaves would return. Notices for runaways represent a fraction of all slaves who ran away from their owners.

Black American slaves escaped their bondage for a variety of reasons. Although a few ran away to avoid being sold, and others to prevent a flogging, or because they had received a whipping, in the main it appears that most slaves in North Carolina fled to restore familial ties that had been broken as a result of the sale of family members. Some fugitives ran away, or at least owners believed, they had run away to other slaveholding states to visit or to kidnap members of their families. Another group of runaways absconded simply to find freedom in the North. But whatever their immediate purpose, ultimately they were running for freedom. Hundreds of runaways were harbored by family members, and it was during these times that they often enticed their loved-ones to abscond as well. Most slaves left their owners by foot—being aware that horses and boats provided faster means of transportation, but that they were also cumbersome.

Slaves seized the opportunity to run whenever it availed itself to them. Their flight did not rest upon seasonal conditions; they ran every month of the year. And although companionship, no doubt, was desired by runaway slaves, most of them escaped their enslavement alone, avoiding possible betrayal and apprehension. Slaves tended to run away from areas in the state where the black population was more heavily concentrated, primarily in the eastern and coastal counties of North Carolina. Slaveowners in North Carolina provided an incentive to citizens of the state, by offering rewards to apprehend and return their fugitive slaves. Slave flight presented a number of problems for slaveowners and non-slaveholders, and much of the frustration involved the expense of recovering slaves. It was a life and death game that slaves played at the expense of their owners in a quest to be free.

Notes

1. See, for example, the dozens of "Bills of Sales" for slaves in the Bertie County Slave Papers, 1744 to 1815, North Carolina Division of Archives and History, Raleigh, North Carolina. See also Chapter 3, 30n. Hundreds of advertisements for the sale of slaves also were found in North Carolina newspapers during the period 1775 to 1840. For a general discussion, see Norrece T. Jones, Jr. *Born a Child of Freedom*, Chapter 2.

2. Many owners were very explicit about who their slaves were going to visit. See, for example, the *North Carolina Gazette*, August 1, 1777 for Sam, who was headed to Maryland or Virginia to see his sisters and brothers; *North Carolina Journal*, March 6, 1793 for James Porterfield's notice, who was informed that his slave Harper was going to see his mother who lived near the Roanoke River, September 25, 1793 for Ned who was reportedly destined for Bath, North Carolina to see his brother. *Fayetteville Gazette*, May 21, 1793, in which W. McNaughton specified that his slave, Jame, had left Cumberland County en route to Salisbury to see his mother; *North Carolina Circular*, July 10, 1805; *Carolina Federal Republican*, January 16, 1813; *Edenton Gazette*, June 9, 1818, October 16, 1820, October 23, 1820, December 18, 1820; *The Star*, October 27, 1826 for Jack who was raised in Norfolk, Virginia, but made his destination Columbia, South Carolina; *New Bern Spectator*, March 7, 1829, May 2, 1829, August 1, 1829 for the thirty-year old fugitive Tom, who ran from Lenoir County to Slocumb's Creek in Craven County to visit his relatives; *People's Press*, May 7, 1834; *Charlotte Journal*, June 10, 1836; *Wilmington Advertiser*, October 5, 1838 for John who fled from Governor Edward Dudley's plantation in New Hanover County to see his mother and sister in Washington, North Carolina; *Fayetteville Observer*, March 20, 1839 for the female runaway Edy who ran in 1839 to join her brother who fled in 1835; and *North Carolina Standard*, April 10, 1839 for Lucy who lurked about a plantation on which her husband lived in Wake County.

3. *Edenton Gazette*, October 16, 1820; *Free Press*, May 30, 1828; *Carolina Centinel*, September 6, 1823. For other examples of male slaves who attempted to get back to their families, see

the *North Carolina Gazette*, October 6, 1775; *State Gazette of North Carolina*, February 7, 1788, March 30, 1793 for Isaac, who escaped from his owner in Chowan County to be with his wife in neighboring Perquimans County; *Newbern Gazette*, December 22, 1798 for Peter, who once belonged to Governor Richard Caswell. According to his master, Peter had fled to neighboring Duplin County; *North Carolina Minerva*, July 22, 1805; *Wilmington Gazette*, December 15, 1807, November 15, 1808, June 19, 1810; *Edenton Gazette*, July 16, 1811 for a black Methodist preacher who ran away from his Craven County owner Myles O'Malley, and was seen at the Methodist Camp Meetings because his wife was there; *The Star*, March 25, 1814; *Carolina Federal Republican*, May 30, 1815, July 6, 1816; *Raleigh Register*, November 14, 1817, January 19, 1821; *Warrenton Reporter*, March 2, 1827 for a man who had two wives; *Elizabeth City Star and North Carolina Eastern Intelligencer*, May 27, 1826 for Joe; *Warrenton Reporter*, March 2, 1827 for a slave who had two wives in Warren County; *Miner's and Farmer's Journal*, May 10, 1834; *The Statesman and Third Congressional District Advertiser*, February 7, 1835; *Raleigh Register*, November 29, 1836 for Richard who fled from Buncombe County to be with his free black wife in Raleigh; *Tarboro Press*, March 18, 1837; *North Carolina Sentinel*, March 29, 1837; *Fayetteville Observer*, March 28, 1838.

4. *The Star*, March 27, 1828; *Free Press*, April 10, 1829; *The Star* March 18, 1830; *North Carolina Minerva*, June 10, 1800. See also the *North Carolina Journal*, March 6, 1797, July 6, 1807; *Raleigh Register*, March 20, 1812 for Robin, who was believed to have gone to Mississippi Territory in pursuit of his wife who was taken by her owner to sell her there, September 17, 1813, and July 24, 1818, in which Joseph S. Pugh disclosed that his fugitive Sip, had been shot, but that he fled to follow his wife to Alabama; *The Star*, January 29, 1829 and October 18, 1837 for Anthony who was in pursuit of his wife who was taken to Mississippi; *Fayetteville Observer* May 1, 1839;

5. *Edenton Gazette*, September 17, 1807, November 24, 1809; *Free Press*, August 22, 1826.

6. See the *Raleigh Register*, July 15, 1814 for Ben and Alice, August 26, 1814 for Charles and Pompey; *The Star*, April 5, 1816, December 6, 1816 for Adam. For examples of runaways

who fled to other slaveholding areas to undoubtedly return to family members, see the *State Gazette of North Carolina*, January 28, 1791; *North Carolina Journal*, October 1, 1793, June 11, 1798, January 18, 1802, and March 29, 1802 for Peter and Fanny, who were purchased in Norfolk, Virginia; *Raleigh Register*, April 13, 1807; *The Star*, September 14, 1809, October 5, 1809, September 21, 1815, December 15, 1815, and April 26, 1816 for the runaway Sam, who was purchased in Portsmouth, Virginia and was headed back there; *Western Carolinian*, May 14, 1822, March 23, 1824, and May 29, 1827, in which John Mayhew of Iredell County advertised that his slave, Abraham, who had been lanced, was trying to get back to Virginia. This marked the second time that he had tried to return to Virginia. See also the *Free Press*, February 3, 1827 for Moses and Nat, and September 8, 1827; *Greensborough Patriot*, August 24, 1836

7. *Edenton Gazette*, September 24, 1807; the notice for March is in the *Star*, August 12, 1814.

8. *North Carolina Gazette; or Impartial Intelligencer*, August 5, 1797; *Wilmington Gazette*, April 9, 1801, January 9, 1800; *Elizabeth City Star and North Carolina Eastern Intelligencer*, May 27, 1826. For other instances of concealment of runaways by family members, see the following: *Wilmington Gazette*, January 9, 1800 for Manuel, who was harbored by his wife in New Hanover County, January 20, 1803 and June 19, 1810 for the female runaway Harriet, who was harbored by her parents at Town Creek Bridge in New Hanover County; *The True Republican and American Whig*, June 20, 1809.

9. See the *Carolina Centinel*, November 7, 1818 for Jack. The notices for Moses, Clara, Penny, and Nancy, are in the *Wilmington Gazette*, May 5, 1803; *True Republican & Newbern Weekly Advertiser*, February 9, 1811; *Carolina Centinel*, December 30, 1820; and *Catawba Journal*, February 7, 1826, respectively.

10. See for example, Herbert Gutman, *The Black Family in Slavery and Freedom, 1750-1925* (New York: Vintage Books, 1976), see chapter 7 especially; Blassingame, *Slave Community*, chapter 4; Peter Wood, *Black Majority*, 182; Thomas L. Webber, *Deep Like the Rivers: Education in the Slave Quarter Community, 1831-1835* (New York: W.W. Norton and Company, Incorporated, 1978), 115. For studies that have emphasized the

importance of familial ties as motive for slave flight, see Kay and
Cary, "Slave Runaways in Colonial North Carolina," 12-13; Mullin,
Flight and Rebellion, 109-110; Julia Floyd Smith, *Slavery and
Plantation Growth in Antebellum Florida, 1821-1860*
(Gainesville: University of Florida Press, 1973), 62; Joe Gray
Taylor, *Negro Slavery in Louisiana* (Baton Rouge: The Louisiana
Historical Association, 1963), 181-82, *Negro Slavery in
Louisiana*; Orville W. Taylor, *Negro Slavery in Arkansas*
(Durham: Duke University Press, 1958), 215-17, *Negro Slavery
in Arkansas*; James Benson Sellars, *Slavery in Alabama*
(University, Alabama: University of Alabama Press, 1958), 266,
and Charles S. Syndor, *Slavery in Mississippi* (New York: D.
Appleton-Century Company, Incorporated, 1933), 103-104,
hereinafter cited as Syndor, *Slavery in Mississippi.*

11. *New Bern Spectator*, November 8, 1833; *People's Press*,
November 13, 1835.

12. *North Carolina Journal*, July 10, 1797. See *The Star*, July
4, 1823 for Ned, and *Hillsborough Recorder*, May 17, 1820 for
Jim.

13. See the *Raleigh Register*, November 21, 1826 for these
four slaves. The notice for Cuff, David, and Moses is in the
Carolina Centinel, July 20, 1822; *State Gazette of North
Carolina*, March 2, 1793. For other slaves who attempted to
leave the state via ocean-going vessels, see *Hall's Wilmington
Gazette*, September 7, 1797 for John who was en route to
Wilmington to board a vessel to leave the state; *Edenton
Gazette*, January 12, 1810, October 7, 1817; *Carolina Federal
Republican*, July 6, 1816, July 5, 1817; *Carolina Centinel*, March
27, 1819, July 22, 1820, March 7, 1834; *New Bern Spectator*,
April 18, 1834.

14. *The Star*, August 16, 1827. The notice for Peter is in the
Raleigh Register, October 21, 1834. Brantly advertised for Davy
in the *Raleigh Register*, August 4, 1808 and also *The Star*, July
20, 1809. For the other slaves in route to Ohio, see the *Raleigh
Register*, April 12, 1814 for Will, June 7, 1825 for Ben,
September 29, 1826; *Miner's and Farmer's Journal*, April 10,
1832; *The Star*, April 8, 1814; *Western Carolinian*, September
11, 1821. Notices for slaves bound for Pennsylvania are in the
Raleigh Register, June 3, 1800, October 20, 1820, January 9,
1829; *Edenton Gazette*, June 5, 1820, March 2, 1810, *Western*

Carolinian, June 28, 1825; *People's Press*, August 21, 1833. Advertisements for the fugitives headed to New York are in the *Raleigh Register*, January 9, 1829; *Edenton Gazette*, March 2, 1810; *Carolina Centinel*, July 26, 1833; *New Bern Spectator*, June 18, 1831; *Wilmington Gazette*, January 13, 1816. The notice for Jack, a Craven County slave who was "accustomed to the sea" and headed for New England, is in the *North Carolina Gazette; or Impartial Intelligencer*, March 23, 1793. For an excellent discussion on northern flight, see Larry Gara, *The Liberty Line: The Legend of the Underground Railroad* (Lexington: University of Kentucky Press, 1961), Chapter 3. See also, Hilty, *Toward Freedom for All*, 89-100. William Still, a free black contemporary of the antebellum period chronicled the stories of slaves who fled North during the late 1840s and 1850s and found freedom, William Still, *Still's Underground Rail Road Records*, rev. ed (Philadelphia: J.W. Keeler & Co., 1883).

15. See *The Star*, July 27, 1821 for Robbin. The notice for Sam is in the *Raleigh Register*, June 28, 1816. See other examples in the *Edenton Gazette*, January 27, 1808 for Dolphus, who was said to be "a very disposed Negro, who went off without provocation," November 9, 1811, in which Frederick Creecy wrote that he would not chastise his runaway, Harry, if he returned in thirty days, November 12, 1821, February 24, 1831; *Carolina Federal Republican*, January 2, 1813; *Raleigh Register*, January 23, 1818, June 22, 1822; *Free Press*, April 26, 1831 for the slave Will, who ran away from Edgecombe County without a cause, and was believed to have been lurking in Edgecombe and Halifax counties; *New Bern Spectator*, April 18, 1834 for the fugitive Wile, who left his Craven County owner headed "North," running "without provocation and purpose," according to his owner William P. Biddle.

16. See the *North Carolina Minerva*, May 28, 1804 for Richard Tomosson's notice for Ephraim, in which he offered fifty dollars in reward money for his fugitive, and thirty dollars for his horse; *Raleigh Register*, November 14, 1817 for John B. Mebane's notice offering twenty dollars for his runaway, Tom, and ten dollars for the horse. For instances in which other slaves fled by horseback, see the *North Carolina Gazette*, March 13, 1778; *North Carolina Journal*, January 16, 1793; *The True Republican and American Whig*, June 20, 1809; *Raleigh Register*, January

29, 1813; *Edenton Gazette*, May 9, 1820; *American Recorder*, August 31, 1821 for Ned, whose owner promised a reward of five dollars each for him and the horse.

17. For the fugitives who left their owners by boat, see the *North Carolina Gazette*, April 3, 1778 for Salem, a Craven County slave who had reportedly "gone down the river" in a boat; *State Gazette of North Carolina*, July 8, 1791 for the twenty-five year-old slave Jack, and an unnamed slave, who took a canoe and sail.

18. For similar findings in other states, see Windley, "Profile of Runaway Slaves," 175-77; Mullin, *Flight and Rebellion*, 192n.

19. See for example, Kay and Cary, "Slave Runaways in Colonial North Carolina," 33; Sellers, *Slavery in Alabama*, 267, who contended that: "More advertisements for truant slaves appeared between May 1 and October 1 than during the other seven months of the year." See also Taylor, *Negro Slavery in Louisiana*, 184; Orville Taylor, *Negro Slavery in Arkansas*, 225; Syndor, *Slavery in Mississippi*, 103-104.

20. See Windley, "Profile of Runaway Slaves," 179; Mullin, *Flight and Rebellion*, 192n.

21. The phrase "stole themselves" refers to runaway slaves and was used by Peter Wood; see Wood, *Black Majority*, 239.

22. Johnson, "Runaway Slaves and the Slave Communities in South Carolina," 418.

23. The notice for Jim and Solomon is in the *Carolina Watchman*, January 12, 1833. *North Carolina Gazette; or Impartial Intelligencer*, February 24, 1798 for Jack and Tamer; the advertisement for Nancy, her children, and the other slaves is in the *People's Press and Wilmington Advertiser*, October 13, 1837. See also the *North Carolina Journal*, January 18, 1802, March 29, 1802 for Peter and Fanny who were purchased in Norfolk, Virginia and fled to return there, September 13, 1802; *The Star*, February 24, 1815; *Raleigh Register*, July 15, 1814. For females who absconded with their children, see the *Carolina Federal Republican*, June 6, 1812 for Louisa who ran away with her fifteen-month-old infant girl in March, 1812. Louisa, according to her owner, John House of Pitt County was headed for Washington, Beaufort County where she once lived. House also pointed out that the fugitive's husband was in Washington; *Raleigh Register*, May 19, 1820 for Henry Potter's notice for

Sooky and her child who ran from him in Wake County two days after he purchased her and her child. See the *True Republican & Newbern Weekly Advertiser*, June 12, 1811 for Sophia, who absconded with her two daughters, aged eight and five; *The Carolinian*, January 14, 1815 for Sylvia who likewise ran off with her two children, four and two years of age. In addition, see the *Newbern Gazette*, April 25, 1801; *The Star*, January 1, 1819 for Sarah, a thirty-five year old Edgecombe County woman, who left her owner on November 30, 1818, carrying her three children. Absalom Sessions placed an advertisement in the *Wilmington Gazette*, January 23, 1801 for Peggy, a New Hanover County woman who fled with her three children. For other instances of parents fleeing with children, see the *North Carolina Gazette; or Impartial Intelligencer*, October 26, 1793; *Raleigh Register*, October 3, 1806; *Carolina Federal Republican*, August 1, 1812; the *Western Carolinian*, February 26, 1822; and Fayetteville's *Carolina Observer*, May 29, 1823.

24. Dew's notice is in the *Newbern Gazette*, August 25, 1798. For the number of slaves held by Dew in 1800, see the *Second Census of the United States, 1800: Edgecombe County, North Carolina, Population Schedule*, microfilm of National Archives manuscript copy, North Carolina Collection, University of North Carolina Library, Chapel Hill.

25. Alexander's 1816 runaway notice is in the *Raleigh Register*, May 3, 1816; the 1822 advertisement was published in the *Western Carolinian*, May 7, 1822. Also see *Fourth Census of the United States, 1820: Mecklenburg County, North Carolina, Population Schedule*, microfilm of National Archives manuscript copy, North Carolina Collection, University of North Carolina Library, Chapel Hill.

26. Edmund Hatch's notices for his slaves who fled in groups are in the *Carolina Federal Republican*, April 3, 1813; *North Carolina Gazette*, October 1, 1796; *Carolina Centinel*, June 13, 1818 for Joe, John, America, and Andrew, July 11, 1811, October 1, 1826, October 14, 1826; and *Hall's Wilmington Gazette*, August 30, 1798. Hatch, as noted earlier, was labeled a "notorious" slaveowner. In 1810, he owned twenty-two slaves; and in 1830, that number had increased to forty-two. See the *Third and Fourth Censuses, 1810 and 1820: Jones County,*

North Carolina, Population Schedule, microfilm of National Archives manuscript copies, North Carolina Collection, University of North Carolina Library, Chapel Hill.

27. Clitherall's notice is in the *Wilmington Gazette,* January 20, 1803.

28. See Merrens, *Colonial North Carolina,* 85-92.

29. See Donald R. Lennon and Ida Brooks Kellam, *The Wilmington Town Book, 1743-1778* (Raleigh: Division of Archives and History, North Carolina Department of Cultural Resources, 1973), xxx; Department of State, *Return of the Whole Number of Persons in 1800;* Department of State, *Return of the Sixth Census,* 42.

30. Department of State, *Return of the Whole Number of Persons in 1800;* Department of State, *Compendium of the Enumeration of the Inhabitants and Statistics of the United States, 1840,* 41-42.

31. *Wilmington Gazette,* September 24, 1801. For owners who promised a reward, but did not specify the amount, see the *Fayetteville Gazette,* October 12, 1789, September 25, 1792, May 21, 1793; *Raleigh Register,* October 13, 1815, March 29, 1816, and May 31, 1816; *Milton Spectator,* November 7, 1832; *Miner's and Farmer's Journal,* November 10, 1832; *Oxford Examiner,* October 4, 1832, December 10, 1832; *Carolina Watchman,* February 2, 1833, and March 29, 1834; *North Carolina Standard,* April 7, 1836; *Raleigh Register,* January 29, 1838; *Fayetteville Observer,* March 7, 1838.

32. See, for instance, the *Carolina Observer,* February 27, 1817, September 7, 1831, April 28, 1835, May 5, 1835; *Cape Fear Recorder,* July 21, 1830.

33. See the *People's Press,* June 17, 1835 for John.

34. See Frey, *From the Rock,* 163-64; Crow, *The Black Experience,* 75-78.

Summary and Conclusions

Slave flight and all of its accompanying problems plagued North Carolina citizens. Slaveowners fought to secure legislation to combat this annoying dilemma. It was a problem that forced owners to often dig deeply into their pocketbooks. Some slaveowners hired professional slave catchers, and what they called "nigger" dogs to track down their human property. Slave desertions proved to be extremely costly in a number of ways. Runaways robbed their owners of labor. We do not know how long slaves were in flight; as a whole, we do not know what happened to them while they were in flight; it is extremely difficult to determine if they were apprehended, or if they returned of their own accord; but we do know that a great many slaves enjoyed some measure of freedom for long periods of time.

Whether their desertion from slavery took the form of "petit marronage"—that is absence for short periods of time, or that of "grand marronage," characterized by flight for years—running away was a form of resistance, regardless of immediate goals. The length of time between the slave's escape and the publication of the runaway notice, give us some idea about the minimum number of days that they were in flight. Some owners waited weeks, or even months before placing a notice in the newspaper for their runaway. The majority of owners were careful to list the date of their slave's desertion. And when the ad was finally placed in the newspaper, they sometimes advertised for weeks, months, and occasionally years. Based on the information provided by slaveowners in the fugitive advertisements, it is clear that on the average, slaves had been in flight nearly forty days before the notice appeared for them. This does not include the weeks and months of advertising that ensued. But regardless of whether they were away for two

211

weeks, four weeks, months, or even years, the period of time should not detract from an appreciation of the slaves' desire to wrestle a degree of power from their owners. Flight, whether "petit" or "grand," was a challenge to the slaveowner's power and authority. Fugitives who visited relatives, and possibly returned to their owners shortly thereafter, runaways who fled to avoid a flogging, or because they were whipped, and those who escaped because they feared being sold, should not be dismissed as having engaged in frivolous behavior.

The fact that the North Carolina General Assembly session after session enacted legislation to deal with runaway slaves, only testifies to the seriousness of the problems that runaways caused. Slaveowners faced the problem of concealment of their fugitives by other slaves, free blacks, and even whites. They were also confronted with the problem of the enticement of their slaves by blacks and whites. And they had to deal with sea captains who sometimes hired runaway slaves and conveyed them out of the state to freedom. In 1792, the North Carolina General Assembly made it a capital offense to convey slaves out of the state. From 1715 to 1840, the state legislature built upon the legal framework that governed runaway slaves. An elaborate set of laws was enacted during these years at the behest of slaveowners, and non-slaveholders as well, to combat slave flight.

Slaves tended to run away from counties in the eastern section of the state where the black population was heaviest. Counties, such as, Craven, Edenton, and New Hanover, contained majority black populations. Slaves who fled in these counties, and to these counties were often harbored by other blacks—slave and free. Wilmington and Edenton, for instance, were known throughout the state as sanctuaries for runaway slaves. These counties were also situated on or near the coast of North Carolina. This afforded slaves an opportunity to leave the state in ocean-going vessels. Runaways also found employment in the shipping industry in these counties.

The runaway notices contain specific information about slaves which make it relatively easy to construct a physical profile. First of all, slaveowners indicated the name of their runaways, in most cases. The advertisements also disclose some information about the African-born and West Indian-born slave populations in North Carolina. Unlike Virginia and South

Carolina, very few foreign-born slaves were represented in the runaway population in North Carolina. Slaveowners were quick to point out certain physical markings that foreign-born slaves possessed, in an effort to distinguish them from creole slaves. Male slaves were more likely to run away. They fled at a rate of more than four and a half times that of female slaves. Male slaves were hired out more frequently than their female counterparts, and the fact that they possessed occupational skills that often carried them beyond the farms and plantations, increased their chances of flight. Familial obligations, basically, explain why female slaves did not runaway as often as men.

Almost half of the slave runaways were between 20 and 29 years of age. Fugitives between 30 and 39 constituted the second largest category. The fact that many of these slaves had been owned by more than one master partially accounts for these age groups being highly represented in the runaway population. They were familiar with many areas of North Carolina, and also with other slave states. Many of these slaves parted with family members as a result of being sold. Their aim was to re-establish familial ties, while some other fugitives escaped to be free.

There is little doubt that complexion played a significant role in how slaves were treated by whites, how they perceived each other, and in their ability to pass as free, and to pass as white. Almost half of the fugitives for whom information was provided about complexion, were reportedly "yellow," "light," "bright," or "mulatto." "Mulatto" does not denote color, but as the offspring of black and white parents, these slaves were extremely "light" in complexion. Owners indicated that many of the slaves could easily pass as white. Fifteen percent of all runaways in this sample were mulattoes. The large number of very light-skinned fugitives gives us some indication about the extent to which miscegenation occurred in North Carolina. Although the North Carolina General Assembly outlawed marriage between the races in an effort to reduce the number of mulatto children in the state, blacks and whites continued their sexual relations, and there were even interracial marriages. These obviously gave rise to the mulatto population in the state.

Farm and plantation labor was often dangerous. Slaves suffered from cuts, bruises, burns, and a number of other physical disabilities that were associated with their occupations on and off the farms and plantations. The axe, scythe blade, and cotton gin all took their toll on slaves. Runaways could be identified by whip marks, cropped ears, and brands. According to the owners, nearly 12 percent of the North Carolina fugitives had visible scars on their bodies that could readily identify them. Slaveowners often included minute detail concerning their fugitive's anatomy. These included descriptions of their toes, and other parts of the body that required closer examination by would-be apprehenders. Owners also revealed that some slaves suffered from diseases and other physical problems. Slaves could be identified by smallpox pustules, warts, and sores. Rheumatism, ruptures, tuberculosis, and gonorrhea formed some of the diseases and disabilities often reported by slaveowners.

The runaway advertisement is by far the best source for an analysis of the clothing worn by slaves. Some fugitives were poorly clad, while others had on adequate clothing for the season they fled. A number of fugitives were "well-dressed." A little more than 15 percent of the slaves who fled carried additional clothing with them. These were men and women who sought complete freedom from their owners and slavery.

From the runaway notices, we are able to gauge the kind of personalities that slaves had. The real value of these notices is that they tell us something about the mental, physical, emotional, and spiritual make-up of slaves in North Carolina. Slaves presented themselves in a variety of ways. Many looked "humble," wore smiles, and were often described as having non-threatening dispositions. Other runaways, according to their owners, possessed "grum," "sullen," temperaments, while another group of fugitives was "bold" and "proud" in their appearance. We also know something about the slave's proficiency in English, and how they spoke in general. A few African-born fugitives, for instance, spoke no English at all; others reportedly spoke "broken English"; and a third group was proficient in the use of English. West Indian-born fugitives often spoke two or more languages.

In their descriptions of creole slaves, owners tended to describe the manner in which slaves communicated orally. Slaves were often described as "slow" speakers, "quick and abrupt," in their conversation, "free" spoken, "loquacious," "bold and assertive," and in a number of other ways. Some slaves stuttered or stammered, and had other speech impediments. The notion that stuttering was an affliction most characteristic of skilled slaves, because of their daily contact with whites, is not supported by this research. Twenty-two percent of the 120 fugitives who had speech impediments in this sample were skilled. The question is, how do you explain the affliction in those slaves who were not skilled? Based on what we know about the etiology of stuttering today, most slaves who had this disfluency possessed a neurophysiological problem.

This research supports recent investigations by scholars that there was no such thing as a "typical" slave personality. Slaves did not respond in the same manner to their enslavement. There is no question that the "Sambo" personality did exist among slaves in North Carolina, and throughout the South as well, but the evidence is extremely weak to support the notion that this was the dominant personality trait. Fugitives were described as "artful," "keen," "shrewd," "intelligent, "cunning," and "defiant." Slaves were ambivalent in their relationships with whites; they were defiant of white authority; and many ran away from their owners on several occasions. Slaveowners permitted North Carolina citizens to kill their slaves if they resisted. Some owners legally outlawed their runaways. They were often intractable slaves who were not only a constant threat to the owner, but to the survival of slavery as well.

Slaves ran away from their owners for a number of reasons. It appears that most runaways fled to restore family ties because they were often severed by the sale of its members. The extent to which families were separated is evident by the fact that 33 percent of the fugitives had two or more owners. Some slaves fled to avoid being flogged, while others ran because they feared being sold. Another group of slaves ran to relieve themselves of slavery altogether. These were men and women who ran North, or passed as free in North Carolina. Slaves fled every month of the year, proving that the desire for freedom burned constantly—not just when climatic conditions favored flight. The overwhelming majority of slaves fled by foot, rather than by horse or boat, to reduce the chances of being apprehended. Most slaves chose to flee alone, as opposed to running off in groups. Individual flight minimized the possibility of discovery and apprehension. As an incentive to whites to apprehend and return runaway slaves, most slaveowners offered a reward. Owners offered less in reward money for women and elderly slaves.

The incidence of slave flight in North Carolina was similar to that in Virginia and South Carolina. This can be attributed to the nature of slavery in these three states. The major difference between flight in North Carolina and the phenomenon in Virginia and South Carolina, was the large number of foreign-born slaves in the runaway populations in the latter two states. North Carolina, unlike Virginia and South Carolina, was not a major importer of slaves directly from Africa or the West Indies. The state's participation in the external slave trade was reflected in the small number of African- and West Indian-born fugitives in the runaway population. The proportion of males and females in the runaway populations in the three states was similar. And so was the average age of both male and female runaways. The percentage of fugitives who performed skilled tasks, and the diversity of occupations in which slaves were involved, were also comparable. Slaves in these three states left their owners for the same reasons. The connection between these three states (especially Virginia) can be seen in the fact that owners reported that at least 165, or 6 percent of the fugitives were headed for Virginia and South Carolina.

The real value of this study is that it has resurrected a group of slaves, and given them life. We now know more about how North Carolina slaves looked, and the many ways they presented themselves in the face of white authority. We can cite names, ages, complexion, the physical afflictions from which slaves suffered, and so much more. Answers about fugitives have been provided in studies on slaves in Virginia and South Carolina, but not for North Carolina. One of the objectives of this study was to place slave flight in North Carolina on a level with that in Virginia and South Carolina.

It was hard to accept the idea that slaves in the "Tarheel State" did not respond to their condition in slavery in ways similar to those in other states. This study has shown, that indeed, slaves in North Carolina fought to secure psychological and physical freedom from the horrors of slavery. Many slaves achieved these objectives by "stealing themselves," finding freedom for whatever length of time.

Bibliography

Primary Sources

Manuscripts

William R. Perkins Library, Duke University, Durham, N.C.

Dismal Swamp Land Company Papers
Robert Menzies Papers

North Carolina Division of Archives and History, Raleigh, N.C.

Bertie County Slave Papers, 1744-1815
Chowan County Slave Records, Criminal Action Concerning
      Slaves, 1767-1829
Pettigrew Papers
Richard Street Papers

Microfilm

Fourth Census of the United States, 1820: Mecklenburg County,
      North Carolina, Population Schedule. Microfilm of
      National Archives manuscript copy. North Carolina
      Collection, The University of North Carolina Library,
      Chapel Hill.
Second Census of the United States, 1800: Edgecombe County,
      North Carolina, Population Schedule. Microfilm of
      National Archives manuscript copy. North Carolina
      Collection, The University of North Carolina Library,
      Chapel Hill.

Third and Fourth Censuses, 1810 and 1820: Jones County,
North Carolina, Population Schedule. Microfilm of
National Archives manuscript copy. North Carolina
Collection, The University of North Carolina Library,
Chapel Hill.

Printed Primary Sources

*Annals of the Congress of the United States, 7th Congress, 2nd
Session*. Washington: Gales and Seaton, 1851.

*Annals of the Congress: The Debates and Proceedings in the
Congress of the United States, Second Congress, October
24, 1791 to March 2, 1793*. Washington: Gales and
Seaton, 1849.

Catterall, Helen T. ed. *Judicial Cases Concerning American
Negro Slavery and the Negro*. 4 volumes. Washington:
Carnegie Institute of Washington, 1929.

Clark, Walter, ed. *The State Records of North Carolina. Names
of Heads of Families, 1790 Census*. Goldsboro: Nash
Brothers, Book and Job Printers, 1905.

Cooper, Thomas and David J. McCord, eds. *The Statutes at
Large of South Carolina*. Columbia: A.S. Johnston, 1840.

Devereux, Thomas. *Cases Argued and Determined in the
Supreme Court of North Carolina From December Term,
1826 to June term, 1826*. 4 vols. Raleigh: Gales and Son,
1829.

Donnan, Elizabeth. *Documents Illustrative of the Slave Trade to
the United States*. 4 vols. Washington: Carnegie Institute
of Washington, 1935.

Elliot, Jonathan. *The Debates in the Several State Conventions,
or the Adoption of the Federal Constitution together
with the Journal of the Federal Convention*. 4 vols.
Washington: Published under the Sanction of Congress.

Ford, Worthington Chauncey, ed. *Journals of the Continental
Congress, 1774-1789*. Washington: Government Printing
Office, 1904.

Hening, William D., ed. *The Statutes at Large, Being A
Collection of All the Laws of Virginia. Philadelphia:
Thomas Desilver, 1823*.

Iredell, James. *Laws of the State of North Carolina. Edenton:* Hodge and Willis, 1791.

_____. *Reports of Cases at Law, Argued and Determined in the Supreme Court of North Carolina, from December Term, 1845, to June term, 1846, both.* 6 vols. Raleigh: Weston R. Gales, 1846.

Journal of the Convention, Called by the Freeman of North Carolina, to Amend the Constitution of the State, which Assembled in the City of Raleigh, on the 4th of June, 1835. Raleigh: J. Gales and Son, 1835.

Martin, Francis-Xavier. *The Public Acts of the General Assembly of North Carolina.* 2 vols. Newbern: Martin and Ogden, 1804.

Moore, Bartholomew F., and Asa Biggs. *Revised Code of North Carolina.* Boston: Little, Brown and Company, 1855.

Peters, Richard, ed. *The Public Statutes at Large of the United States of America.* Boston: Charles C. Little and James Brown, 1850.

Proceedings and Debates of the Convention of North Carolina Called to Amend the Constitution of the State, Which Assembled at Raleigh, June 4, 1835. Raleigh: J. Gales and Son, 1836.

Return of the Whole Numbers of Persons Within the Several Districts. Philadelphia: Childs and Swaine, 1791.

Ruffin, Thomas and Francis L. Hawks. *Reports of Cases Argued and Adjudged in the Supreme Court of North Carolina, During the Years 1820 and 1821.* Raleigh: J. Gales and Son, 1823.

Taylor, J.L. *Cases Adjudged in the Supreme Court of N. Carolina From July Term 1816, to January Term 1918, Inclusive.* Raleigh: J. Gales, 1818.

The Carolina Law Repository, Containing Biographical Sketches and Eminent Jurists; Opinions and Reports of American and Foreign Jurists; and Reports of Cases Adjudged in the Supreme Court of North Carolina. 2 vols. Raleigh: Joseph Gales, 1816.

United States Census Office. *Schedule of the Number of Persons within the Several Districts of the United States, 1830.* Washington: Duff Green, 1832.

U.S. Department of Commerce, Bureau of the Census. *A Century* of *Population Growth: From the First Census of the United States to the Twelfth, 1790-1900*. Washington: Government Printing Office, 1909.

_____. *Historical Statistics of the United States: Colonial Times to 1970*. Washington: Government Printing Office, 1976.

U.S. Department of Commerce. *Negro Population, 1790-1915*. Washington: Government Printing Office, 1918.

U.S. Department of State. *Census for 1820*. Washington: Gales and Seaton, 1821.

_____. *Compendium of the Enumeration of the Inhabitants and Statistics of the United States, from the Return of the Sixth Census*. Washington: Blair and Rives, 1841.

_____. *Return of the Whole Number of Persons Within the Several Districts of the United States*. Washington: William Duane, 1802.

Newspapers

American Recorder (Washington), 1815-1825
Cape Fear Mercury (Wilmington), 1775
Cape Fear Recorder (Wilmington), 1816-1832
Carolina Beacon (Greensborough), 1836-1837
Carolina Centinel (New Bern), 1818-1835
Carolina Federal Republican (Newbern), 1809-1818
Carolina Gazette (Rutherfordton), 1836-1840
Carolina Observer (Fayetteville), 1816-1835
Carolina Patriot (Greensborough), 1837-1839
Carolina Watchman (Salisbury), 1832-1840
Catawba Journal (Charlotte), 1824-1827
Charlotte Journal, 1835-1840
Edenton Gazette, 1800-1831
Edenton Intelligencer, 1788
Elizabeth City Gazette, 1807-1808
Elizabeth City Star and North Carolina Eastern Intelligencer, 1825-1833
Encyclopedia Instructor (Edenton), 1800
Fayetteville Gazette, 1789-1793
Fayetteville Gazette, 1820-1822
Fayetteville Intelligencer, 1809-1811

Fayetteville Observer, 1836-1840
Free Press (Halifax and Tarboro), 1824-1835
Freeman's Echo (Washington), 1829
Greensborough Patriot, 1826-1835
Halifax Minerva, 1829
Hall's Wilmington Gazette, 1797-1798
Herald of Freedom (Edenton), 1799
Herald of the Times (Elizabeth City), 1836
Hillsborough Recorder, 1820-1840
Hornet's Nest (Murfreesboro), 1812-1813
Milton Gazette and Roanoke Advertiser, 1824-1831
Milton Intelligencer, 1818-1820
Milton Spectator, 1831-1840
Miner's and Farmer's Journal (Charlotte), 1830-1835
New Sentinel (New Bern), 1837
Newbern Gazette, 1798-1804
Newbern Herald, 1809
New Bern Spectator and Literary Journal, 1828-1835
Newbern Spectator and Political Register, 1836-1840
North Carolina Centinel (Fayetteville), 1795
North Carolina Chronicle (Murfreesboro), 1827
North Carolina Chronicle; or, Fayetteville Gazette, 1790-1791
North Carolina Circular (New Bern), 1803-1805
North Carolina Gazette (New Bern), 1775-1778
North Carolina Gazette, or Impartial Intelligencer, and Weekly Advertiser (Newbern), 1794-1798
North Carolina Intelligencer, and Fayetteville Advertiser, 1805-1809
North Carolina Journal (Halifax), 1792-1810
North Carolina Journal (Fayetteville), 1836-1840
North Carolina Minerva (Fayetteville and Raleigh), 1796-1821
North Carolina Miscellany (Edenton), 1832-1833
North Carolina Sentinel (New Bern), 1836-1837
North Carolina Spectator and Western Advertiser (Rutherfordton), 1800-1835
North Carolina Standard (Raleigh), 1834-1840
Oxford Examiner, 1830-1838
People's Press (Wilmington), 1833-1835
People's Press and Wilmington Advertiser, 1836
Political Press (Wilmington), 1814-1815

Raleigh Register, 1799-1840
Roanoke Advocate (Halifax), 1829-1833, 1840
Southern Telescope (Greensborough), 1837
State Gazette of North Carolina (Newbern and Edenton), 1787-1799
Tarboro Press, 1836-1840
The American (Fayetteville), 1813-1818
The Carolinian (Newbern), 1814-1815
The Farmer's Reporter (Winston-Salem), 1836-1837
The Harbinger (Chapel Hill), 1833-1834
The Morning Herald (New Bern), 1807-1809
The North Carolina Mercury and Salisbury Advertiser, 1798-1801
The Post Angel, or Universal Entertainment (Edenton), 1800
The Star (Raleigh), 1808-1835
The Star and North Carolina Gazette (Raleigh), 1836-1840
The Statesman and Third Congressional District Advertiser (Washington), 1834-1835
The Tarboro Scaevola, 1837
The True Republican or American Whig (Wilmington), 1809
The Whig (Washington), 1835-1839
The Wilmington Chronicle and North Carolina Weekly Advertiser, 1795-1796
True Republican and Newbern Weekly Advertiser, 1810-1811
Warrenton Reporter, 1824-1840
Washington Gazette and Weekly Advertiser, 1806-1808
Washington Herald, 1827
Washington Whig and Republican Gazette, 1840
Western Carolinian (Salisbury), 1820-1840
Western Star of Rutherfordton, 1840
Wilmington Advertiser, 1837-1840
Wilmington Centinel and General Advertiser, 1788
Wilmington Gazette, 1799-1816
Wilmington Weekly Chronicle, 1840
Yadkin and Catawba Journal (Salisbury), 1824-1834

Secondary Sources

Books

Allport, Gordon. *Personality: A Psychological Interpretation.* New York: Henry Holt and Company, 1937.

Aptheker, Herbert. *American Negro Slave Revolts.* New York: Columbia University Press, 1943.

_____. *Nat Turner's Slave Rebellion.* New York: Humanities Press, 1966.

Arndt, William B. Jr. *Theories of Personality.* New York: Macmillan Publishing Company, Incorporated, 1974.

Arnold, Robert. *The Dismal Swamp and Lake Drummond: Early Recollections, with Vivid Portrayals of Amusing Scenes.* Norfolk: Evening Telegram Print, 1888; Murfreesboro, NC: Johnson Publishing Company, 1968.

Barbara, Dominick A. *Your Speech Reveals Your Personality.* Springfield, IL: Charles C. Thomas, Publisher, 1958.

_____. *A Practical Self-Study Guide for Stutterers.* Springfield, IL: Charles C. Thomas, Publisher, 1983.

Bassett, John S. *Slavery and Servitude in the Colony of North Carolina.* Baltimore: The Friedwell Co., Printers, 1898.

Bentley, Elizabeth Petty, comp. *Index to the 1800 Census of North Carolina.* Baltimore: Genealogical Publishing Company, Incorporated, 1977.

_____. *Index to the 1810 Census of North Carolina.* Baltimore: Genealogical Publishing Company, Incorporated, 1978.

Berlin, Ira. *Slaves Without Masters: The Free Negro in the Antebellum South.* New York: Pantheon Books, 1974

Blassingame, John W., ed. *Slave Testimony: Two Centuries of Letters, Speeches, Interviews, and Autobiographies.* Baton Rouge: Louisiana State University Press, 1977.

_____. *The Slave Community: Plantation Slavery in the Antebellum South.* rev. ed. New York: Oxford University Press, 1979.

Brickell, John. *The Natural History of North Carolina.* Dublin: James Carson, 1737; Murfreesboro, NC: Johnson Publishing Company, 1968.

Brigham, Clarence S. *History and Bibliography of American Newspapers, 1690-1820*. 2 vols. Worcester, MA: American Antiquarian Society, 1947.

Carlisle, Jock A. *Tangled Tongue: Living with a Stutterer*. Toronto: University of Toronto Press, 1985.

Cecil-Fronsman, Bill. *Common Whites: Class and Culture in Antebellum North Carolina*. Lexington: The University Press of Kentucky, 1992.

Corbitt, David L. *The Formation of the North Carolina Counties, 1663-1943*. Raleigh: State Department of Archives and History, 1950.

Cornelius, Janet Duitsman. *"When I Can Read My Title Clear": Literacy, Slavery, and Religion in the Antebellum South*. Columbia: University of South Carolina Press, 1991.

Gara, Larry. *The Liberty Line: The Legend of the Underground Railroad*. Lexington: University of Kentucky Press, 1961.

Crow, Jeffrey, and Flora J. Hatley. *Black Americans in North Carolina and the South*. Chapel Hill: The University of North Carolina Press, 1985.

_____. *The Black Experience in Revolutionary North Carolina*. Raleigh: Department of Cultural Resources, Division of Archives and History, 1977.

Drewry, William. The Southampton Insurrection. Washington: The Neale Company, 1900.

Elkins, Stanley. Slavery: *A Problem in American Institutional and Intellectual Life*. Chicago: The University of Chicago Press, 1968.

Escott, Paul D. *Slavery Remembered: A Record of Twentieth-Century Slave Narratives*. Chapel Hill: The University of North Carolina Press, 1979.

Feist, Jess. *Theories of Personality*. New York: Holt, Rinehart, and Winston, 1985.

Fogel, Robert W., and Stanley L. Engerman. *Time on the Cross: The Economics of American Negro Slavery*. Boston: Little, Brown and Co., 1974.

Foner, Laura, and Eugene O. Genovese, eds. *Slavery in the New World: A Reader in Comparative History*. Englewood Cliffs, NJ: Prentice-Hall, Inc., 1969.

Franklin, John H. *The Free Negro in North Carolina, 1790-1860*. Chapel Hill: The University of North Carolina Press, 1943; New York: W.W. Norton, 1971.

Frey, Sylvia. *Water from the Rock: Black Resistance in a Revolutionary Age*. Princeton: Princeton University Press, 1991.

Genovese, Eugene. *Roll, Jordan, Roll: The World the Slaves Made*. New York: Pantheon Books, 1974.

Green, Evarts, and Virginia D. Harrington. *American Population Before the Federal Census of 1790*. New York: Columbia University Press, 1935.

Gutman, Herbert. *The Black Family in Slavery and Freedom, 1750-1925*. New York: Vintage Books, 1976.

Hilty, Hiram. *Toward Freedom for All: North Carolina Quakers and Slavery*. Richmond: Friends United Press, 1984.

Hopkins, Donald. *Princess and Peasants: Smallpox in History*. Chicago: The University of Chicago Press, 1983.

Inscoe, John C. *Mountain Masters, Slavery, and the Sectional Crisis in Western North Carolina* Knoxville: The University of Tennessee Press, 1989.

Irwin, Ann. *Successful Treatment of Stuttering*. New York: Walker and Company, 1980.

Jackson, Ronald Vern, and Gary Ronald Teeples. *North Carolina 1830 Census*. Bountiful, UT: Accelerated Indexing Systems, Incorporated, 1976.

Johnson, F. Roy. *The Nat Turner Story*. Murfreesboro, NC: Johnson Publishing Company, 1970.

Johnson, Guion G. *Antebellum North Carolina: A Social History*. Chapel Hill: The University of North Carolina Press, 1937.

Johnston, James H. *Race Relations in Virginia and Miscegenation in the South, 1776-1860*. Amherst: University of Massachusetts, 1970.

Jonas, Gerald. *Stuttering: The Disorder of Many Theories*. New York: Farrar, Strauss and Gioux, 1977.

Jones, H.G., Julius Avant, eds. *Union List of North Carolina Newspapers, 1751-1900*. Raleigh: State Department of Archives and History, 1963.

Jones, Norrece T. Jr. *Born a Child of Freedom, Yet a Slave: Mechanisms of Control and Strategies of Resistance in Antebellum South Carolina*. Hanover, NH: University Press of New England, 1990.

Jordan, Winthrop. *White Over Black: American Attitudes Toward the Negro, 1550-1812*. Chapel Hill: The University of North Carolina Press, 1968.

Kiple, Kenneth F., and Virginia H. King. *Another Dimension to the Black Diaspora: Diet, Disease, and Racism*. Cambridge: Cambridge University Press, 1981.

Lane, Ann J., ed. *The Debate Over Slavery: Stanley Elkins and His Critics*. Urbana: University of Illinois Press, 1971.

Lefler, Hugh Talmadge, and Albert Ray Newsome. *The History of a Southern State: North Carolina*. Chapel Hill: The University of North Carolina Press, 1973.

Lemmon, Sarah McCulloh, ed. *The Pettigrew Papers*. Raleigh: State Department of Archives and History, 1971.

Lennon, Donald R., and Ida Brooks Kellam. *The Wilmington Town Book, 1743-1778*. Raleigh: Division of Archives and History, North Carolina Department of Cultural Resources, 1973.

Littlefield, Daniel. *Rice and Slaves: Ethnicity and the Slave Trade in Colonial South Carolina*. Baton Rouge: Louisiana State University Press, 1981.

Longfellow, Henry W. *The Complete Poetical Works of Henry W. Longfellow*. Boston: Houghton Mifflin Company, 1902.

Mannix, Daniel, and Malcolm Cowley. *Black Cargoes: A History of the Atlantic Slave Trade*. New York: Penguin Books, 1976.

Markel, Norman N., ed. *Psycholinguistics: An Introduction to the Study of Speech and Personality*. Homewood, IL: the Dorsey Press, 1969.

Masterson, William H., ed. *The John Gray Blount Papers*. Raleigh: State Department of Archives and History, 1965.

Mencke, John. *Mulattoes and Race Mixture: American Attitudes and Images, 1865-1918*. UMI Press, 1976.

Merrens, Harry Roy. *Colonial North Carolina in the Eighteenth-Century*. Chapel Hill: The University of North Carolina Press, 1964.

Miller, Randall M., and John David Smith. *Dictionary of Afro-American Slavery*. Westport, Connecticut: Greenwood Press, 1989.

Newton James, and Ronald L. Lewis, eds. *The Other Slaves: Mechanics, Artisans and Craftsmen*. Boston: G.K. Hall & Co., 1978.

Oates, Stephen. *The Fires of Jubilee: Nat Turner's Fierce Rebellion*. New York: Harper and Row, Publishers, 1975; Mentor Books, 1976.

Overstake, Charles P. *Stuttering: A New Look at an Old Problem Based on Neurophysiological Aspects*. Springfield, IL: Charles C. Thomas, Publisher, 1979.

Owens, Leslie H. *This Species of Property: Slave Life and Culture in the Old South*. New York: Oxford University Press, 1976.

Petty, Gerald M., comp. *Index of the 1840 Federal Census of North Carolina*. Ann Arbor: Edwards Brothers, Incorporated, Printers, 1974.

Postell, William. *The Health of Slaves on Southern Plantations*. Gloucester, MA: Peter Smith, 1970.

Potter, Dorothy Williams, comp. *Index to 1820 North Carolina Census: Supplemented from Tax Lists and Other Sources*. Baltimore: Genealogical Publishing, Incorporated, 1978.

Powell, William S. *The Proprietors of Carolina*. Raleigh: The Carolina Charter Tercentenuary Commission, 1963.

_____. *Ye Countie of Albemarle in Carolina: A Collection of Documents, 1664-1675*. Raleigh: State Bureau of Archives and History, 1959.

_____. *The North Carolina Gazetteer*. Chapel Hill: The University of North Carolina Press, 1968.

_____. *North Carolina Through Centuries*. Chapel Hill and London: The University of North Carolina Press, 1989.

Price, Richard, ed. *Maroon Societies: Rebel Slave Communities in the Americas*. Garden City, NY: Anchor Press/Doubleday, 1973.

Rawick, George P. *From Sundown to Sunup: The Making of the Black Community*. Westport, CN: Greenwood Publishing Company, 1972.

_____. *The American Slave: A Composite Autobiography: North Carolina Narratives*. Westport, CN: Greenwood Publishing Company, 1972.

Riper, Charles Van. *The Nature of Stuttering*. Englewood Cliffs, NJ: Prentice-Hall, Inc., 1971.

Savitt, Todd L. *Medicine and Slavery: The Diseases and Health Care of Blacks in Antebellum Virginia*. Urbana: University of Illinois Press, 1978.

Schlesinger, Arthur, ed. Frederick Law Olmsted, *The Cotton Kingdom* New York: Random House, 1984.

Sellars, James Benson. *Slavery in Alabama*. University, AL: University of Alabama Press, 1958.

Shurkin, Joel N. *The Invisible Fire: The Story of Mankind's Triumph Over the Ancient Scourge of Smallpox*. New York: G.P. Putnam's Sons, 1979

Smith, Billy G., and Richard Wojtowicz. *Blacks Who Stole Themselves: Advertisements for Runaways in the Pennsylvania Gazette, 1728-1790*. Philadelphia: University of Pennsylvania Press, 1989.

Smith, Julia Floyd. *Slavery and Rice Culture in Low Country Georgia, 1750-1860*. Knoxville: the University of Tennessee Press, 1985.

_____. *Slavery and Plantation Growth in Antebellum Florida, 1821-1860*. Gainesville: University of Florida Press, 1973.

Stampp, Kenneth. *The Peculiar Institution: Slavery in the Ante-Bellum South*. New York: Alfred A. Knopf, 1956.

Still, William. *Still's Underground Rail Road Records*. rev. ed Philadelphia: J.W. Keeler & Co., 1883.

Stowe, Harriet Beecher. *Dred: Tale of the Great Dismal Swamp*. 2 vols. Boston: Phillips, Sampson and Company, 1856.

Syndor, Charles S. *Slavery in Mississippi*. New York: D. Appleton-Century Company, Incorporated, 1933.

Taylor, Joe Gray. *Negro Slavery in Louisiana*. Baton Rouge: The Louisiana Historical Association, 1963.

Taylor, Orville W. *Negro Slavery in Arkansas*. Durham: Duke University Press, 1958.

Taylor, Rosser. *Slaveholding in North Carolina: An Economic View*. Chapel Hill: The University of North Carolina Press, 1926; Negro Universities Press, 1969.

The Federal Writers' Project of the Federal Works Agency: Works Projects Administration. *North Carolina: A Guide to the Old North State*. Chapel Hill: The University of North Carolina Press, 1939.

Walker, David. *David Walker's Appeal in Four Articles; Together with a Preamble to the Coloured Citizens of the World, but in Particular, and Very Expressly, to those of the United States*. Edited by Charles M. Wiltse. New York: Hill and Wang, 1956.

_____. *Walker's Appeal: An Address to the Slaves of the United States of America*. Edited by William Loren Katz. New York: Arno Press and the *New York Times*, 1969.

Starke, Barbara M., Lillian O. Holloman, and Barbara K. Nordquist, eds. *African American Dress and Adornment* Dubuque, Iowa: Kendall/Hunt Publishing Company, 1990.

Watson, Alan D. *Wilmington: Port of North Carolina*. Columbia: University of South Carolina Press, 1992.

Webber, Thomas L. *Deep Like the Rivers: Education in the Slave Quarter Community, 1831-1835*. New York: W.W. Norton and Company, Incorporated, 1978.

White, Deborah. *Ar'n't I a Woman: Female Slaves in the Plantation South*. New York: W.W. Norton and Company, Incorporated, 1985.

Williamson, Joel. *New People: Miscegenation and Mulattoes in the United States*. New York: The Free Press, 1980.

Wood, Betty. *Slavery in Colonial Georgia, 1730-1775*. Athens: University of Georgia Press, 1984.

Wood, Peter. *Black Majority: Negroes in Colonial South Carolina from 1670 through the Stono Rebellion*. New York: Alfred A. Knopf, 1974.

Wynne, Frances Holloway, comp. *Wake County, North Carolina Census and Tax List Abstracts, 1830 and 1840*. Fairfax, VA: Frances Holloway Wynne, 1985.

Yetman, Norman R. *Voices from Slavery*. New York: Holt, Rinehart and Winston, 1970.

Articles

Aptheker, Herbert. "Maroons within the Present Limits of the United States." *Journal of Negro History* XXIV (April 1939): 167-184.

Bishir, Catherine. "Black builders in Antebellum North Carolina." *North Carolina Historical Review* LXI (October 1984): 423-61.

Brown, Alexander Crosby. "The Dismal Swamp Canal." *The American Neptune* IV (July 1945): 203-21.

Censer, Jane T. "Southwestern Migration among North Carolina Planter Families: The Disposition to Emigrate." *Journal of Southern History* LVII (August 1991): 407-26.

Chase, Judith W. "American Heritage from Ante-bellum Black Craftsmen." *Southern Folklore Quarterly* 42 (1978): 135-58.

Counihan, Harold J. "The North Carolina Constitutional Convention of 1835: A Study in Jacksonian Democracy." *North Carolina Historical Review* XLVI (October 1969): 335-64.

Crow, Jeffrey J. "Slave Rebelliousness and Social Conflict in North Carolina, 1775-1802." *William and Mary Quarterly* XXXVII (January 1980): 79-102.

Eaton, Clement. "A Dangerous Pamphlet in the Old South." *The Journal of Southern History* II (August 1936): 323-34.

Egerton, Douglas R. "Gabriel's Conspiracy and the Election of 1800." *Journal of Southern History* (May 1990): 191-214.

Green, Lorenzo. "The New England Negro as Seen in Advertisements for Runaway Slaves." *Journal of Negro History* XXIX (April 1944): 125-46.

Harper, C.W. "House Servants and Field Hands: Fragmentation in the Antebellum Slave Community." *North Carolina Historical Review* LV (Winter 1978): 42-59.

Heuman, Gad. "Runaway Slaves in Nineteenth-Century Barbados." *Slavery and Abolition* 6 (December 1985): 95-111.

Higginbotham, Don, and William S. Price, Jr. "Was It Murder for a White Man to Kill a Slave? Chief Justice Martin Howard Condemns the Peculiar Institution in North Carolina." *William and Mary Quarterly* 36 (October 1979): 593-601.

Higgins, Robert W. "The Geographical Origins of Negro Slaves in Colonial South Carolina." *South Atlantic Quarterly* LXXXI (1971): 34-47.

Inscoe, John C. "Mountain Masters: Slaveholding in Western North Carolina." *North Carolina Historical Review* LXI (April 1984): 143-73.

Johnson, Michael P. "Runaway Slaves and the Slave Communities in South Carolina, 1799-1830." *William and Mary Quarterly* 38 (July 1981): 418-41.

Kay, Marvin L. Michael, and Lorin Lee Cary. "Slave Runaways in Colonial North Carolina, 1748-1775." *North Carolina Historical Review* LXIII (January 1986): 1-39.

McLean, Robert C., ed. "A Yankee Tutor in the Old South." *North Carolina Historical Review* XLVII (January 1970): 51-85.

Meaders, Daniel. "South Carolina Fugitives as Viewed Through Local Newspapers with Emphasis on Runaway Notices, 1732-1801." *Journal of Negro History* 60 (1975): 288-319.

Morgan, Philip. "Colonial South Carolina runaways: Their Significance for Slave Culture." *Slavery and Abolition* 6 (December 1985): 57-78.

Morris, Charles Edward. "Panic and Reprisal: Reaction in North Carolina to the Nat Turner Insurrection, 1831." *North Carolina Historical Review* LXII (May 1985): 29-52.

Olwell, Robert A. "'Domestick Enemies,': Slavery and Political Independence in South Carolina, May 1775-March 1776." *Journal of Southern History* 55 (1989): 21-48.

Peek, Phil. "Afro-American Culture and the Afro-American Craftsman." *Southern Folklore Quarterly* 42 (1978): 109-34.

Phifer, Edward. "Slavery in Microcosm: Burke County, North Carolina." *Journal of Southern History* XXVIII (May 1962): 137-65.

Powell, William S. "Carolina in the Seventeenth-Century: An Annotated Bibliography of Contemporary Publications." *North Carolina Historical Review* XLI (January 1964): 74-104.

Prude, Jonathan. "To Look Upon the 'Lower Sort': Runaway Ads and the Appearance of Unfree Laborers in America, 1750-1800." *Journal of American History* (July 1991): 124-59.

Stavisky, Leon. "The Origins of Negro Craftsmanship in Colonial America." *Journal of Negro History* XXXII (July 1947): 417-29.

Taylor, Rosser H. "Slave conspiracies in North Carolina." *North Carolina Historical Review* V (1928): 20-34.

White, Deborah. "Female Slaves: Sex Roles and Status in the Antebellum Plantation South," *Journal of Family History* (Fall 1985): 248-61.

Wood, Peter H. "Whetting, Setting, and Laying Timbers: Black Builders in the Early South." *Southern Exposure* VIII (Spring 1980): 3-8.

Theses and Dissertations

Brinn, Susan. "Blacks in Colonial North Carolina, 1660-1723." Master's thesis, The University of North Carolina at Chapel Hill, 1978.

Callahan, Benjamin F. "The North Carolina Slave Patrol," Master's thesis, The University of North Carolina at Chapel Hill, 1973.

Ervin, Eddie Marie. "Runaway Slaves in Antebellum North Carolina." Master's thesis, North Carolina College at Durham, 1946.

Leaming, Hugo P. "Hidden Americans: Maroons of Virginia and the Carolinas." Ph.D. diss., 2 vols. University of Illinois at Chicago Circle, 1979.

Lempel, Leonard. "The Mulatto in United States Race Relations: Changing Status and Attitudes, 1800-1940." Ph.D. diss., Syracuse University, 1979.

McGeachy, Katherine Ann. "The North Carolina Slave Code." Master's thesis, The University of North Carolina at Chapel Hill,

Raper, Derris Lee. "David Walker's Appeal and Nat turner's Insurrection on North Carolina." Master's thesis, The University of North Carolina at Chapel Hill, 1969.

White, Deborah. "Ain't I A Woman?" Female Slaves in the Antebellum South." Ph.D. diss., University of Illinois at Chicago Circle, 1978.

Windley, Latham. "Profile of Runaway Slaves in Virginia and South Carolina." Ph.D. diss., University of Iowa, 1974.

INDEX

Africa, 7
African-born slaves, 67-69,
72, 126, 127, 141,
142
Ages of Runaways, 73-78
Alabama, 10
Alexander, Zenas
(slaveowner), 190
Alston, William
(slaveowner), 11
Average age of runaways,
76
American Revolution, 7-8
199, 201
Artful slaves described by
slaveowners, 101,
129, 130, 137, 139-
143, 150,
160n, 165n, 166n,
Atta (slave), 82
Augustus, Sarah (ex-slave),
42
Austin (slave), 83
Average age of runaways,
76
Baker, Blount (ex-slave),
43
Barbados, 4, 167
Bess (slave), 85

Bill (slave), 125
Black population, 5-8,
18, 40
Blassingame, John, 132
Blount, John Gray
(slaveowner), 48-49
Boats, escape by, 183,
208n
Body build of slaves, 88-89
Bold, confident slaves, 125-126
Branding of slaves, 92-93
Brister (slave), 150
Broken English, spoken by
slaves, 125-127
Burns, received by slaves, 89,
90, 93, 94
Burrington, Governor George,
population estimates in
North Carolina, 6-7
Census districts, 12-17
Chapel Hill, 72, 129
Climatic conditions, 183-184
Clothing, 32, 65, 99-103,
additional clothing taken
by slaves, 101, 102, 125,
129, 177, 181
Coastal towns, as sanctuaries
for runaways, 45, 47
Colonization Society, 129,
160n

"Common" whites,
    as harborers of
    runaways, 44-45
Complexion, 32, 65, 79,
    80, 83, 85, 86, 88,
    89, 126, 103
    descriptions of slaves
    black, 79, 80, 82, 83,
        86, 89, 91, 95,
    bright, 79, 80, 82, 83,
        85
    brown, 79, 80, 82
    dark, 79, 80, 83
    light, 79, 80, 82, 83
    mulatto, 79, 80, 82,
        83, 85
    yellow, 79, 80, 82, 83,
        85
Concessions and
    Agreement, 4
Constitutional Convention
    of 1835 in North
    Carolina 42; of
    1787 in
    Philadelphia, 50
Conveyance of runaway by
    shipowners, 48
County populations, 17-21
Cullen (slave), 85
Cotton gin, 90
Crasson, Hannah (slave),
    43
Craven County, 42, 66, 68,
    79, 82, 92, 130,
    137, 152, 154, 171,
    176, 181, 192, 193,
    205, 206
Countenance, 123-126,
    descriptions of 128,
    129, 137, 150,

Creole slaves, 67-69, 73
Cropped ears, 39, 92,
Dawson, Anthony (ex-slave), 43
Dew, William (slaveowner),
    192
Diseases, 65, 95-98
Dudley, Governor Edward,
    48
Edenton, 12, 45, 48, 49,
    124, 129, 130, 140, 151
Ellis (outlawed slave), 36
English, slave proficiency
    in, 123, 126-128, 159n
Familial bonds, as
    motivation for slave
    flight, 173-176
Family flight, 187
Federal Fugitive Slave Law,
    51
Federal Census of 1790, 8
Female slave, escape with
    children, 71, 21n
Flight by foot, 183
Floggings, 91, 180
    as motivation for flight,
    179
Fort, Ricks (slaveowner), 102,
    176
Free blacks, 29, 30, 40-46, 49,
    52 58n, 60n, 66, 76,
    85, 97, 191, 195
Free states, as point of
    destination for
    runaways, 99, 181-182,
    183,
Fugitive Slave Clause, 51-
    52
Fundamental Constitutions,
    4

Gabriel's slave conspiracy, 39

Georgia, 10, 91, 165, 175, 183

Genovese, Eugene, 138

Great Dismal Swamp, 33, 35, 54n, 55n

Group flight, 184, 187
   composition of, 189

Haiti, 31

Haitian Revolution, 38, 39

Harboring of runaways by slaves, free blacks, and whites, and relatives, 30, 43, 44, 48, 49, 64, 178-179, 180, 191

Harnett, Cornelius (slaveowner), 79

Hatch, Edmund (slaveowner), 92, 93, 190, 209n

Haynes, Herbert (slaveowner), 11

Height, descriptions of by slaveowners, 65, 88, 96

Hill, Whitinall, 11
   see also Whitmill Hill, 181

Horseback, flight by, 131, 183

House servants, 143, 144, 149, 150, 167,168

Immigration of blacks to North Carolina, 7

Insurrection scare of 1802, 39

Kay, Marvin L. Michael, 7-8

King Charles II, 3

Literate slaves, 41, 141, 142, 144, 146n

Locke, John, 4

Lords Proprietors, 3

Lurking by runaways, 36, 42, 61n, 95, 203, 209

Maroon societies, 33, 35

Maryland, as point of destination for runaways, 177, 178, 185, 189

Massachusetts, 50, 185

Meritorious services, 10

Miscegenation, 80, 82

Mississippi, 10, 91, 185,

Mulattoes, 80, 82, 83, 86,

Mullin, Gerald, 132, 143

Nat Turner's slave insurrection, 41

Natural increase, of slave population, 7, 8

Naval stores, 6, 22, 25, 193

"Negro" clothing, 100

Newbern, 12, 45, 48, 79,

Neurophysiological disorder, as cause of speech impediments, 137-138

Northern flight, as point of destination for runaways, 182-185

North Carolina General Assembly, 10, 30, 31, 40, 80, 91, 153

North Carolina Slave Code, 32-33

Occupational hazards, 89-90

Occupational skills, 71

Oral hygiene, 93

Origins of slave flight in
    North
    Carolina, 190-194
Outlawry legislation, 36, 52
Overstake, Charles, 137,
    164n
Pass system, 31, 83, 86,
    144
Passing as free, 83
Patrol system, 37-43,
    patrollers, 38, 39, 59n
Pennsylvania, as point of
    destination for
    fugitives, 50, 180-181
Pepper, Dick (slave), 150,
    169n
Perkins, Samuel H., 35
Permission to kill slaves,
    153
Pettigrew family, 96
Piety (slave), 83, 85, 93
Pregnant female runaways,
    93, 98-99
Previous owners, 44, 75,
    99, 178
Quakers, 10, 24n
Rewards for runaways, 198
Runaways,
    female, 71-73, 88, 89,
        92, 93, 98-103,
        131, 133, 134, 140,
    male, 36, 48, 50, 75,
        88-90, 93, 99-101,
        103, 133, 134, 140
Sambo, 126, 129, 138, 151,
    155
Shoes, 98, 100, 125
Shooting of runaways, 50,
    90, 93, 94, 153
Skilled artisans, 66

Slave Code of 1741,
Slave crimes, 29
Slaveholding families, 11, 12,
    22
Slave population,
    estimates and census
    accounts, 5-7, 10, 12, 17,
        42, 43, 45, 72,
        73, 86, 191, 195,
        196
Smallpox, 95-96
South Carolina, 4-8, 11,
        21, 22, 30, 31, 50,
        51, 91, 92, 126,
        133, 143, 184,
        199
    Negro Act of 1741 in,
        31, 54n,
    Stono Rebellion in, 31
Speech impediments, 123
Stuttering, 132-134, 136-138,
        162n
Theft of runaways, 49-50
Theories of personality, 123
Tobacco, 17, 22
Virginia, 3, 4, 7, 8, 11, 30,
        33, 35, 39 41, 42,
        53
    as point of destination
    for runaways, 75, 83,
        125, 129, 136, 144,
        152
Wake County, 79, 137,
        150, 175, 179, 181
West Indies, 7, 21, 92, 128,
        143, 185
Whip marks, 91, 93, 151
Windley, Latham, 67, 91,
        133, 143

Wilmington, 33, 40, 45, 46,
    runaways boarding
    vessels at, 47, 174;
    slaveowners warn
    captains not to convey
    runaways from, 48

With a pass, 86-88